SERPENTS IN THE MANGER

SERPENTS IN THE MANGER
Overcoming Abusive Christianity

JERRY L. HARRIS PH.D

MELODY J. MILAM PH.D

BARRICADE BOOKS INC. / NEW YORK

Published by Barricade Books Inc.
61 Fourth Avenue
New York, NY 10003

Copyright © 1994 by Jerry L. Harris and Melody J. Milam

Printed in the United States of America.
Designed by Cindy LaBreacht.

Library of Congress Cataloging-in-Publication Data

Harris, Jerry L.
    Serpents in the manger: overcoming abusive Christianity / by Jerry L. Harris and Melody J. Milam
    p. cm.
ISBN 1-56980-017-0: $24.00
1. Fanaticism—Controversial literature. 2. Christianity—Psychology—Controversial literature. 3. Religious addiction—Christianity—Controversial literature. 4. Control (Psychology)—Religious aspects—Christianity—Controversial literature. I. Milam, Melody J. II. Title. III. Title: Abusive Christianity.
BR114.H37 1994
261—dc20   94-25588
                                              CIP

ACKNOWLEDGMENTS

Throughout the three years we labored on Serpents, several people have generously assisted us, cheerfully tolerated our obsession with the project, and graciously endured our complete submersion in the work. To these, our friends and loved ones, we extend our deepest gratitude for their support: Erin Milam, Deborah Harris, Bobby J. Potter, Tamara Hanby, Nancy Didrickson, Joel R. Butler, Ronnie Ellis, Tim Campbell, Sharon Rush, Paul Scofield, Kim Roselle, Bill Mills, Sammy Campbell, and Jim Browder.

We would like to especially thank our editor, Kathryn Jones, for making the book easier to read and more understandable, and our agent, Natasha Kern, for her helpful insights.

Many names and inconsequential details have been disguised to protect those individuals whose stories appear in the manuscript. We wish these people love and complete recovery along with the hope that their experiences may help others.

CONTENTS

Christianity, Science, and Psychology

"To everything there is a season,
and a time to every purpose
under the heaven.

. . .

A time to keep silent,
and a time to speak."

ECCLESIASTES 3

Since the Bible was written from a first century view, Christianity adopted a first century view. The world was perceived as flat with four corners, heaven above and hell below. This world was considered the center of the universe with the sun revolving around the earth. Those who select a strict literal interpretation of the Bible calculate the earth was created somewhere between 4,000 and 5,000 years ago.

As the scientific view of the world progressed, theologians were troubled by the perspectives developed by the physical sciences. The earth was not perceived as flat but round; there was no literal heaven above or a literal hell below; the earth was an insignificant planet, revolving around an average star in a galaxy containing a billion stars in a universe containing billions of galaxies. Man was not perceived by this new science as having been literally created out of clay but as having evolved into the complex being that has the power to think and be self-aware. The scientific world view of the Bible is, as it should be, first-century.

The same could be said of the psychological perspective of the Bible, as interpreted by conservative Christians today. The psychological perspective is one of control of the children of God by power and threatened abuse. The children of God must believe, obey, and/or follow the teachings of Christ or they will at worst suffer in hell or at best not be among the chosen at the resurrection. That is, they will not receive eternal life, which may not be abusive but certainly is neglectful.

This psychological perspective is one of control and rigidity. One must comply or love will be withdrawn and punishment given. Concepts are black and white, right and wrong; there are the chosen and the lost; and there is a God who miraculously intervenes in nature and saves some people but lets others perish. We must invoke this God to save us and care for us lest He punish us. He will listen to all prayers and grant or not grant based upon some divine wisdom we do not understand.

This simple psychological world view is first-century. Although we are approaching the twenty first century, we have psychologically progressed very little. We still think in terms of black and white. We are still exclusive: the Baptists, the Catholics, the Jews. We are not a brotherhood of man. We still punish and withdraw love. We wonder why our culture is so violent. We blame guns, the breakdown of the family, family dysfunction, as we carefully look past the church on the corner. The church where Jesus died for our sins, a human/deity blood sacrifice. Where sinners are punished eternally, some children of God are saved, some children of God are lost. Those that will be saved must believe, follow, and obey. There is no other way. All other ways will be eternally punished in the fires of hell.

Too many families still follow this Abusive Christian Model. We threaten our children and punish our children. We withdraw love and punish them when they do not obey. We punish students in our schools. We punish prisoners. We punish church members who fall. We continue to worry about the violence in our culture. We grow angry and upset at anyone who has the audacity to point out this first-century psychological world view and openly state that it is abusive and violent. We fear and strike out at what is different or what threatens our thoughts and our sacred beliefs.

We divide ourselves: Baptist, Buddhist and Jew. Islam and infidel. We hope "they" don't move into our neighborhood. We must rise above this first-century psychological world view. We must understand that one does not cure abuse by being abusive. Punishment rarely works. We all are children of God: red, yellow, black, and white. We must learn to treat each other as brothers and sisters, and not threaten, manipulate, and cajole others to adopt our point of view. We may not be right. The strongest faith is the faith we have in our inner strength and in each other. We must teach ourselves and our children a new love, without violence, death, and punishment. We must show love, and not simply preach it as we punish in the back room. A new love that thinks in terms of helping rather than punishing, understanding rather than converting, and acceptance rather than compliance. A new love that is not only given to the select and those who adopt our views, but to those who are different and believe in different ways.

In working toward this new and nonabusive approach in Christianity, we must look at the abusive aspects and understand them fully. We must understand the influence of archaic psychological perceptions and how those perceptions influence us now. Based upon current psychological knowledge and theory, we believe the first-century model to be dysfunctional and abusive. At worst, it can lead to dysfunctional, abusive and violent behavior.

We certainly do not wish to cast aspersions on all of Christianity. Many people receive help in many ways by kind, loving, generous acts of Christians and their churches. However, there is a dark side to Christianity. A side we think has been harmful to many people. It is that side we wish to explore.

If you have been harmed by this "dark side" of Christianity, we hope this book will help you understand and recover from your injuries. If you have left organized religion because of your injuries, we hope we can rekindle your interest in the spiritual side of your personality. It is there.

We do not intend to point out abuses without pointing out options. People can change and belief systems can change. Changes are already being seen. To those individuals willing to work for constructive change in Christianity, we hope this book will stimulate your thinking. We invite you on our journey while we explore Christianity as it enters the twenty-first century.

CHAPTER 1

THE DARK SIDE OF THE LIGHT

*"I form the light,
and create darkness:
I make peace,
and create evil.
I the Lord do all
these things."*

ISAIAH 45: 7

How is it possible we came to believe Christianity could hurt people? Christianity was the religion of our childhoods and the tradition of our families. To many of our friends, Christianity was and is "The Light," their hope for the future. Supposedly, Christianity provides moral leadership to our families and our nation. Until recently, the authors of this book did not see Christianity as destructive or abusive. However, as we examined our own lives, and continued working with patients in our psychotherapy practices, we kept coming back to the same questions. Why are these Christians hurting so badly? Why are they confused, abused, and lost?

When we started questioning the teachings that had been part of our own belief system all our lives, it took a while for our minds to metabolize these new realities. We had to be honest enough and free enough with our thinking to give these new ideas a chance. This was difficult. At first, we thought we might be wrong. We considered that we were simply rebelling against authority. We even considered that we were rugged individualists. But in the end, we recognized there are destructive and abusive sides to Christianity.

We want to take you on a pilgrimage of self-healing and discovery—a pilgrimage brought about by our quest for understanding. First, though, let us tell you something about ourselves and how Abusive Christianity has troubled our lives.

JERRY'S STORY

I was reared in a Southern Baptist church. We were there every time the doors were open. I took my religion seriously and by the time I went to college, I had memorized more than one hundred verses from the Bible. While at Oklahoma Baptist University, I decided that God had called me to become a minister, and I was licensed as a minister by my hometown church.

Upon completing OBU, I moved to Fort Worth, Texas, to complete my training as a Baptist minister at Southwestern Baptist Theological Seminary. I moved in with two roommates who were also ministerial students. To me, coming to the seminary was a quest—a quest to seek and to search for what I considered to be the ultimate, for what I considered to be God.

First semester enrollment included classes such as Basic Evangelism—how to get people to join the church, and how to get people to tithe so that enough money could be raised to run the church. Indeed, a church can be big business and one has to raise a considerable amount of money in order to manage a big business. But I felt I was being taught the mechanics of church without the spirit of church. Furthermore, I found that you do not "seek and search" for God. Rather, the denomination defines, within a very narrow range, what is acceptable and what is unacceptable belief. In essence, you are told what to believe, such as the virgin birth and the divinity of Jesus.

Realizing that I did not fit the Southern Baptists' rigid specifications for preaching, I decided to leave the ministry. I could not, in good conscience, be a Southern Baptist minister. I once had felt that I had "the call from God," now I decided that "call" was probably a wrong number. I decided to go into some other field of work.

After I informed my family of my decision to leave the ministry, several things happened. First, I had not realized that my mother's family had prayed, evidently for several generations, for a minister in the family. It seemed I was an answer to these generations of prayer. The final result was a change in attitude toward me from my extended family. There was less acceptance on the part of my relatives and less contact with those relatives. In their eyes, I had destroyed their image of "the minister." I felt guilty, fearing perhaps they were unhappy with my decision. I felt isolated, lonely, abandoned. I could not turn to the family that I had "let down." I could not be honest about my religious beliefs. Those beliefs would *not* be accepted. They would see my "different thinking" as sin. I knew this, because that is what I used to tell people when *their* faith wavered.

When I told my two roommates that I was not going to continue my study for the ministry, our living arrangements changed. They were continuing with the seminary, and they had plans to move to other apartments. I was aware that I was no longer seen as "part of the group," and as such, I was not invited to move with them. There were no angry words; in fact, there were no words at all. I simply was not invited. As a result, I moved out alone, finding a little room off the back of a house. I no longer had the support of family and then I lost the support of my seminary friends. This experience ended up being one of the most depressing and isolating moments of my life.

Since my religious beliefs were in a state of flux and my support group had collapsed, I really did not know where to turn. I could not go to friends in the church, because I knew they would not accept me. Eventually, I turned to bars and started drinking. I was impressed by the people in bars because they accepted me. They really could care less what my background was, and they really did not care what I believed. They were friendly and nice to me and made no demands. They invited me to their houses. They cooked dinner for me. I was absolutely overwhelmed by the thought that I had found people in bars who acted more "Christian" than the people I had just left in church and in seminary. The contrast was powerful and dramatic and, if not for some of those people, my feelings of hurt and rejection would have been much worse.

I felt excluded from my family and friends because my beliefs did not agree with theirs. As I look back, it seems strange that I was an outcast, and not one person I had known had tried in any way to help me. Does exclusion preclude help? I was hurt and angry for several years.

Initially, I thought my family and seminary friends were narrow-minded and unaccepting. Years later, I began to think that the problems were within the belief system of Christianity. Behind the preached love and acceptance are destructive beliefs which alienate and divide people.

At a family reunion in 1993, my family discussed the publication of this book. Bettie, a niece who converted to Catholicism, and I decided that family love and unity were more important than the individual beliefs. Our family is closer now than ever before. To pull together, love and support each other—that is the ultimate in Christian love. I hope this book reflects that spirit.

MELODY'S STORY

When I was in elementary school, my parents had an extremely dysfunctional relationship. My father was planning to go back to school to be a Church of Christ minister. He was cruel, angry, rigid, and authoritarian. He used church doctrines to focus his anger and hostility on others, especially my mother. He was extremely suspicious and jealous of her. He watched her every minute because he wanted to make sure she did everything the Bible wanted her to do. He literally kept her a prisoner in her own home, refusing to let her go out into the world, or even into the yard or to the grocery store, for fear that she would sin. For years, she was not allowed to go anywhere but to church. She could not buy clothes or wear make-up. As a result, she felt trapped and developed a relationship with the man across the street.

This went on for a short period. My father apparently picked up signals of problems and hired a detective, who made recordings of my mother on the phone with this neighbor. My father used these recordings to punish my mother severely. In order to shame our mother, he made these tapes available to me and my sisters, if we wanted to hear them.

He went to the elders of the church where he was a deacon and with them decided to force my mother to confess her sin in public. They let my mother know, with threats of eternal damnation, that this was what had to be done. She complied. My father had the elders come to the house weekly under the guise of holding prayer meetings for her.

I can remember the Sunday she got up in front of the church. I can remember her voice as she talked about her sin and asked the forgiveness of everyone. I can remember the shame of sitting there listening and the humiliation I felt and I knew she must feel.

I was angry. I felt embarrassed, abused, hurt, and fearful. One always thinks about the fear of being in that person's place and I did. I felt with her and for her. I was nine years old.

My father, the deacon, the Christian, was unable to forgive her. He had very little insight into the fact that he had set up this situation, and sought to punish her further for her sins by leaving the family. I was the only one old enough to understand or to realize what had happened.

Mother took my sisters and me and joined another Church of Christ. Because she was a divorced woman, she found that there were new restrictions on her. She could not date, see other men, sleep with other men, or remarry without "forcing another man into adultery," according to the Church of Christ doctrine.

My mother felt uncomfortable with these dictates. She was unable to live the life they demanded. She was lonely and she wanted to remarry. So, after going to the church for a short time, she stopped attending. Yet she very gladly took us every Sunday morning, Sunday night, and Wednesday, if we wanted to go, and encouraged us in that.

Immediately after she had missed church for a few weeks, the elders wrote her a letter saying she was "disfellowshipped." No one ever offered her help or said a word to her. Nineteen others in the congregation received similar letters.

Instead of letting it drop there, the elders continued to punish. I had become an assistant Sunday School teacher. I was teaching a class of three-year-old children and was dedicated in my service to the church. One Sunday, as my sisters and I were sitting in church, the elders very loudly and clearly said that our mother was to be "disfellowshipped." Everyone knew that meant thrown out, excommunicated, social sanctions. No one from the church was to communicate with her or socialize with her or relate to her in any way. She was to be isolated and punished for her refusal to attend church.

The insensitivity of that act still appalls me. I can only wonder what they must have been thinking to have performed such a humiliating act in front of us—her children. We were angry, hurt, and shocked because we weren't even warned. It was an angry, punishing, insensitive, unnecessary act.

Afterward, my feelings about the church began to change. I no longer saw it in a positive light. I began to act out with other kids in my group. I began to skip church services. I began to ride in the preacher's car with the preacher's son during the sermon after we had slipped the keys out of the preacher's coat pocket. I lost my desire to participate. Not long after that, I completely abandoned my efforts at attending church. And I "threw the baby out with the bath water." I lost my spirituality.

I became angry at religion and avoided anything religious or spiritual. I felt empty and looked to fill my emptiness by getting into intense but unhealthy relationships with anyone who came along. I married and divorced several times—each time to an individual as spiritually empty as I was. I also refused to expose my children to religious training for fear they would be injured.

I eventually argued with my father and went seven years without seeing him. He had been dead for several years before I was able to forgive him for what he had done. Eventually, my anger subsided and I began to meet people who had healthy happy spiritual lives both outside of and within Christianity. I talked to them and began studying their beliefs. I studied other religions and, soon recognizing that a loss of spirituality was usually accompanied by feelings of emptiness, learned to fill my emptiness by choosing very carefully my own combination of beliefs, ones that could not be hurtful or destructive to myself or to anyone else. Through this search, I learned the difference between religion and spirituality and the necessity of meeting spiritual needs. Since that time, one of my daughters has joined me in my pursuits, the other still searches.

You know the old saying that all therapists *are* therapists because they are crazy. It may be true. We (Harris and Milam), were so neurotic by the time we finished undergraduate school that we both decided to become mental health professionals. We needed the help!

Over the years of dealing with our own injuries and working with people in pain, we became vaguely aware that others had gone through experiences similar to ours. But we avoided pursuing any line of questioning that would have exposed those issues. Maybe we were afraid of what we would discover. Maybe we were afraid to reopen old wounds that had never fully healed. Maybe we were afraid to tread on such sacred ground.

But there came a point when we could no longer ignore our own injuries or the stories we were hearing. There was too much of a pattern, and we had been trained to recognize patterns in people's lives. Finally, we had to listen to and really hear what our patients were telling us and confront what we were finding in our lives. We came face to face with the fact that Christianity is full of destructive beliefs and practices.

The individual story that really convinced us that mainstream Christians and Christian churches can and do abuse people was brought to us by a young couple seeking help. They came to us because they had been devastated by "counseling" from their conservative Christian minister.

John and Mary Jane were a bright young couple, strongly religious and devout in their faith. As newlyweds, they tried and failed to conceive a child. For years they tried everything, going from one fertility clinic to another. Finally, Mary Jane became pregnant. Their intense joy soon turned to pain, however, when Mary Jane had a miscarriage. Confused and hurt, they turned to their minister for consolation and help in dealing with their loss. Not understanding how this could have happened to them, they trusted their minister to help them find answers and strength.

His answer was: "You are being punished by God for something you have done!" Devastated, they searched their memories for an offense serious enough to have resulted in the death of their child. Now even more confused and deeply injured by the minister's words, they sought help from professional counseling. Eventually, they decided to change their religious affiliation, but not before honestly considering the minister's ideas and suffering greatly from his words.

The abuse here is direct and flagrant and should be recognized as such by anyone. The minister was obviously callous and severely lacking in empathy for the plight and pain of others. His belief that God is involved in the affairs of people in a punishing way is a common belief in Christian religion. Such a belief is abusive and can be used to manipulate, control, and injure. This belief, along with their minister's judgment, devastated this couple so much that they sought professional counseling.

John and Mary Jane's story is not uncommon. Abusive Christianity and the results of Abusive Christianity find expression in many different and varied behaviors in people. On the surface, some of these behaviors seem to be in direct contradiction to the beliefs and ethics found in Christianity, such as violence, family violence, child abuse, sexual abuse, sexual "acting out," and other sexual problems.

People will ask, "How in the world could Christianity be responsible for violence and sexual acting out?" Violence can result directly from beliefs of punishment. Sexual acting out can result from dynamics which are set into motion by Christian beliefs. These beliefs can create the very problems that Christian preachings frequently attack!

Consider the story of Sheila, the daughter of a conservative Christian minister. During her high school days, she was the picture-perfect Christian young lady. Sheila was very active in the church, which made her father very proud. She decided to go to a Christian college to prepare for work in church music.

When Sheila started college, several traumatic events happened in rapid succession. Her boyfriend of three years convinced her to begin a sexual relationship even though they did not plan marriage for several years. After their initial sexual encounter, the boyfriend quickly lost interest in Sheila and they broke up. Hurt and confused, Sheila had no one to talk with. She certainly could not tell her family about the sexual relationship. She dated other men and started to sexually act out, which increased her shame and confusion. She paid no attention to birth control; in fact, she knew very little about birth control or about sex. After a few months, she became pregnant. She had no idea who the father was.

Sheila did not believe in abortion, so she knew she could not keep the pregnancy from her parents. She went home and told her parents the whole truth. They were devastated. Her father was enraged. In a fit of anger, he slapped his daughter and told her to leave.

In the following weeks, Sheila's father openly rejected and condemned his daughter. He stated she was not welcome in church, and she was "not to ever come back inside the Lord's house again." Eventually, her father refused to speak to her. We came to know Sheila after she sought help following an attempted suicide.

This sad story reflects several ways Christian beliefs can lead to or result in abusive and destructive behaviors. The following behaviors, in our opinions, are the result of Abusive Christianity and will be discussed in the book:

- Perfectionistic behavior.
- Abandonment after sexual relationships.
- Guilt, shame, and fear.
- Lack of communication.
- Sexual acting out.
- Lack of sexual knowledge.
- Violent and angry parental behavior.
- Punishment.

These are a few of the abusive and destructive behaviors that we will examine on our journey to understanding and recovering from

Abusive Christianity. You may discover yourself along the way, or recognize your friends and family members.

Before we begin our exploration, though, we want to make one point about our approach to the subject of Abusive Christianity. You do not cure abuse by being abusive, and we will not take an abusive stand against Christian religion. Rather, we intend to point out the destructive aspects of commonly accepted Christianity. Our own lives, along with work with patients and individuals who have shared their stories with us, form the basis of our position. That is, we believe that Christian religion advocates beliefs and practices which ultimately hurt people. There is a dark side to "The Light."

WHAT IS ABUSIVE CHRISTIANITY?

Abusive Christianity is Christianity that hurts people, and we think that Christian beliefs and practices are a major source of abuse in our culture. By Christianity, we are referring to the "down the street" churches, such as Apostolic Churches; Assembly of God; Southern, Fundamental, General, Missionary, and Primitive Baptists; Catholic; Christian Science; Church of Christ; Holiness; Churches of Jesus Christ of Latter-Day Saints; Nazarene, and most charismatic, fundamental, evangelical, and gospel churches.

These religions espouse certain beliefs. They believe God is currently involved with man and has chosen to reveal himself to man via His Son, Jesus, the Christ. Other beliefs typical of these religions are:

- Jesus was divine
- There is a Holy Spirit.
- There is a heaven and there is a hell.
- In order to go to heaven, you must be "saved," and to be saved you must believe certain doctrines or perform certain acts (such as baptism).
- God is involved with people.
- God is responsible for all the good in the world.
- God can and will reward you for your behavior. Success is not due to your hard work. God gives success.

- God punishes people, or "allows" punishment to happen, because of their bad behavior or to "teach them a lesson" or for some mysterious reason which "only He understands."
- God is in control of your life and your future.
- God is to be feared, because He has the power to send you to hell, and He has control of your future.
- The Bible is the unerring, divinely inspired Word of God.
- The Bible is the ultimate authority.

One does not have to look far to find examples of abuse within most religions. The recent book *Toxic Faith* by Arterburn and Felton is chock-full of examples of devil worship, cult activity, and even murders that were committed because some individual believed that God "told me to do it." When we narrow the field to Christianity, abuse is still easy to find. Oral Roberts comes quickly to mind. It is so obvious "televangelists" are abusive that we do not intend to address this issue at length. Oral Roberts has not actually done anything illegal—at least that we are aware of. However, he *was* talking, in a vision, to a 900-foot Jesus who was going to take him "Home" unless people sent in millions of dollars in donations.

Hopefully, most people laughed about the 900-foot Jesus. Personally, we wondered why he did not just round it off to an even thousand feet! Far less humorous is the fact that thousands of individuals sent in money—in many cases, money they could not afford to send.

These people are abused by their own belief system, expecting that God will do something special for them or for their loved ones if they contribute money. So they respond by sending in thousands of dollars, hoping for health, wealth, happiness, or favor from God.

Further, they are abused by belief in an individual they think they can trust. These "Christian ministers" promise their listeners will receive blessings from God. These promises are from a "man of God," so people trust them. The evangelist is the one that benefits most. These "televangelists" have taken literally millions of dollars from trusting individuals, all with the blessings and in the name of Christianity. It is almost as if people think that God could be bribed or "bought off."

Consider this comparison: A headline in the local paper (*The Fort Worth Star-Telegram*) on March 12, 1991, stated in large bold letters, "**WOMAN, 82, CHARGED $17,136 FOR $500 JOB**." Some "businessmen," and we use that term lightly, devoid of both morals and compassion, charged an elderly lady more than $17,000 for yard work worth less than $500. People were indignant about this woman's abuse.

However, if the elderly woman had mailed her money to any one of the TV evangelists to buy favors from God, no one would have said a word. The news media would probably have little interest in that story. If people will not confront this type of blatant abuse—that is, these televangelists taking literally millions of dollars from people who cannot afford it—they certainly will not confront the abuses they see in conventional everyday Christianity.

This reflects the way our society currently thinks and behaves. People do not want to be seen as standing against "Christianity," even if it is abusive! *The tacit rule is: Do not confront abuse when it is from Christian organizations.*

Not only large organizations perpetrate abuse. Well-meaning people also condemn, manipulate, or hurt others because of the destructive nature of their Christian beliefs. Parents abuse their children, churches abuse their followers, families withdraw love and support, individuals are depressed, angry, fearful, anxious, withdrawn, upset, perfectionistic, and are dysfunctional in a myriad of other ways, all because of the abusive nature of certain beliefs and practices commonly found in Christianity. These concepts are being preached and "pounded into" (a term that Jerry's minister used while trying to teach him religious concepts) these abused individuals by their well-meaning parents and by well-meaning, but nonetheless dysfunctional preachers and Sunday school teachers.

Further, many sexual dysfunctions result from the fearful, constrictive, and negative nature of Christian sexual ethics. A March 20,

1992, story by the Associated Press reported that seven Chicago priests had been removed from parishes or indicted because of complaints they sexually abused children. Note that the seven only included those who had been caught, only included Catholic denominations, only included the Chicago area, and only included child sexual offenders. What are the real numbers for the whole country? What if the study were expanded to include all denominations? And what if the study were expanded to include all other sexual behaviors not condoned by Christianity? Would there be anyone left to do the study? In our own city, local assistant district attorneys assure us that an inordinate number of ministers are charged with sexual abuse crimes.

We know the world is full of "perverts" and a number of them will be found in Christianity. However, we are convinced that abusive Christianity can set up and facilitate this type of sexual dysfunction along with many others.

There are many concepts in Christianity which we believe are abusive. By "abusive," we mean that these ideas directly hurt people, can be used to hurt people or set into motion behaviors and attitudes which end up damaging people and their relationships. Some of these concepts are:

- Heaven and hell.
- Original sin.
- Salvation.
- Prayer as magic.
- The Holy Spirit.
- God controls people and their lives.
- Punishment for sin.
- Anger leads to punishment.
- Sex is sinful.
- Masturbation is wrong.
- God is "male" and only men should be in positions of authority.
- Homosexuality is a sin.
- God withdraws love and punishes with anger or hell.
- The world can be broken down into good and bad.

This does not mean that if you believe in any of these concepts, you are automatically abused or will abuse others. The way these beliefs are presented to people may be abusive, or frequently, these beliefs structure how a person thinks and deals with the world. This thinking and approach to life may be destructive or abusive.

These concepts form a system of beliefs by which people can live their lives and raise their families. That is, they form a basis, or a model, upon which a family system can function. For instance, consider the concepts of original sin and punishment. Families which function according to this Christian model may see their children as "bad" (sinners) simply because of the concept of original sin. The child is not seen as a good child who happens to be behaving in a bad manner. The Christian concept is that people are born into sin: "We are all sinners." This idea does not distinguish the person from the behavior. The child is simply *bad*. Furthermore, these "bad" children should be punished, which is consistent with Christian beliefs, as opposed to being understood and lovingly corrected to help them change their behavior. What you believe influences how you behave. If you believe that children are bad, then you will act that way. You will punish them.

This concept of dividing people into "good and bad" and "punishment for all sinners" is as common in our culture as it is ineffective. Consider the discipline in our school systems and our prison systems, both of which use punishment. We all know how ineffective they have been in teaching morality and facilitating change. Prisons seem to teach prisoners two things: to be better and more efficient criminals, and to be more violent. Not only does punishment not work, it often makes conditions worse. However, punishment for sins is one of the most basic beliefs of Christianity. This belief formed the basis for the use of punishment in our culture, and this belief alone causes widespread abuse and dysfunction.

Pointing out abuses found within and caused by Christianity is a very sensitive area, and we are certain these ideas will be controversial. We also know this book will make certain people very angry. We do not wish to hurt or offend people. Indeed, we both work in professions which help people. In our attempt to help, there will be some who are offended and hurt. For us to suggest that the ideas and practices of Christianity have hurt people and are currently hurting people will probably not endear us to the followers of Christian religion.

However, we feel the time is right to look at abuse within Christianity. People are becoming more sensitive to the ideas and issues of abuse, and it is time they realized that religious beliefs, specifically Christian beliefs, can be dangerous. What you believe can, indeed, hurt you and cause you to hurt others.

WHO IS AFFECTED BY ABUSIVE CHRISTIANITY?

Christianity dominates our entire culture. The destructive aspects of Christianity directly hurt people, or lead people to hurt others. The people who commit this type of abuse usually have been victims of abuse. They have been exposed to or manipulated by destructive ideas and beliefs. They, in turn, internalize these destructive beliefs and they identify with the person that taught them the abusive concepts. They use that person as a model and they abuse others in the same style of behavior. So the abuse grows like the proverbial snowball rolling downhill.

Religions, with angry and aggressive theologies, have caused people to act out in a hostile and aggressive manner throughout history. A good example of this, outside of the Christian faith, is the Islamic belief of Jihad, or holy war. Inside the Christian religion, we have the notorious examples of The Inquisition and the burning of "witches" and other "unholy" people in the early history of the United States. Our forefathers believed that witches were "evil" or possessed by the devil. Given that belief and the belief that God was "at war" with Satan, then the appropriate treatment would be punishment or to put that unholy individual to death. Our forefathers' behavior was consistent with their beliefs.

Christian abusers believe they know "The Truth," and they are doing the "Right Thing." They believe this to be in the best interest of the "lost soul" involved or in the best interest of God's holy church. They do not perceive their behavior as abusive because they are following the will or orders which they strongly feel are ordained by God.

In all probability, the people who burned witches were not mean or bad people. They were influenced and controlled by a destructive belief system. They truly believed in demons and that these demons were incarnate evil—that individuals who were "possessed by demons" were dangerous. These demon-possessed individuals were condemned by God anyway, so it made sense to sacrifice them.

A more modern example of the same type behavior is the church minister who commits adultery or is discovered to be homosexual. The church members will probably expect the minister to leave the church. They do not try to help or understand. Tolerance is not consistent with their belief system. They will withdraw fellowship as a form of punishment, believing that is "the right thing to do." The members will not see themselves as lacking love, understanding, or compassion. They will see themselves as "right."

This concept of doing the "right thing" and punishing or "getting rid of evil people," reaches beyond the impact of the local Christian churches. The primary source of values in our culture is the Judeo-Christian ethic. Almost anyone who has been reared in our culture is affected by this abusive Christian concept. All of us are subjected to principles which are influenced by Christian thought. For example, public schools act on the concept of punish and then banish (by expelling) errant students. Unacceptable people in our society are banished to prisons where the atmosphere is punishing. These same principles are found in Christian churches today.

The notion of original sin influences our belief about the basic nature of people. If we believed they are basically good, or positive and growth-oriented in nature, all we would need to do is to stay out of the way and they would develop into good persons. We would tend to treat people as if they would learn from their mistakes. We would treat them with respect, kindness, and consideration. We would love and encourage them.

However, if we thought that man was evil, bad, and basically sinful, then we would treat adults and children accordingly. We would discipline them and punish them to rid them of their evil and sinful ways. According to Christianity, the basic nature of man is that he is born in sin. He *is* a sinner, an evil creature and he needs to be changed, to be saved. (The statement that "*he* is born in sin" is common of the prejudice against women in Christianity. In this instance, it may have worked in their favor. Men are violent in larger numbers and punished by prison in larger numbers.) If that sinner is not saved, he or she faces everlasting punishment in hell according to Christianity. It doesn't get much more punishing or abusive than that!

Christians have taught these beliefs for centuries. Instead of loving and helping those that have gone astray, we "cast stones" at the sinners. We banish and punish. This belief of punishment for sins is one of the basic beliefs which fuels child abusers.

Abusive Christianity also defines our culture's sexual ethics. Take, as an example, the movie ratings. Explicit sexual interaction, even between "married couples," is taboo on the screen and will receive a triple-X rating. However, violence is much more acceptable. The cinematic screen can show brutal, vicious violence and murder and receive an R rating. Movies do not receive triple-X ratings for explicit violence. This bizarre ethic leads to the insane belief that normal, consensual, marital sex is worse than brutal violence and murder.

In Christianity, this is true. Christian history is saturated with violence, from the destruction of entire cities for immoral behavior to the violent death of Jesus. Man is so evil (original sin) that God's Son had to die a violent death so man would not be punished forever by that same God.

It's so ironic—Christianity does not consider threatening people with the everlasting damnation and destruction of hell as violent, because that is what Christians believe! Christians do not view this violent threat as immoral. Violence is acceptable in our culture, partly because it is part of the Abusive Christian Belief.

Sex is evil, but violence is acceptable. No wonder people in our culture are confused about sex and violence!

WHY THIS SUBJECT HAS NOT BEEN ADDRESSED

No one seems to want to confront Abusive Christianity! This surprises us, because many people seem to understand that a great deal of abuse parades around under the guise of Christianity. When we told people we were writing a book on Abusive Christianity, many responded, "Well, it's about time." Most comments have been positive and encouraging, and many individuals took advantage of the opportunity to tell us their stories of fears, anger, pain, and psychological injuries caused by Abusive Christianity.

With so much material available, why have not more books been written on this subject? Books on every other type of abuse flood bookstore shelves.

It is obvious to us that little is written about Abusive Christianity because of the anticipated negative reaction from Christians. Like their neighbors. Their co-workers. Their friends. Their families. They are afraid of abuse from the followers of Christianity. Many Christians are very angry people, and remember—they believe in punishment!

Several people have commented that we will be the "Salman Rushdies" of our community. We also heard reactions like: "You will be run out of town on a rail by the Southern Baptists!" "Do you plan to live in this area?" "God help you, the fanatics sure won't!" "God can certainly handle it, but can the people?"

One of our patients, Susan, had been reared in a very conservative Pentecostal religion. Susan had attended several therapy sessions when she changed jobs and, as a result, had no insurance. She needed help with personal problems but did not have the finances to afford counseling. She was asked, in lieu of payment, if she would be willing to share her religious beliefs. She was so excited that she called her mother. With no prompting, and no knowledge of the topic of this book, her mother said in a threatening manner, "You are going to talk to your therapist about our religion, aren't you?" Susan said she felt immediately "dirty... filthy." She feared she would be a disgrace to the family if she talked about her religion. From her mother's reaction, she clearly was forbidden to talk about her religion.

Secrecy is one of the standards of dysfunctional families, and Susan's family was dysfunctional. Claudia Black, in her book *It Will Never Happen to Me,* outlines the four rules of dysfunctional, addicted families as: DON'T TRUST, DON'T TALK, DON'T FEEL, and ACT LIKE EVERYTHING IS OKAY. Susan's family certainly followed those rules. If she broke the rules, by breaking the secrecy, Susan feared her family would reject her.

In Susan's family, adhering to Christian rules came first. "To mother, religion comes before anything, including me," she said. She felt secondary to her mother's religion, and she knew her life, her different ideas, and views would not be tolerated. Her attitude was, "I am wrong if I don't agree with Mom and the church's religion."

Given the power of the printed word, if people are afraid to talk about Abusive Christianity, how much more afraid would they be to write about it? Or, upon reading a draft of this book, one publisher commented, "How do you feel about being crucified?"

Emotions always run high when people question the beliefs and practices of any religion, especially Christianity. Two decades ago, as a student at Southwestern Baptist Theological Seminary, Jerry did a research paper on the different Christian religions. He identified 2,200 different Christian denominations. All of these religions were "Christian," but their separateness shows that they do not agree with each other. Frequently, within a single denomination, liberal and conservative elements not only disagree with each other, but are in "turf battles." These internal battles are destructive, angry, and abusive.

To call Christianity to account for its abuses would be to draw anger from all these elements. It is not a task to be taken lightly, and quite frankly one that may prove dangerous. All of the Baptists, both liberal and conservative, may attack us! They may even, God forbid, call in the Methodists.

However, it is the nature of people to question. We will not shy away from the task because of fear or controversy. We will present ideas and concepts that may be disagreeable to some people. However, we think we must ask these questions and face the abuse buried within Christian religion.

THE HALO EFFECT

People see what they want to see. This bias is called the "halo effect." When something is widely accepted as good, right, and correct, even trained observers tend to distort their perceptions to fit this standard. In our society, most people see Christianity as good and as the hope for our future. Therefore, the halo effect demands that people will distort their perceptions to see Christianity as "good and correct," regardless of the abuses that may occur. Many people, consistent with the "halo effect," parade around in the theater of Christianity acting as if everything is wonderful and beautiful. That is what their bias mandates. But one does not have to look far to see that much pain, agony, and misery are still growing from the roots of Christianity.

We ask you to set aside any halo effect and follow us in our journey, a journey which may be frightening for some and enlightening for others. A journey which, we promise, can have a happy ending. We will be challenging beliefs that you have been comfortable with all your life. We will be talking about issues most people think are sacred, such as salvation, prayer, personal relationship with God, original sin, the nature of God, punishment, good and evil. We will be talking about how Christianity can enter the twenty-first century, and in a happy and satisfying manner.

We do not ask you to agree with all the ideas and concepts presented in this book. All we ask is for you to think about them. If you are confident in your faith, there is certainly no danger in thinking. If you are a victim of Christian Abuse or an abuser because of what you have been taught to believe, we hope this book will help you.

WHAT CAN BE DONE

Jack Ryan, the protagonist in Tom Clancy's military thriller *Clear and Present Danger*, states,

> Either you stand for something, or you don't, ... Any jackass could be against things, like a petulant child claiming to hate an untasted vegetable. (p. 498)

Spirituality is an essential and vital part of the human experience. However, as Christians, we must also stand against abuse wherever it exists. We must stand against those ideas and concepts which contribute to human misery regardless of their source and for those abused individuals who have abandoned spirituality in their lives because of Christian abuse.

Many victims of Abusive Christianity are angry with God and religion and do not want to have anything to do with either. Along with toxic and abusive Christianity, they also give up spirituality. They give up the part of themselves which helps them feel connected to people and the world around them. In essence, they give up a large part of being human. Many of these abused individuals are attracted to eastern religions or fringe religions. Some even end up in toxic cults and are abused again. Some end up making money, sex, power, or organizations their religion in an attempt to fill their spiritual needs.

The recovery from abuse, whether caused by religion or not, is spiritual in nature. Christian religions divide and injure people. The spiritual unites and heals people. *It is the spiritual nature of man that is damaged by Abusive Christianity.* The recovery from this abuse will need to be spiritual. There is no abuse in genuine spirituality. It is a force which pulls people together. However, we must warn that any endeavor which involves people can end up being abusive.

One major difference, and there are many, between religion and spirituality is that religion is divisive. Religion tends to divide people and to classify people. You are either a Baptist, a Catholic, a Methodist, or some other religious classification. But you are different from, and do not agree with and are not similar to, an individual with a different classification. You may not like that person, and probably would not associate with that person simply because of religion.

Jerry recalls that as a young Baptist, he was taught to fear Catholics and to certainly not befriend them. Catholics were dangerous people. When John F. Kennedy became president, there was a great deal of fear in the Baptist Church that the country might be controlled by Rome. The fear was that people who believe differently than you are potentially dangerous to you and especially to your belief system. Many Christian ideas and concepts teach us to fear and not tolerate people who are different from us. So for a long time, Jerry was afraid of Catholics. He would not even talk about Jews!

On the other hand, spirituality brings people together. We believe spiritual needs should be met in healthy ways. A major purpose of this book is to help define what is Abusive Christianity and what is healthy spirituality.

We want to make it clear that Christianity and spirituality are not the same. Religion is a means by which we attempt to meet our spiritual needs. *Many times religion is actually counter to spirituality.* This is sad since so many people depend upon organized Christian religions to meet their spiritual needs.

We will attempt to provide options for meeting spiritual needs. The reason many people aren't "spiritually starved" is that unconsciously they discover endless ways to express their spirituality. You may be surprised at what you are already doing to meet your spiritual needs. There are healthy, natural, and fulfilling experiences which not only touch and nurture your spirit but help keep your body healthier, too.

If you have been confused about your Christian experience, we hope this book will help you better understand your feelings about what has happened to you, why abusive beliefs proliferate in Christianity and what you can do to heal and nurture the spiritual part of yourself that has been wounded. If you have felt isolated, you will find that you are not alone.

CHAPTER 2

DEFINITION WITHIN THE DARKNESS
Abusive Christianity

*"For now we see
through a glass, darkly;
but then
face to face..."*

I CORINTHIANS 13: 12

A buse occurs when one person injures, hurts, or mistreats another person. Abuse, then, is a function of unhealthy human interaction. During the past decade, therapists have focused a great deal of attention on the causes of this unhealthy interaction, including the study of alcoholic and addicted families, neglectful and abusive families, and the impact these families have upon their children. Very little focus has been given to the beliefs and practices of Christianity as a source of and cause of abuse.

DYSFUNCTIONAL FAMILIES

John and Linda Friel, in their book *Adult Children: The Secrets of Dysfunctional Families*, list these characteristics found in dysfunctional families:

1. Physical, emotional, or sexual abuse/neglect and vicarious abuse.
2. Perfectionism.
3. Rigid rules, life style, and/or belief systems.

4. The "No Talk Rule" / Keeping "The Family Secrets."
5. Inability to identify and/or express feelings.
6. Triangulation (a communication pattern using one person as intermediary).
7. Double messages/double binds.
8. Inability to play, have fun, and be spontaneous.
9. High tolerance for inappropriate behavior/pain.
10. Enmeshment. (see Friel and Friel, pp. 74-75)

Even at first glance, it is obvious that many of these characteristics are found in Christian beliefs and in Christian families which suggests that dysfunction occurs in these families.

In looking at dysfunctional families, theorists typically study the belief system of the family, the interactions between family members, or the system of rules found in the family. They especially study the interaction between the mother and father, because that is the model of behavior the children generally follow. Family interaction is based, in part, upon the parents' beliefs and the rules they follow in dealing with each other and their children. If there is neglect or abuse, the source will be found in these rules, beliefs, and family interactions.

The tools of our journey are ideas, concepts, and theories. One should understand the use and limits of the tools, so we must examine and understand what we mean by "theories." We will then build a basic theory about neglect and abuse. For the sake of discussion, we will build a theory including different types of neglect and abuse, arranging these types in a hierarchy, even though there are inherent problems with this type of hierarchy.

As a general rule, abuse is worse than neglect because of the psychological damage it does to the child. However, there are situations in which gross neglect is worse than mild abuse, and therein lies the problem. The hierarchy cannot be rigid. Regardless, as a general rule, abuse is more psychologically damaging and harder on children than neglect. The continuum presented here ranges from no abuse or neglect to severe physical abuse and death of the child.

After examining these concepts and building our theory, we will apply these ideas to Christianity.

CONTINUUM OF NEGLECT-ABUSE

1. NO NEGLECT OR ABUSE. This is the perfect family. It is emotionally available and open, caring, and loving.

2. EMOTIONAL NEGLECT. This parental system is emotionally not available for the children. The parents are emotionally absent. The parents either work all the time or they are involved with hobbies or other ventures.

3. PHYSICAL NEGLECT. This parental system intentionally neglects the physical care the children need.

4. VERBAL ABUSE. This parental system yells at or verbally demeans the child. We use the term "emotional abuse," meaning the child can be abused by the emotional tone alone. "Content abuse" is when the content of the message is abusive.

5. PHYSICAL ABUSE. This is when the parental system abuses the child by hitting, slapping, or in some way physically assaulting the child.

6. SEVERE ABUSE. This is when the parental system severely physically abuses and physically injures the child, often resulting in death.

REIFICATION

Reification is difficult to understand. It is rare that we think about how we think, but that is precisely what we are going to do here. So, slow down, relax, and get ready to think about how you think.

There is a big difference between real life and all of these nice theories constructed to help us understand life experiences. People frequently become confused between the theories and real life experiences. Why is this important? Because people fight and argue over words, ideas, concepts, and doctrine, which they mistakenly accept as reality. The world of reality and the world of words are not the same.

In the English language, the word "is" contributes to this confusion. That word leads us to think we are dealing with reality, with real life, and not simply with concepts, ideas, and theories. At times, people become perplexed, confusing ideas and concepts with real life experiences. This confusion is called "reification." The verb is "to reify."

To use a simple example, consider the statement, "This is a chair." Technically, that statement is incorrect. Chair is the word, the term, we use to describe an object you sit on. We frequently confuse the term "chair" with the object. As if that were not difficult enough to understand, this confusion becomes even worse when we use abstract terms such as "love," "abuse," or "God."

Real life experiences and feelings are nonverbal. Ideas and concepts are made up of words. We become aware of the difference between ideas and experiences when we have an experience that does not lend itself to words, such as the joy of music or the taste of strawberries.

When people "get in touch" with their experiences, there are generally very few words and thus little to argue over. Experiences pull people together, unite people. Words and ideas about those experiences often cause debate and differences of opinions. Words can often ruin meaningful experiences, much like religion can often destroy spirituality. While visiting a psychiatrist friend in California, Jerry had an experience that illustrated this point.

> I was once in California with a friend who is a psychiatrist. We were watching the sun set over the ocean as the clouds and sun painted the sky with a variety of magnificent shapes and colors. The sky, ocean, and clouds were beautiful beyond words. The experience was wonderful and peaceful. The psychiatrist, in his typically analytical way, started describ-

ing and trying to label all of the colors and shades of colors. There were several colors he debated about with himself. "Is it purple, magenta, or a deep red?" I became annoyed with this need to label. For me, the experience was shattered by this debate.

People can argue whether God exists or "Is God love?" "Is He omnipotent?" "Is He omniscient?" All Christian denominations say, "God *is* omnipotent." "The Bible is divinely inspired." They claim to have "The Truth." The material in this book is not "The Truth" about reality. You must judge if these theories fit you and your experience. If the ideas apply to you, use them; if not, at least you will have been exposed to a different perspective. No scientific theory is "The Truth." It is only theory.

The terms in our hierarchy of abuse are easy, separate, and distinct. They are: The Perfect Family, Emotional Neglect, and Physical Neglect. However, putting into terms one's own experience of neglect is not always so easy, separate, and distinct. We have to be careful not to reify these labels. Remember, *reify means to confuse the experience with the label.* Experience is much more complex. In reality, emotional and physical neglect will overlap.

THE PERFECT FAMILY

Now, let's begin to construct the theory, the Continuum of Neglect/Abuse. For the theory to begin at the starting point, there must be a Perfect Family where the parents are always available. These perfect parents are attentive to their children, always emotionally open, and respond to them in a consistently caring manner. They know how to deal with anger in a nondestructive manner, intimately sharing their personal issues of hurt and fear in a way that does not injure their children or cause pain, fear, or feelings of rejection and abandonment. They are able to deal with these emotional issues and not repress them. As a result, they get to know and understand each other at deeper and deeper levels, growing closer and closer in a nonpossessive manner.

We frequently recommend that our patients read the self-help books on codependency and dysfunctional families. One complaint we hear about this literature is, "Everyone is codependent," and "All families are dysfunctional to one extent or another." This is another example of reification—confusing the model or theory with reality. Families are families and our theories are the best we can do at this point. Theories frequently break down at the extremes. However, the theory of the Perfect Family does represent a goal. It is important to attempt to understand ourselves and our families so we can grow closer and more intimate.

EMOTIONAL NEGLECT

To some extent, there will be Emotional Neglect in every family. It is simply impossible for a parent to be emotionally available, at all times, in every circumstance, and there are no Perfect Families, except in theory. Emotional neglect, or a lack of emotional availability on the part of the parent, is the first step in our hierarchy of neglect and abuse.

Parents may be unavailable simply because they may be ill, have other children with needs, and have work pressures or other concerns. If such lack of emotional availability creates feelings of abandonment in a child, and it certainly can, then everyone is from a dysfunctional family. It depends on the experience of the child involved. It is probably safe to assume that almost everyone has some type of psychological injury due to emotional neglect from their family of origin. In some cases the theories make it appear that everyone needs therapy.

Many excellent books have been written about the effects of dysfunctional families on children and how these children subsequently develop as adults. We have included a list of recommended readings at the end of this book, to cover many areas of abuse and neglect and the effect on adults reared in such environments.

In short, to the extent that your parents were not emotionally available to you, you developed as a survivor and as an adult probably will have some problems. We will call these problems "psychological injuries."

PHYSICAL NEGLECT

When the physical needs of the child are not being met, the critical questions are: Why are they not? Is it intentional? Are the parents spending money on themselves and neglecting the needs of the child? To some extent the neglect will either be willful on the part of the parents or a product of the circumstances of the parents.

Both situations can have a powerful impact. In the case of willful Physical Neglect, there is a likelihood that there will also be Emotional Neglect, and the psychological injury will be more extensive. A person reared in this environment is likely to experience more difficulty with relationships and self-concept.

Regina initially sought help with marital problems. Over the past few years, her feelings for her husband diminished. She felt distant and estranged from him. She was active in her church and found herself attracted to a man who was a member of the same church. They worked closely on a committee together . No one else knew about their emotional involvement. Even though their relationship was not sexual, she was too ashamed to talk to anyone about it, and she especially would not talk to anyone at church.

Regina's personal history was interesting. She referred to her father as a "good man." He was never at home because he had to work all the time. Her father's job required that he dress very well and drive a nice car. Financially the rest of the family suffered. Even though it was never talked about, Regina felt very neglected by her father. As a child, some of her schoolmates made fun of her poor dresses, while pointing out her father's obvious affluence. Physically, emotionally, and financially, her father was not there for her. This neglect hurt Regina and the hurt showed in her adult relationships.

The person who is a victim of poverty while coming from a caring and an emotionally available family is still a victim of poverty. There will be scars. But the trauma will be less difficult to cope with, as a general rule, than the child who also suffers Emotional Neglect along with Physical Neglect.

Our history is rich with individuals who were reared in very poor environments, but received the psychological support and nurturance, or had the individual tenacity, to rise above their environment and accomplish great things. Chances are good these individuals received emotional and psychological support and nurturance somewhere— perhaps from friends, neighbors, teachers, relatives, or church.

The child who is willfully neglected physically and emotionally is not without hope. But without help from someone, he or she is certainly at a greater disadvantage than the child who has caring and available parents. If we increase the neglect, chances are great we will increase the complexity and depth of the psychological injuries.

The "lack of physical availability" simply means that the parent or parent surrogate is not there. That is, the parents are not physically available to the child even though the child may be adequately cared for. Situations which create this are varied and complex. The parents may be deceased. The child may be adopted and miss his or her natural parents. The child may be reared by the state. All of these situations can create psychological injury.

There is one situation which demands special attention. That is the child who is very well physically cared for, but the parents are rarely home. The child may be reared by maids or by a nanny and be very well cared for financially, but the parents are not physically available. The parents may work all the time or work two jobs. These circumstances can scar the child. The critical question is to what extent the child experiences Emotional Neglect due to the parent's absence and the neglect causes psychological injuries.

PSYCHOLOGICAL INJURY

Our culture is not very understanding about "psychological injuries." We understand physical injury because we can see those scars. We cannot see psychological injuries—there is no scar in your brain—but they are nonetheless real.

How can we know that these childhood "injuries" carry over to adulthood? We know because if you were neglected or abused as a child, these injuries will show in your attitudes, feelings, and behavior. The childhood trauma created psychological defenses and behaviors (often unconscious) by which you attempted to cope with the neglect and abuse. These defenses and coping behaviors are now a part of how you protect yourself from people and the neglect and abuse you feel you may receive from them. The childhood injuries will especially show in your intimate relationships.

Let's say that your family of origin was emotionally neglectful. That is, as a child, you did not receive the attention and the positive affection and nurturing that you needed. You will develop "psychological scars" from those childhood injuries. These injuries could include a lack of trusting that people really love you and will be emotionally available to you, a fear of closeness, or perhaps some difficulty with self confidence and self-esteem. You may experience these scars as a feeling of emptiness or a feeling of loneliness. You may feel depressed, unhappy, sad, guilty, helpless, and hopeless to some extent.

These psychological injuries may only be serious enough to help us empathize and understand the feelings of those in worse situations. In "normal" situations, these scars will probably not create debilitation in adult life. As we increase the trauma in our scale of neglect and abuse, the injuries and the symptoms suffered will increase.

The more minimal the family dysfunction, the fewer the psychological scars and resulting individual symptoms. With increased abuse, the scars become more extensive.

VERBAL ABUSE

The parent or caregiver who verbally demeans or insults a child so as to induce fear, hurt, or a negative emotional reaction in that child is inflicting verbal abuse. It generally increases trauma and psychological injury to the child a step above neglect alone. A parent yelling and saying demeaning things to a child is certainly not emotionally available to the child. On top of not being emotionally available, the parent is actively engaged in verbally hurting the child. Furthermore, verbal abuse is willful—the commission of an act, not an omission, as is neglect. Thus, verbal abuse is generally more traumatic to the child than simple neglect alone.

Any type of abuse, as a general rule, will cause more psychological damage and psychological scarring to the child than will neglect. This is not to minimize neglect. The trauma depends upon the sensitivity of the child and how the child will react in a given situation.

EMOTIONAL ABUSE VS. CONTENT ABUSE

This is a very easy discrimination to make, but nonetheless an important one. Example: Jerry has an Australian cattle dog named Pepper. This strange animal is highly responsive to emotional tones in voices. If he hears an angry voice tone, even on television, he manages to lower his entire bulk and creep along inches off the floor, slinking away to seek refuge under his protective coffee table. It does not matter what is said or to whom the message is directed. Pepper responds to emotional tone, even if the content of the message is positive.

Conversely, people can respond in a negative manner to a message, even if the emotional tone in which the message is given is positive. If the message carries a negative content, the response to the message will be stressful and negative. Examples of this are a physician disclosing a very serious illness to a patient, or authorities delivering the message that a loved one has been injured in an accident. The emotional tone of the message will be neutral or even caring. The content of the message elicits hurt, fear, or pain.

Therefore, people can respond to the content of the message or the emotional tone of the message. Content abuse, which is abusive if one believes the message, regardless of the emotional tone or jesting demeanor of the deliverer, would include statements such as "you are worthless," "you are stupid," "you are nothing but a failure," "you are no good."

As a general rule, the emotional tone and the content of the verbal message are consistent. However, in Christian religion one frequently hears a message in a very loving and caring tone, but the content of the message is truly frightening and distressing. This type of abuse we will call "Content Abuse."

PHYSICAL ABUSE

Physical abuse, in its milder forms, is difficult to identify and define. One definition could be any physical contact with a child that is unwanted by that child or that will induce fear, hurt, anger, or some other negative emotion. Is spanking a child physical abuse? The motives of some parents may be positive and their intentions good, but they hurt their children nonetheless. Does it depend on how hard you spank the child? Should schools spank children? To debate these questions would be a book in itself.

When we look into the more severe forms of physical abuse, none of us has difficulty identifying the abuse. We have worked with children who have been severely beaten, shot at by their parents, and subjected to electrical shock. No question—that's abusive. Furthermore, there is no way for a child to suffer severe physical abuse without significant psychological scars. Without question, this type of abuse is the most damaging and the most severe.

In the city where we live, Fort Worth, two children in recent years have been murdered by their parents or by people living with the biological parent. Another child was chained and starved until he was brain dead. In jail, his parents complained when their first meal was late. Yes, abuse can extract the ultimate price from the child— death. There is no greater family dysfunction than that.

CHRISTIAN ABUSE

Christian Abuse is generally verbal abuse and emotional abuse, although in certain situations, it can become physical abuse. Christian Abuse happens when one individual causes harm, a negative emotional reaction (fear, intimidation, rejection) or psychological injury to another individual, and the motivation behind the abusive act is Christian doctrine, belief, or practice.

An example could be a preacher who causes fear and terror in a child "in need of salvation," by using threats of no life after death, hell, and/or eternal suffering. Another example would be the father who demeans, yells, and perhaps physically abuses his daughter because of an unwed pregnancy. In these examples, the Christian Abuse is an abusive attempt to force people to "change their ways," or to manipulate a person into believing what is seen as proper doctrine or belief. Christian Abuse may be an attempt to shame or punish another individual for evil acts.

Christian Abuse, then, is an act by a person which compromises, or psychologically or physically injures, another person. We recently saw a tape of one "evangelist" who was having people fax in prayer requests. He was "laying hands" on the fax machine making sure they understood "the more you give, the more your reward." We recall Oral Roberts saying he needed some "quick money," or the Lord would call him home. These are examples of blatant Christian Abuse.

A less dramatic form of Christian Abuse comes closer to home. Almost daily, people are subjected to messages to "accept Jesus as their Savior." They are not simply presented the information and left to make a rational decision. They are abused—manipulated with fear, false hope, guilt, and shame to accept and obey the tenets of the religion.

Christians, with good intentions, chastise and condemn young unwed mothers, drug abusers, homosexuals, people of different ethnic groups (at least they do not invite them into their churches), people with different beliefs, people who drink, gamblers, prostitutes, unbelievers, and on and on. These people are not welcome in the church, unless, of course, they believe the proper doctrine, change, clean up, and dress nicely. The church could—and, in our opinion, should—be a haven of help for the poor and the downtrodden, the drug abusers, and the prostitutes. After all, aren't those the types of people that Christ helped?

Jerry had a friend in Fort Worth who was a street minister. No, he never stood in any street to preach. He went to bars. He helped alcoholics, prostitutes. and runaway kids—people who are unwelcome in traditional church. When some of thesee people attempted to go to a local church, they were asked to leave. They were not dressed appropriately. They looked like street people because they were street people. They were told they would make the members "uncomfortable." This type of Christian Abuse is one of the most painful abuses. It is one of rejection/abandonment because people look different.

Christian Abuse goes beyond neglect but includes it, simply because when you abuse, you neglect. Religious dogma can also predispose a person, say a parent, to be neglectful. In the doctrine of the church, the rules are the rules and they are not open for examination or for compromise. There is no way to remain "emotionally available" to the needs of a child, say, to dance or wear make-up, if your rigid rule system forbids it.

Take the example of an adolescent who is starting to date and is now going "steady." Petting is becoming more and more sexual and the young couple is "getting carried away." If the youngster knows that the position of the church is "no sex before marriage," and his or her parents believe that doctrine, he or she will probably figure the parents will not be "emotionally available" to listen to fears and struggles with the issue. We have heard countless parents, good parents, simply say "that's wrong," and then sit back and cross their arms as if saying "case closed." This Christian Abuse destroys emotional availability and communication.

When an individual, a parent, or helper is involved in preaching doctrine and supporting doctrine to their children and/or followers, it is not easy to remain "emotionally available;" generally the parents are too emotionally involved with their beliefs *and* their child. Yet the child needs a loving, caring parent who will listen and be sensitive to the child's needs, thoughts, and beliefs. Then the parent can help the child develop his or her position, which, in the final analysis, is generally close to what the parent believes.

However, if the parent or helper tells the adolescent to "change your ways" and "accept the truth," we can give you an absolute guarantee: That person is *not* understanding and "emotionally available." The child is expected to change, and that is that. On an emotional level to the developing child, that is neglect, bordering on abuse, frequently Christian Abuse. The general response from the child will be rebellion.

We have chosen the terms "Christian Abuse" and "Christian Neglect" to use in these situations for two reasons. First, this type of abusive attitude has its roots in the rigid, autocratic, and massive rule system found in Christian churches. Second, we strongly feel that attention needs to be drawn to the type of authoritarian, demanding, and abusive attitude frequently found in Christian churches. Thus the term *Christian* Abuse. These conservative Christian beliefs create neglectful and abusive situations which divide and tear apart families as well as churches.

DEFINITIONS OF ABUSE IN CHRISTIANITY

ABUSIVE CHRISTIANITY—A generic term used to describe all abuses in Christianity.

CHRISTIAN ABUSE—The action taken by an individual who uses destructive Christian beliefs and practices in an attempt to intimidate, emotionally manipulate, or control others so their behavior and beliefs will be consistent with the abuser's belief system. This includes members in Christian religions presenting destructive beliefs and dogmas to people in an attempt to "convert" them.

DESTRUCTIVE CHRISTIANITY—Those beliefs and concepts, generally held by conservative Christians, but found to some extent in all Christian churches, which are inherently abusive and damaging to people, or which form the basis for Christian Abuse.

ABUSIVE CHRISTIAN MODEL—The influence that the historical relationship between God/Christ and Man has had on our personal development and the behavior of the family and institutions in our culture.

DESTRUCTIVE CHRISTIANITY—DESTRUCTIVE CHRISTIAN BELIEFS

We want to stress the following point: Christians and Christian ministers are *not* sadistic brutes who wander about looking for another person to abuse; at least, most of them are not. They are good people with good intentions who are trying to help people. Their behavior is based upon their beliefs, and it is their destructive beliefs that lead them into Christian Abuse.

The term "Destructive Christianity" is used to refer to the beliefs, the practices, and the theology of Christianity. We believe they are inherently abusive, or by their very nature, lead people to abuse others. By "inherently abusive," we mean that if a person tries to literally live by these beliefs, that person will experience pathology or dysfunction. Either the individual behavior will tend toward the irrational and unrealistic, or the behavior in the family will tend to be irrational, unrealistic, lacking in intimacy, punitive, and abusive. We will discuss these abusive beliefs and practices at length in Chapter 3.

Destructive Christian Beliefs include:
- Original sin.
- Salvation by the blood of Jesus Christ.
- The Holy Spirit, Satan, and demons.
- Heaven and hell.
- Hell and eternal punishment.
- Only "true" believers go to heaven.
- God punishes people with accidents and illness for not doing His will (righteous anger).
- God "saves people" when accidents illness, and disasters happen.
- God answers prayers and grants requests.
- God is a He and women are inferior.
- Concepts pertaining to sex, marriage, and divorce, such as contraception and homosexuality.
- Rigid and unrealistic rule systems of conservative Christian churches.

These concepts tend to be bizarre and at times violent, such as "washing in the blood of the Lamb." They tend to set up abuse toward children (original sin and punishment) and prejudice toward women. In some situations, the beliefs induce an overly positive attitude of hope—expectations of salvation—where action and honest fear might be more appropriate. When salvation and magic do not occur, confusion and anger set in. In essence, these beliefs and concepts can lead to victimization and abuse; as psychotherapists, we have seen numerous situations where people have been injured by these beliefs.

The major reason to differentiate between Christian Abuse and Destructive Christianity is that it is possible—in fact, probable—that the perpetrators of Christian Abuse end up being abused and victimized themselves by the abusive concepts of their theology. We call this Destructive Christianity.

The effects of Destructive Christianity can be dramatic and pervasive, as when the Catholic position on birth control causes children to be born to people in many different cultures who do not really want or need children and often leads to thousands of children being born into starvation and gross poverty.

Christian concepts are so common and so much a part of our culture that we resist seeing them as abusive. We also resist seeing the extent to which this abuse has taken place and currently takes place in our culture.

Destructive Christian Beliefs are basically what we have termed "Content Abuse." The ideology and statements are destructive and abusive if you understand and believe them.

ABUSIVE CHRISTIAN MODEL

Sigmund Freud, in his book *The Future of an Illusion,* introduced the concept that God is a projection of a father figure. This allowed people to understand God. People of the first century projected characteristics of their earthly fathers upon God. If Freud was correct, the parental model or family system model of the first century should have also been projected on the characteristics of God and how God treated people. We believe it was. In fact, this first-century parental model is still in existence today. It permeates our families, schools, and courts.

Our interest here is the family and we will focus on issues which have influenced family relations. We strongly believe Christian influence has contributed to attitudes, beliefs, and models leading to neglect and abuse within families today.

All families function according to a system of rules. All families have some sort of philosophical basis from which they interact with each other; for example, children are good versus children are evil, or people are basically positive versus people are basically negative. Parents have a basic belief about the nature of man and what must be done to make people change.

Families act upon these unconscious internal rules and beliefs. When we look at an abusive family, the abusive parent must have a set of internal rules. It is doubtful that parents are aware of these internal rules which allow them to abuse their children or other people. They are even less aware of the origin of these rules and beliefs. In all probability they learned these rules during childhood from parents and care givers.

These parents are following some model of behavior that was abusive. What sort of model of family behavior would exist if the original model was based upon conservative Christian beliefs? How would those families behave? How would they treat their children? What would they talk about, and what would they refuse to talk about? What would they expect of their children? How would they discipline their children? What would be their concept of love?

In building a model, let us look at some of the basic beliefs of conservative Christianity. Christian religion starts by placing man as a sinner. People are born in sin and are in need of salvation by God. It follows that if people are sinners and deserve eternal punishment, they must be bad or defective in some way, and their only hope is "salvation." This "salvation" is accomplished through a belief in Jesus Christ, and without salvation people continue in sin and face "everlasting hell." According to some Christian beliefs, the unbelievers go to hell and suffer and burn forever after they die. Under some Christian views, people are bad, evil, and worthy only of punishment. Or people should be ashamed of their origins. This concept places human beings in a very negative light.

JUDEO-CHRISTIAN RULES

Using the Judeo-Christian model, the model found in most conservative churches today, let us examine the rules that are supposed to govern Christian lives. Even though most of these rules originated in the first century, they are still in effect today and are still followed by many families:

- Children are born in sin.
- People are worthy of and deserve punishment and hell.
- People must follow the rules, believe, or perish.
- Punishment is very severe—eternal pain and suffering.
- Rules are rigid and not negotiable.
- Rules cannot be questioned.
- Certain topics cannot be discussed (topics in this chapter, for instance).
- Issues are black or white, good or bad.
- Perfection is expected.
- Control and conformity are highly valued.
- Love is conditional upon conformity. If not, love is withdrawn and punishment is anger and pain.
- God is Love, but believe or perish—double messages.

We believe these were typical family rules in the first century. These rules were projected onto God and became the way God would treat people. These rules are very close to the characteristics of the dysfunctional family listed by Friel and Friel at the first of this chapter. Also projected in this first-century system were rules about women, homosexuals, masturbation, and segregation (confusion of tongues) that we consider dysfunctional and prejudicial today. This rule system, part of what we call the Abusive Christian Model, may be the prototype of all dysfunction in families and much dysfunction in our culture. It has certainly had enough time to become embedded in our culture—almost two thousand years!

THE DYNAMICS OF THE MODEL

The dynamics of a family include how the rules are put into effect. How do the people behave and treat each other? Back to our Judeo-Christian model. How did God treat people? How did God treat His Son? Even though the Judeo-Christian system is supposed to be the system He initiated and punishment in hell is the punishment He originated, God evidently did not want people to burn in hell. So, in the Old Testament, God set up a system of blood sacrifice to atone for the sin of people. An animal, a lamb, would be killed and the blood would atone and wash away the sins of man. This type of practice is certainly violent and cruel. We cannot understand why God would want blood. Was this blood to appease Him? Or to bribe Him to be kind? Or was it a payment of the best things? Today animal sacrifice is frequently referred to in describing the sick and cruel practices of "devil worship."

At some point, God decided to send His Son to earth, specifically to be killed, to be murdered, sacrificed by the authorities at the time. His blood would then atone for the sins of all people. Belief in Jesus could save humankind from hell and everlasting suffering. If people did not believe in Jesus, they would be condemned to a fate of everlasting suffering after their death. It does not take a genius to see this is a very violent, bloody system in which humans must certainly be evil.

In the early 1900s Freud shocked the world by stating God was only a projected father image. Freud made it acceptable to step outside the primitive fear of eternal punishment and question God. We would like to step outside that fear at this point and examine some of the violence found in this Abusive Christian Model.

In reading the Old Testament, it is easy to see that God was conceived as a God of anger and wrath. God knew the destiny of human beings in the world. Of course, people had free will. But Adam and Eve really had only two choices. God must have known what would happen if Adam and Eve made either choice. God was the deity setting the contingencies.

He (assuming the traditional male perception of God, which is a prejudice) knew what would happen. Now, given one still believes this, the only logical conclusion is that God elected a system in which potentially He would participate in the murder of His own Son. God knew this beforehand. That act, of course, would be the epitome of abuse in a family. For reasons we do not know, God did not choose some other system of management of people. God chose not to stop a violent system that he created. If He could not stop it, He is not God, by definition. So that leaves us with the concept that He chose the type of system that would end up in the murder of His own Son, and He participated in that brutal action.

We are not going to offer any more theological options as to why things are the way they are. Hopefully, God knows. But if one were told such a story about an earthly father who followed a practice that killed and bled animals and eventually resulted in the death of his own son, one would think this family was crazy and dysfunctional beyond words. Outside of the religious context, one would have no problems in saying this was indeed the sickest of families, probably involved in some type of destructive cult. In our culture, the father would be seen as mentally ill.

To push this line of reason even further, how egocentric (assuming an ego) of a deity to want people to believe in certain ideas and to believe in "His Son," or this deity would punish those people by sending them to eternal hell. They would burn in punishment forever, simply because they did not believe what He wanted them to believe. Or, because they did not do what He wanted them to do. Also, what a perverse and convoluted way to save them, by setting up the murder of His Son. Could not an omniscient God think up a better plan?

This family system proceeds to condemn any future children (we are the "children of God") to everlasting pain if the rules are not rigidly followed. This is the model, or the system, that has had such a large impact on our culture and our concepts of the family, right and wrong, work, punishment. This is the Abusive Christian Model.

ANGER AND LOVE AS OPPOSITES

We will discuss this model throughout the book and expand upon and give examples of families that follow this model. The old model is structured around anger and love being opposites. When God loves you, everything is fine. If you do not obey, God withdraws His love and punishes violently with his anger. This first-century model is a set-up for abuse.

OLD DYSFUNCTIONAL MODEL

Love _____Anger/punishment

NEW MODEL OF LOVE

Love/Anger_____Indifference

Only recently, with the advent of the writing about dysfunctional families, have psychotherapists been able to understand dysfunction and to understand a healthy new model of family interaction. This new model sees love and anger as being very close to each other. You become angry with the ones you love, but you do not hurt the ones you love. You help them. This is the alternative model to the Abusive Christian Model.

A family following this new model would not hurt their children. They would help them. A family following the Abusive Christian Model would expect their children to obey. The rules would be rigid and there would be punishment, in some instances violent and angry punishment. This Abusive Christian Model is sick.

As professionals involved in mental health and the psychological health of families, we would hope to help family systems move away from the Abusive Christian Model. If that model is followed in our culture, we could be condemned to a culture that is angry, violent, and willing to sacrifice people for doctrine and willing to hurt people because those people simply do not agree with them and are different from them.

We believe it is time, and that the atmosphere is open, to ask the questions: What influence has the Christian model had on our psychological development and the developments of our attitudes about people and solutions to problems? Could this belief system contribute to child abuse? Could it contribute to an attitude of war? Could it contribute to neglect, fear of discussing certain topics, and emotional constriction in people? Could it set up perfectionistic and unrealistic values which lead to depression and despair? Could it contribute to sexually acting out by being so oppressive, rigid, and constricted? Could it facilitate violence? In essence, could this system of belief cause psychological injury to people which leads to further injury and pain? We believe the answer is "Yes" to each of these questions. The Abusive Christian Model, which is found in many Christian churches and influences many families in a violent and destructive way, must change.

Back to our original list of questions for this section. Abusive Christian families would behave according to God's rules, of course. Who wants to volunteer to go to hell? They would expect their children to be "saved," and if not "saved" at least to "do right" and "live right." If their children were wrong, they would punish them. They would talk about "right" things and not talk about "wrong" things. Wrong things would include sex, drugs, and questions about God. They would expect their children to be perfect or to strive for perfection. They would love their children when the children did what they were told to do. They would punish them and be angry with them when the children did not do what they wanted them to do. All in all, this sounds like the typical American family, and these families need help.

CHAPTER 3

HARSHNESS AT THE HANDS OF GOD

*"The Christian Army
is the only army I am aware of
where they shoot their own wounded."*

—A WOUNDED CHRISTIAN SOLDIER

Bonnie and Clyde met at a small Church of Christ and, like their outlaw counterparts, rode off on a whirlwind romance. The beautiful wedding raised the church to new heights in spirituality, its members said. At first, the young couple seemed a perfect picture of Christian marriage.

Clyde, a successful contractor, donated considerable time and money to the church and was very close to the young minister. When the marriage began to falter, the minister and Clyde grew even closer and prayed together. But Bonnie and Clyde divorced.

Bonnie no longer felt welcome in the small church. The minister was noticeably agitated, if not aloof. Several church members told her that since divorce was not acceptable, it would be best if she left the church. In her despair, Bonnie became involved with another member of the congregation. William was married but had not lived with his wife for several years. This also was totally unacceptable to the church, and the young minister vocally condemned the sins of Bonnie and William.

Bonnie pressured William to divorce. The minister pressured Bonnie and William to stop seeing each other. They felt they were falling "deeper and deeper into sin."

Bonnie is quite sure it was the pressure of "the sin" that drove William to suicide. She said she wishes she had "never known about

God." The minister had little compassion for Bonnie and told her, "You are not a child of God." Bonnie's parents were "very religious," and after the death of William, she felt she could not live with them. When Bonnie came to counseling, she was thinking of suicide. "I am already in hell," she said.

The lives of these people became intertwined in a bizarre journey directed by their internal "maps." One of the most interesting concepts in behavioral psychology is the idea that everyone has different types of maps in their heads—a theory known as "cognitive maps." They are the paths and guideposts each of us has inside that direct us how to behave and how we think we should behave.

You probably have a geographic map of the route from work to home, home to school, and then to mother's or sister's house. Some people have a geographic map that is so good, they can take a turn into an unknown area and still "know" where they are. Others are easily lost and seem to have a poor map or no internal map at all. See how the internal maps—drawn from the Abusive Christian Model and Destructive Christian Beliefs introduced in the last chapter—set in motion and maintained the momentum of these catastrophic events that affected the lives of Bonnie, Clyde, and William.

Each of us has concrete maps. Concrete maps represent physical objects and places. Where did you park your car? What is the arrangement of your home or work area? Where did you leave your car keys? Where are your shoes? Remember, you must pay attention in order to construct a map of where your keys may be located. If you "unconsciously" put them down while concentrating on something else, there may be no map.

Each of us has abstract maps. Abstract maps exist in thought rather than in matter. What is beauty, justice, or love? What is God? You have a "map" of behaviors and thoughts which coincide with these concepts. Abstract maps may be vague or unconscious. For example, one person's perceptions of love, beauty, and justice may differ greatly from another person's. That is one way to say individual maps differ. It would be unusual if they were identical. As individuals, each of us observes circumstances from slightly different perspectives, and we all behave in slightly different ways.

Let's use "love" as an example. Your definition of love would reflect your thoughts about love. Now, let's define a map, not only as your thoughts, but also as your actions when you love someone. Your definition is what you believe. Your map is what you do. Your definition of love and your actions when you love someone could be different. People who define love as a caring relationship may find themselves abusing their children. Their definition and map of love differ.

People may not be fully aware of their cognitive maps. For example, those of you who were abused as children may feel there is no love in a relationship unless there is abuse. These characteristics are required for your map of love. However, they probably do not fit your definition of love.

Bonnie, Clyde, William, and the Church of Christ minister were not fully aware of the way their own internal maps directed their lives. The destination of each person was to be "a good Christian." The "roads" to reach that destination were the rules. The rules, based upon Destructive Christian Beliefs, demanded that standards be met. Those standards included the beliefs that divorce is wrong, sexual relations should exist only within marriage, and sin requires harsh punishment and rejection. The individual maps then directed each person's behavior, such as the minister's rejection of Bonnie and Bonnie's pressure on William to divorce and marry.

When you have a map, you follow it. Independent thought is not required, you simply follow, and by following, you will "automatically" reach your goal. Christian religion provides us with a model from which we derive "maps" about reaching heaven, being a good parent, and being a good Christian. We use Christian beliefs with our personal experiences to develop our own unique map. Some people are able to lie or cheat in business, yet still consider themselves "good Christians." Maps drawn from Destructive Christian Beliefs can be difficult to understand, and at times, inconsistent.

In the last chapter, we constructed a theory which described abuse. We also established a hierarchy of abusive situations. On a personal level, you already had a definition of abuse. However, you must keep in mind that your definition and your map may be different. If you yell at your children to "correct" them, you will not perceive your yelling as abusive. In this situation, yelling at your children to correct them is not included in your unique definition of abuse.

SIDE TRIP

Maps guide us from point A to point B. Imagine a trip from Chicago to Las Vegas by car. You will drive through towns and areas that you know very little about. However, you can still navigate from Chicago to Las Vegas, if you follow the map.

We often guide people from point A to point B in Christian beliefs. For example, you want to guide a "lost" friend to salvation. There is a process to be followed to achieve salvation. However, with good intentions, you may inadvertently guide the friend into areas with undesirable implications.

MAPS: GEOGRAPHIC AND COGNITIVE

Lost soul————Salvation
SIDE TRIPS
Lost soul—emotional manipulation
threats of hell
guilt and fear
conformity at any cost
rigidity of options
exclusivity
Superiority of options over others
—————Salvation

For example, in order to lead someone to "salvation," you may use emotional manipulation such as guilt or fear. The person has to conform to what you say for being "saved" to be possible. There are many "side trips" to the Christian belief system and practice. Many of those side trips are abusive, or lead people to neglect or to abuse others. Look at your beliefs objectively and be willing to examine areas or "side trips" that you may not have questioned before.

Using our example of Bonnie and Clyde, the side trips include the minister's anger, rejection, and manipulation of Bonnie in an attempt to "bring her back to God." The effects of Abusive Christianity brought Bonnie into counseling where she confronted her manipulation of William in an attempt to legitimize their relationship, and William's guilt and shame, which brought about his eventual suicide.

Bonnie was able to examine her beliefs and the resulting side trips. For example, in order to be a "good Christian," she had to be married. Living with William was living in sin. She was caught up in a side trip of pain and rejection, which stemmed from the condemnation by her church and minister.

Some of our most difficult journeys are our inner journeys into our beliefs. In order to grow personally and intellectually, we must be willing to think independently. We must be willing to examine our ideas, our behaviors, and our maps. We must be willing to compare our ideas and maps to those that are different. We tend to defend our religious beliefs before we consider alternatives.

In this chapter, we will examine some of the abusive and destructive beliefs and practices which are found in conservative Christianity. We will compare what we know about abuse and neglect with beliefs of conservative Christian religion.

THE RULE SYSTEM: MUSCLE-BOUND CHRISTIANITY

Reared in conservative Christian churches, neither of the authors was allowed personal freedom under our families' religious beliefs. We made a list of rules we had to follow in order to avoid being involved in sin. These rules are still common in many conservative Christian churches.

THOU SHALT NOT:

- dance.
- play cards (dominoes maybe).
- drink alcohol.
- smoke.
- indulge in mixed bathing (swimming).
- have long hair (men only).
- wear too much make up (women only).
- wear provocative clothing (including shorts).
- listen to certain music.
- watch certain shows.
- think sexual thoughts.
- tell dirty jokes.
- laugh at dirty jokes.
- use or listen to vulgar language.
- bet or gamble.
- visit other churches.
- date outside your religion.
- believe in evolution.
- take philosophy classes.
- have sex or touch yourself sexually or masturbate.
- get pregnant.
- do *anything* to excess.
- do anything suggestive.
- think (we were only permitted to believe).
- be lazy.
- be a bad witness.
- get angry, unless it is righteous.
- lie.
- wear too much jewelry.
- draw attention to yourself (women only).
- take a leadership role if you were a woman.
- talk back to authorities.
- put yourself first.

- think angry or negative thoughts about your parents.
- question the rules.
- take pride in yourself or in your accomplishments (remember "Pride goeth before a fall").
- call our dance band a "dance band"—we called it a "jazz band."
- celebrate Christmas or birthdays.
- make a joke about religious beliefs or rules.

THOU SHALL:

- obey your parents.
- obey your elders.
- go to church.
- bring others to church.
- date within your religion.
- tithe.
- put God first.
- read the Bible daily.
- pray daily.
- put others before yourself.
- witness to others.
- save sex for marriage.

...and on and on and on. To be a "good Christian" required that you be something besides a human being. The rules were inflexible; you must follow them to avoid "sin." If you do sin, there may be severe consequences. As the Abusive Christian Model pointed out, punishment and withdrawal of love come before reconciliation.

For example, we noted earlier the example of Sheila, a devoted church member who became pregnant while in high school. She was active in the church youth group, made up of a dozen young people who were socially close. After she got pregnant, Sheila stopped coming to church and stopped attending the youth group. Her friends wondered what had happened to Sheila. A rumor that she had become pregnant and was "out of town" circulated. No one remembers seeing Sheila again or recalls anyone asking about her again. She was simply gone. Sheila was sacrificed because of the rules.

There are rules about everything, such as no mixed bathing. Here is the story of Paul, told in his own words:

> "Mixed bathing" is a very curious term. You are not taking a bath. You are swimming. I can remember first hearing the rule and thought, "That is certainly easy to understand!" I thought "no mixed bathing," meant a bath. They said it would arouse the passions and did I ever agree! Taking a bath with a woman would have been just a little too much fun. When I found they were talking about swimming, I was shocked. At church camp, we could not swim together, men and women, boys and girls. Swim, fine, but not together. Needless to say, I was disappointed. But, my attitude was, "They know best."

Paul was taught not to question authority. In his map, he simply followed the rules.

Misguided attempts to follow these rigid rules can lead to confusion and to simplistic thinking. In the early 1990s, fears arose about satanic (a Judeo-Christian concept) "drug" music, such as some of the "heavy metal" music. Crusaders have fought against this music as causing teenagers to use drugs and worship evil. But to blame music for drug abuse or other social ills is short-sighted. The music may be a symptom, but it is certainly not a singular cause. The problem is drug dependence and anger, and the causes are numerous, such as addiction-illness, family problems, and teenagers' attempts to fill a void created, in many instances, by a lack of love and discipline.

At times, the rules seem to be against having any fun at all. There was an incident in California where music from Sausalito was wafting across the bay and bothered the neighbors in an affluent San

Francisco neighborhood. They complained to the mayor of Sausalito. The mayor's response was something like, "There are those individuals that live in morbid fear, that someone, somewhere, somehow, will manage to enjoy themselves." This would seem an especially appropriate comment about many constrictive rules that are still common in Abusive Christian churches.

Some of the rules make sense and it may be appropriate to include these in your map of a "good" person. For example, there are rules against smoking and drinking alcohol. Drinking can be pleasurable in moderation, but if done to excess, destructive habits may develop.

THE DAMAGE OF THE RULES

Muscle-Bound Christianity can psychologically damage individuals in several areas. An excessively tight rule system promotes an attitude of control, control, control. This control is applied by demanding that individuals submit to the rules; forget about reconciliation. The punishment for nonconformists is condemnation or even expulsion from the church or their families.

Further, excessive and unrealistic rule systems can instill shame in individuals. Strict rules foster an attitude of "anti-thinking"—you should not think, only believe. Closely associated with anti-thinking is the attitude that you should give up control of your life and subject yourself to what is taught by the authorities. Finally, this type of Christianity promotes the concept that rules are more important than people. People can be sacrificed for the rules.

Certain individuals and denominations impose their interpretation of the Bible and of Christianity upon their members. They do not allow individual freedom and do not encourage independent thinking. What "God given" right have they to impose their beliefs on others with threats of condemnation?

RULES PROMOTE THE FOLLOWING DYSFUNCTIONS

condemnation
shame and guilt
rebellion

anti-thinking
control by others
rules over people
loss of pleasure

Muscle-Bound Christianity promotes guilt and shame in lieu of normal human impulses to play, enjoy life, and express sexuality. One Christian religion will not allow people to celebrate their birthdays, because it is not Biblical. As a result of the rules of Muscle-Bound Christianity, people can develop fears of their own personal impulses. If they are enjoying themselves, they must be living in a state of sin, they think.

It is interesting to note that adolescents in rebellion follow strict peer rules. The adolescents simply change the content of the rules. They dress alike, wear their hair alike, and think and talk alike. They have been trained to follow rules but not encouraged to think independently. So, when they rebel, they generally find a clique group, a "subculture," and rebel according to those acceptable rules of behavior.

Christian religion teaches individuals to follow rules and to behave accordingly. If the adolescent changes peer groups and becomes involved in the drug culture, where will he or she stop following those rules? Drug use? Prostitution? Theft? Recreational sex? Robbery? Where do you stop rebelling? Following the rules can make one vulnerable to different sub-cultures. It can distort one's ability to make independent judgments concerning reality. Muscle-Bound Christianity contains so many rules that when the rules break down the adolescent may have no rules to follow.

In making judgments, you must think objectively. Muscle-Bound Christianity suppresses independence and conditions people to relinquish control of their lives to rigid rules. These rules, established by the church, are innocently followed by the believer without question. This is the behavioral pattern established in Christians. As a result, individuals, especially adolescents, are vulnerable to the behavioral demands of their peer group. Many adolescents have been damaged by blindly following their peer group in the same style that Muscle-Bound Christianity leads people to give up control of their lives. In a worst-case scenario—that is, a radical rebellion—the adolescent may apply this behavioral pattern to the drug culture.

As we have discussed, nonconformity often results in expulsion from church or from family. These rejected individuals, conditioned to follow the rules, are left handicapped and alone, often without the ability to successfully function on their own.

THE SEVEN SINS OF SALVATION

Within the concept of salvation lies a damaging paradox of Christianity. It is often acceptable to break the rules of common sense in order to pursue the rules of the Christian belief system.

FIRST SIN: EMOTIONAL MANIPULATION/THREATS OF HELL. The urgency of salvation overcomes normal social restrictions on abuse. Witnesses for Christ, in their efforts to "save souls," frequently manipulate people with fear, guilt, and shame. Then they often add threats of hell and everlasting damnation. If business used these manipulative practices, there could be grounds for lawsuits. The story of Jerry illustrates some of these abuses:

> As a child I got saved six times because after I'd get saved, I'd go out and I'd have bad thoughts and I'd think, "Oh my God, it didn't work. I don't want to go to hell, I don't want to die and burn in hell," and I believed all this stuff so I'd go back and be saved again. In fact, the minister once told me, "Hey, you can only be saved one time." If I'd been brighter I'd have said, "Can you give me a better definition of what saved is? Because do you realize that my entire life and death for eternity hangs on this shit and I want to know." They couldn't do it. They told me "you will know." They told me to "believe" and yet they told me in such a way that it was not clear what

I had to do. So what it did was induce more fear. I was afraid to go to sleep at night. It was awful. They should not do that to kids.

Jerry felt victimized by those who tried to save him. As a child, he understood they were trying to help, but the concept of salvation was abstract and difficult to understand. Powerful feelings of fear and worry captured him. As a child, he became insecure in his beliefs and afraid. As an adult, he felt anger and resentment at his childhood religious experience.

Salvation is an excellent example of a Destructive Christian Belief. Where there is a belief in the need for salvation, people will tell children about death, sin, punishment, hell, and salvation by faith. They will be told they are lost sinners and will never experience eternal life unless they believe in Christ. Whatever needs to be done to get them to believe is acceptable.

This is not the same as telling a child, "If you walk out in front of a speeding car, you will be killed or badly injured." The reality there is obvious. However, not so obvious to a child is the concept of a "spiritual god" threatening pain and punishment as a result of not following his rules or "not playing his game." This is an example of Christian Abuse resulting from a Destructive Christian Belief.

This abuse is brought on by well-intentioned Christians who manipulate emotions to pressure people into accepting beliefs in order to gain salvation. The virtual reality of eternal death and suffering can be fearful to an adult; it is devastating to a child.

SECOND SIN: ORIGINAL SIN. The concept of original sin holds that all people are conceived in sin. Original sin creates the necessity for salvation. The birth of every new baby brings into the world another individual who is "born in sin." Without salvation babies are doomed to an eternal hell.

Abusive Christianity espouses that, because children are born sinners, they must be taught what is "right" and change their wicked ways. It is easy to see where the philosophy of "spare the rod, spoil the child" originated. The concept of original sin, along with the Abusive Christian Model, can lead to abusive child-rearing practices. Parents who love their children will see that their children are properly reared and punished for their sins.

Without the oppression of original sin and its implications, a child may be perceived as positive, loving, and sensitive. Where children are reared with that concept in mind, they will be respected and not manipulated. Children should be protected from emotional manipulation, regardless of the source.

Salvation and original sin are Destructive Christian Beliefs. These beliefs can lead to child abuse when combined with the Abusive Christian Model. And these beliefs can lead to emotional manipulation in order to persuade people into acceptance of religious belief.

THIRD SIN: SALVATION AND CONFORMITY. If, as Christians believe, all nonbelievers are destined to end up in hell, a reasonable assumption would be that all people should be Christians. All people need to be saved. All people need to believe in Christ. There is no other option. Other religious beliefs are false. Therefore, Christian missionaries must be sent to all non-Christian peoples so they can be saved.

Christian religion promotes discrimination against and abuse of those who choose to be "nonbelievers," or who believe in another religion. Why should they be valued and respected by Christians when the Christian belief system deems all other religions to be false?

These beliefs demand conformity to Christian doctrine. No value is placed on difference in beliefs; no value is assigned to creativity, unless it is within the framework of Christianity. Christian values and tradition are expected to be universally embraced.

Conformity, control, rigidity, and constriction are all characteristics of this type of Christian thinking. Other beliefs aren't acceptable. Everyone needs to become a Christian. There is *no* other way.

FOURTH SIN: SUPERIOR AND EXCLUSIVE. Viewed from the Christian perspective, Christianity supersedes all other religions.

Christianity is "the way" and "the truth." All other religions fall into the category of "false beliefs." In this manner, Christianity is perceived by its followers as exclusive and superior. The Buddhists are wrong. The Jews are wrong. The atheists are certainly wrong.

Christianity is also divisive. The Northern and Southern Baptists do not agree with each other, and neither agrees with the Catholics. Each group feels its approach is superior and correct. Therefore, Christianity inherently suffers from being divisive as well as superior and exclusive.

These characteristics are inherent in the belief system. Christianity affirms its superiority in that it can lead people to heaven. It claims that it is the *only* way. Christianity suffers from divisiveness because of the characteristics of superiority and exclusivity. Each denomination believes it is correct, and it is the only true way.

This attitude creates several problems. One problem presents itself in dating relationships. Baptists should not date Catholics. Catholics should not date Jews. Christianity causes a type of religious xenophobia in its members.

This destructive side trip comes at high cost. We will never be a "united" people until we deal with this abusive aspect of Christian religion. We will never unite as "Children of God" as long as this Destructive Christian Belief exerts its power.

FIFTH SIN: RIGIDITY OF OPTIONS. Christian churches espouse rigid and non-negotiable rules. Beliefs become black and white. As an example, winning souls to Christ is a virtue, regardless of the emotional manipulation involved.

Perceptions become very clear when the world is seen in black-and-white terms. You must ask yourself whether the light of Christian concepts blinds you to the abuses Christianity encourages in the name of salvation. So intent on doing right, the Christian becomes incapable of doing wrong, incapable of inflicting injury on those to be saved.

What is the abusive aspect of rigidity? This rigid attitude usually carries over into other thoughts and behaviors. We once worked with a conservative Christian couple that could not agree on the proper way to load a dishwasher. He thought he was right. She thought she was right. Both suffered from this abusive side trip, rigidity.

Christianity, as seen in many churches today, suffers from chronic rigidity. If you are wrong, according to the belief, it does not matter how lucid your argument or how rational your excuse.

Christianity must heal the attitude of rigidity with acceptance and flexibility. Acceptance and flexibility produce attitudes which lead to understanding, and all people desire to be understood. We must be willing to listen. Others may have a point. At the very least they deserve respect.

SIXTH SIN: SALVATION EXPECTATION (MYTH). Salvation brings with it expectations that people should think and behave passively. The "salvation" belief places emphasis upon "being saved." You are saved by your faith. There is nothing anyone can do; it is out of your control. You must remain passive and wait for God's salvation.

Passive thinking rarely carries over into the real world because there are only rare emergencies, such as flood, entrapment in auto and air crashes, and severe medical emergencies where we need to be physically saved. In most situations, waiting to be saved may be the least desirable option. Taking the initiative to save yourself or help yourself is usually a more desirable option.

Conservative Christian religions propose that God is able to deliver you from disaster, disappointment, and loss. In times of trouble, "God will take over and make everything okay." Believers are told that God has a master plan and whatever happens is "His" will. These beliefs are found at the national level. Often, people remark about our participation in a war by saying "God is on our side" or "Pray for our troops."

While teaching a psychology class, Jerry once had a discussion about the possibility of a nuclear war. One student responded, "If God wills it, there is nothing we can do about it." The student personified this "sit and wait" attitude. Does it not make more sense to take the initiative to reduce the number of nuclear weapons and to build agreements that strongly limit their use? Waiting to see what will happen can be dangerous, indeed.

Often we need to take action. Delayed action may exacerbate a bad situation or create new ones. Leaving problems for God to solve, when we need to take control, sets us up for failure. Then we may blame the failure on "God's will" and proceed passively to set ourselves up for more failures.

This passive attitude is often seen in females in abusive marriages. They wait for some "sign" or some external force to "save" them. They are following the map of the salvation myth.

It also can be found in people in a business crisis. They sit and wait for something to happen, for things to "get better." The salvation expectation can lead to magical thinking: "If I am just a good Christian, things will work out."

This passivity also affects couples with marital problems. One husband informed us, "If God can't solve it, what can a marriage counselor do?" The salvation myth leads to the development of an internal map of passivity: "God will make things better," or "things will be okay." This attitude of waiting for salvation has a powerful influence on relationships and intimacy, as we will see in Chapter 4.

It is acceptable to "let go and let God deliver you" if nothing can really be done, but how do you determine that you have no control over a situation? Granted, some events are out of our control and we are truly helpless. However, Christian theology fails to clarify these issues for us, and many times that is a difficult decision to make. Who could have predicted the change brought about by the courage and tenacity of the woman who started Mothers Against Drunk Driving, or MADD? We cannot wait for "things to get better." We must make things get better.

SEVENTH SIN: VIOLENCE/THE BLOOD OF JESUS. Our cities and communities seem to be growing more and more violent. The reasons are complex, but one issue often ignored is the Christian emphasis upon blood sacrifice and, ultimately, the sacrifice of Jesus.

In the ritual of Holy Communion or the Eucharist, the consecrated bread and wine are consumed to represent eating the flesh and drinking the blood of Christ. Step back and overlook the religious interpretation, and this is a graphic picture of barbaric violence. We remember a song sung with gusto in church: "Are you washed in the blood?"

Combine these pictures with the belief that all infidels will be punished with everlasting death, suffering, and hell. These concepts contribute to our acceptance of violence and our increasing tendency to glorify violence. The blood sacrifice of Jesus is the ultimate glorification of violence.

Television shows and movies commonly depict acts of violence, and Christians often protest such programs being shown in their communities and in their homes. But with such brutal and barbaric beliefs, you'd think Christian churches would have a harder time taking a strong stand against violence. These beliefs of blood sacrifice and severe punishment with hell are powerful side trips of Destructive Christian Beliefs. Christianity must transcend the very core of these beliefs based on punishment and violence to lead our shattered culture to peace and reconciliation.

HOLY SPIRIT, SATAN, AND DEMONS

The concepts of Satan, demons, and the Holy Spirit are destructive beliefs that promote three destructive ideas. First, the belief in the Holy Spirit promotes spiritual elitism, while the belief in Satan and demons bestows upon "holy" individuals the right to persecute and banish unholy individuals. Next, it lends itself to the idea of being abandoned by the Spirit. Finally, it confuses psychological boundaries and lends itself to a confusion of responsibilities and feelings. This sets the stage for codependency by teaching the perception that external forces can control feelings and behaviors.

Spiritual elitism is the attitude that I have something you do not have. "I have the Spirit, you do not." Therefore, I am somehow special and honored and you, for some reason, have been left out or are lacking. Many of the television evangelists are "filled with the Spirit," speak in tongues, perform faith healing, and collect millions of dollars for their special services. This elitism lends itself to the abuse, the punishment, and the manipulation of others which masquerades as "doing God's work." Those "chosen by the Spirit" have special knowledge and, as such, special power over others who have not been chosen. For example, book burnings and bannings are performed by devout Christians who, protecting the vulnerable against temptation and exposure to evil, see themselves as God's agents. Similarly, intrusive protests at abortion clinics, harassment, and even violent acts such bombings and murder have been committed by devout Christians seeking to "save" women and unborn lives "in the name of God."

Those who have been chosen can also be abandoned by the Spirit. Rona was "chosen" by the Spirit. She was a "good Catholic mother." Her 15-year-old daughter was the pride of her life, and the entire family was active in their parish. Rona felt she was "filled with the Holy Spirit." She felt God. He was there with her. Then the unthinkable happened. One night, her daughter went for a ride with a boyfriend who had just received his driver's license. Within minutes of leaving the house, her daughter was killed in a traffic accident. Rona was devastated. Her life was wrecked.

She felt she had been abandoned by the "Holy Spirit." She felt constant anger and pain and hopelessness. Never again would she have her daughter and never again would she find "The Spirit."

When Rona became distraught and angry, it was due to the Spirit leaving her. Otherwise, how could she feel like she was feeling, empty and hurting? The Spirit was responsible for her feelings. This was God's fault, not hers!

This leads to the final destructive side trip of this belief. Rona had become enmeshed with her daughter and the Holy Spirit and had taken them into her psychological boundaries. Now they were gone. The destructive aspect began when Rona thought of the Spirit as "out there" and in control of her life. The Spirit was responsible for how she felt.

Any belief which removes personal responsibility for feelings is a destructive belief. Any belief which encourages individuals to consider outside spirits or other persons responsible for their feelings is a destructive belief. This belief confuses psychological boundaries and ultimately leads to enmeshment with other individuals. Along with the salvation expectation, it sets the stage for what is commonly called codependency. The thinking that others can control how you feel, or that the Spirit controls how you feel, is a common confusion in our culture. We believe the underlying source of this type of thinking is Christianity.

People are not "filled with the Spirit," as if some giant spiritual hypodermic was needed to inject "the Spirit" into them. This idea treats the Spirit as an external force or power which invades and controls people. People are responsible for what they feel. The Spirit does not "fill" any more than it "abandons." To believe so is destructive. To believe so is to avoid taking responsibility for one's own feelings and behaviors.

Belief in the Holy Spirit can further lead to unrealistic and simplistic answers, such as, "All Rona needs is to believe in Jesus and be filled with the Spirit." Beliefs like this only give people permission to avoid life's complexities and problems. It is a form of spiritual denial which provides pat solutions to complex social and psychological issues. Then, when those solutions fail, individuals feel they have either sinned or they have been abandoned by the Spirit. Their religious views begin to have no practical significance.

Belief in external control lends itself to psychotic thinking and behavior especially when it includes the concepts of Satan and demons. What these concepts offer is generally destructive and harmful. Satanic Cults, spiritualists that "exorcise demons" for a fee, and incidents such as murder incorporate ideas of demonic control and influence.

Teresa, a beautiful child only 15 months old, was murdered in Fort Worth, Texas, late in June 1992. She was allegedly killed by her father who, evidently thinking his daughter was possessed by demons, ran from the house carrying her and yelling, "Satan be gone. Satan be gone."

The belief in the Holy Spirit, demons, and Satan removes responsibility for behavior from the individual and places responsibility in the realm of spirits. A much healthier belief is that you are responsible for your behavior. Beliefs are psychologically necessary, but belief in external powers which invade and control is destructive. How do we escape this dilemma? Easy. The spirit of God is not separate from people; it is an integral part of people. It is a part of you. It is not injected into a special few, nor is it a case of "some have it, some don't." The Spirit is there, in everyone. Always. All you need to do is believe it and get in touch with it.

PRAYER AND MIRACLES

The Bible describes miracles performed by God. Seas part, plagues visit, cities fall, floods devastate. In one such flood, God allegedly killed the entire population, with only Noah saving the animal kingdom and chosen humans. The Bible teaches that miracles and magical things can happen.

Even today, we hear reports of miracles. Statues in churches shed tears. The "Blessed Virgin" appears in the sky. People pray for health, guidance, and blessings. Television ministers promise cures from illness, avoidance of death, and material wealth, if only you will send them a request—with a donation, of course—"to do God's work." The abuse is obvious.

Yet people send money. They send a great deal of money, hoping that these special individuals will pray for them, and God will grant their request. This belief opens people to easy manipulation and abuse by unscrupulous individuals. Why do you need these intermediaries? If God does answer prayers, He will be as likely to answer your prayer as your minister's, or some television minister's.

Part of our work as therapists is with families of murder victims. In one family, a son had been shot and fought for his life in the intensive care unit at the local hospital for several days before he died. The mother was a devoted Christian church worker. She believed in prayer. She asked God over and over again to let her son live. When her son died, she felt victimized and punished. She had lived a Christian life and had worked long and hard in her church. She frequently helped others. She strongly felt she deserved help from God in her time of need.

Her belief that prayers will be answered has caused her a great deal of psychological injury and turmoil. Her attitude was characterized by the remark, "If prayers are not answered, why pray in the first place?" Explanations by ministers, such as, "God works in mysterious ways" and "We cannot understand God, but He wanted your son with Him," fell on deaf ears. Her questions were not answered.

God does not work that way. There is no magic. To expect God to perform magic is to invite frustration and despair.

Obviously, considering the death and misery in the world around us, God does not intervene to help people in distress. In 1991, central Texas reeled from the mass murder of 23 people in a cafeteria. It is absurd to believe that God would allow so many people to die in misery and fear. It is absurd to believe that He would allow *one* individual to die in such a manner.

A variation of this expectation of magic is when people say, "I guess that is the way God wants it," and then they give up. This is a destructive belief. Very similar to other Destructive Christian Beliefs, belief in prayer and miracles suggests that the power and responsibility to act exist somewhere outside the person. That results in fuzzy ego boundaries, confusion about what is self, and what is separate from self. These characteristics make up the core of what is called codependency. Over the centuries, these beliefs have guided people to feel out of control, under the control of others, and not responsible for what happens to them.

But it is *our* responsibility to act, to change things when we can, to find happiness and peace in illness, to extend kindness to those in need. We must be responsible for our world.

It is easy to get around the destructive elements in these beliefs by acknowledging that the power of God is within you, now and always. It is your responsibility to use that power to act. You can make things happen. You and only you are responsible for how you feel and what you do.

CONSTRUCTIVE ATTITUDES TOWARD MIRACLES
- The power of God is within you.
- You are responsible for what you feel and what you do.
- There is no magic but you can create the miraculous.

HEAVEN AND HELL, BLACK AND WHITE

One of the recurring characteristics of Abusive Christianity is rigid, black-and-white, dichotomous thinking. There's no better example than the conservative Christian concepts of heaven and hell, good and evil, right and wrong.

The concepts of heaven and hell, along with the concepts of right and wrong, can traumatize a young child. The trauma parallels situations where the children face cruel and violent punishment, unless those children do exactly what they "should." In order to go to heaven, children either have to comply with an abstract belief and be certain they have complied, or they become "unbelievers." And "unbelievers" will surely end up in hell.

Thinking that has been influenced by these dichotomous concepts becomes rigid and compulsive. People think they have to comply with the black-and-white values and think they have to force others to comply. They worry about their friends and family members who are "unbelievers," or believers in another faith. They easily become obsessed with concern for family and friends. They must preach the message. Eternal lives swing in the balance.

These Christian concepts allow little or no gray area. In the section on Muscle-Bound Christianity, we listed the rules that were consistent with our religion. There are many "thou shalt" and "thou shalt not" rules in conservative Christian religion. These rules are black and white with little room for discussion and little room for negotiation. These ideas and concepts leave no room for human error.

The conservative Christian groups' attitudes on abortion exemplify this no-room-for-discussion, black-and-white thinking. Perhaps you've have seen the banner that declares, *"Abortion Is Murder."* There it is in black and white, plain and simple. However, reality is rarely that simple.

Many examples can complicate the issue. What about rape? What about the rape of a 13-year-old child who ends up pregnant? What about the poor family, already with numerous children, that is told their next child may be grossly deformed? They have neither the skills nor the resources to care for the child. Are they victims? What of their emotional state and their plight? This is a complex and emotionally loaded issue that calls for soul searching and solid reality testing.

But none of that matters, according to conservative Christian beliefs. The plight of young unwed mothers and the conditions of pregnancy are not as important as adhering to the belief that abortion is murder. The feelings of pregnant young girls are irrelevant. The rule is the rule—a simple creed leaving no flexibility. And the bottom line is, the rule is abusive. Those who break the rules find the power of conservative Christianity is awesome, truly awesome. You can burn in hell. Families can disown children. Families can break apart because of this rule and other similar rigid dichotomous rules. The slogan "Pro-Choice" at least leaves options without rigidity.

This type of thinking inadequately prepares people to deal with cultural and business complexities. It does not prepare people to deal with ethical gray areas. "Right or wrong" becomes the quintessential thinking. It pervades our culture and our lives.

Much of the abuse parents dispense to their children is based on this thinking. Children must do right. Children must obey. How often we therapists have seen children victimized for what is " right." We have seen fathers disown their unwed daughters because they became pregnant. Children and love become secondary. *People can and will be sacrificed for the rules.* They will be punished. Sadly, Abusive Christianity undermines helping, accepting, and understanding.

Another example of this type of thinking is the statement that "drug abuse is wrong." Most people who make these statements exclude two of our most socially destructive drugs: alcohol and tobacco. Hundreds of thousands of people die, suffer accidents and diseases because of these two drugs. But these drugs are "socially condoned," openly sold, and widely used.

Physicians prescribe drugs for illness and disease. If you do not think these are important issues, or relevant to the "drug problem," try sitting in on a group of adolescents who have been recently hospitalized for drug abuse. They quickly point out *all* of our social inconsistencies on "drug abuse." Why is alcohol legal and marijuana illegal? Why are powerful mind-altering drugs legally available when you see a physician? These complex issues do not lend themselves to simple answers or slogans.

Rigid rules may even contribute to drug experimentation in adolescents. The inconsistencies in our social and legal rules certainly do. Children see adults using caffeine (a drug of abuse in pill form in some adolescents), tobacco, and alcohol. These rigid and simply stated rules begin to fall apart. Drugs are not all "bad." They see that. These adolescents become vulnerable to someone who points out these inconsistencies and cajoles them into trying illegal drugs.

This inflexibility also discourages individual thinking and communication. We have already discussed, in the section Muscle-Bound Christianity, the dangers when adolescents believe a doctrine, follow, and do not think. They become vulnerable to the rules of the peer group, including the drug subculture. Their lack of thinking provides the means by which they become followers.

A child who experiments with drugs or becomes pregnant cannot communicate with parents who have rigid, dogmatic rules—cannot confide in them or trust them to help. The child, when most in need of a parent, often finds the parent emotionally unavailable because of his or her beliefs. The child must then make a decision to survive. Alone. The child is aware that he or she will be emotionally abused or sacrificed for the rules.

THE SECOND COMING, ARMAGEDDON

These Christian beliefs include the notion that in the final days of earth, the forces of good and the forces of evil will engage in a battle for supremacy called Armageddon. For centuries, Christians have waited for the literal second coming of Christ and this final battle between good and evil.

Many different Christian sects have "calculated" the date for the second coming. Other groups have engaged in violence, such as that found in the battle between the Branch Davidians and the Alcohol, Tobacco and Firearms agents near Waco, Texas, in early 1993. We will not discuss this belief at length because its destructive and violent nature should be evident to almost everyone.

The Armageddon belief elevates violence to the level of a "Holy War," and is common in conservative Christianity. Combined with the beliefs of Heaven and Hell, the crucifixion, the Passover (where God will "smite" the first born of every family that does not have lamb's blood smeared on their door threshold) and various events when God destroyed the sinful, Armageddon anoints war and violence to the level of the sacred. When this God is angry, this God kills people. Doesn't this give permission for people to go and do likewise? These attitudes, combined with easily available weapons, spell disaster.

We will never diminish violence in our culture with beliefs such as Armageddon in our religions. We will never achieve unity and a spirit of love among all men when bound by abusive and barbarous ideas such as this.

This belief also encourages a fatalistic view of violence and "evil." Why should we do anything about it when God will kill all of them anyway? Or, like some of the cults, why not arm ourselves and help God in His great war against those who do not believe as we do? Physical violence and especially verbal violence become acceptable.

Armageddon is certainly a Destructive Christian Belief. It contributes to truly crazy and violent behavior as seen in destructive cults. It makes violence, especially when the violence is for righteousness, acceptable and good.

PUNISHMENT

Beth, a beautiful young girl, was an inpatient in a locked ward of a psychiatric hospital, trying to beat drug abuse. Her father said he loved her but displayed love consistent with the Abusive Christian model. His daughter was "wrong" in her drug abuse, and in order to motivate her to do "right," he would do anything. He had tried all forms of punishment. Yelling. Slapping. Restriction. Nothing worked. One of the authors was working with the father and daughter in a joint session when the father in a moment of frustration said, "Beth, honey, I love you, but if you ever do drugs again, I will beat the hell out of you."

Punishment forms the core of behavioral control in Abusive Christianity. God punishes sinners; in the Old Testament, often severely. Eternal punishment befalls all unbelievers. With punishment such an integral part of Christianity, the wide use of punishment as a deterrent to wrong-doing in our society is easy to understand. Punishment is as universal as it is ineffective. This common means of behavior control infiltrates schools, prisons, and families.

Yet, punishment generally creates fear and anger in the individual and it assures that the individual will not perform the target behavior ... while you are looking. However, the individual may rebel and fight back, creating even more chaos and confusion. The whole point of the punishment may be lost. Punishing the punisher is a common motive in children who run away.

The means by which this father chose to control his daughter included the threat of physical violence. This frequent theme, found in the Abusive Christian Model, invades our culture and our families as a means of behavior control.

Punishment constitutes the major means of behavior control in most conservative Christian churches, through threats of burning in hell, vengeance from God, and expulsion or rejection by the church and its members. Adam and Eve were exiled from the Garden of Eden. Ministers who sin are asked to leave the church and, at times, to leave the ministry. Since all people are "born in sin," they are destined for eternal punishment unless they repent.

In trying to help Beth and her father, the therapist wrote a script for Beth's father to read to her: "You are my daughter and I love you very much. When I see you doing drugs it hurts me, because I love you. When I am hurt, I usually want to hurt back, but I do not believe in hurting those I love. Your drug use also makes me fear for your future. I don't want you to lose your future. I want to help you. How can I best help you?"

It had not dawned on the father to be emotionally open and available to his daughter, instead of venting his anger on her. He did not know how to be emotionally available and caring toward his daughter when he was angry. He is a typical victim of Abusive Christianity and the punishment-oriented Abusive Christian Model. Caring and positive encouragement are much more powerful modifiers of behavior than punishment, and they are not contaminated with fear, anger, and guilt.

WHY PUNISHMENT DOES NOT WORK (FOR CHRISTIANS OR ANYONE ELSE)

B. F. Skinner, a leader in behavioral theory and research, stated that punishment is the most common means of controlling behavior. It is also the most ineffective and morally indefensible.

In the Old Testament, God killed immoral people as a form of punishment. Obviously, changing human behavior was not the goal. His goal was to show His power, to frighten other people into compliance, and to vent His anger. There was no intention of helping. So goes the punishment in most Christian churches today. It is not designed to help people, merely to hurt them, to vent the righteous indignation of the holy. Calling people sinners and stating they are destined for hell does not help them.

Much has been written on the subject of punishment and much of the research has been conducted with animals, specifically rats and pigeons. It is somewhat deflating to be compared to a rat, but unfortunately, most of the theory is applicable to humans.

Behavioral scientists do not agree on a definition of punishment. We have selected two definitions. First, it is any condition which follows a response and decreases the likelihood that response will occur again. Second, punishment is an aversive stimulus following a response.

The first definition assumes a desire to help the individual eliminate unwanted behavior. The second definition simply states that punishment is an unpleasant event, period. This definition reveals no intention to "help" the individual. Even if there is intent to help the individual change, behavioral scientists would agree, punishment fails as an effective method of controlling human behavior. Extensive research has clearly outlined the problems involved.

PUNISHMENT MUST OCCUR IMMEDIATELY. To be effective, punishment must occur not within minutes, but within *seconds* of the unwanted behavior. It is impossible to punish moral behavior this way. For instance, Beth was not punished immediately upon the use of illegal drugs. It took weeks for her father to discover her beginning drug use and, acting consistently with the Abusive Christian Model, to punish it. So instead of connecting the punishment with the drug use, she probably connected the punishment with her father's *discovery* of the drug use and resolved to be more careful next time about disposing of the evidence.

Unfortunately, this preoccupation with punishment from the Christian belief system has carried over to schools and the judicial system. Needless to say, punishment is ineffective there, too.

When one looks at families, churches, courts, and schools, no punishment occurs immediately. In fact, delivering punishment immediately is virtually impossible in most situations. Can you imagine a group of church members following a couple suspected of adultery, in order to dispense immediate and effective punishment?

PUNISHMENT MUST BE APPROPRIATE TO THE "CRIME." The consequences must be so logical and so natural to the behavior that the individual has no difficulty tying the two together. A cook who touches a hot pan easily recognizes the connection between a hot pan and pain. For Beth and her drug use, the natural consequences might be getting arrested and thrown in jail or in having an overdose and becoming very ill. Her father's slapping her and the excessive restrictions only resulted in her thinking he was cruel and unfeeling.

Is there any situation, other than violent crimes against people, in which banishment represents an appropriate consequence? We have seen churches banish individuals for not attending church, divorce, drinking alcohol, and dancing, just to mention a few instances. This inappropriate punishment only led to anger, resentment, depression, and rebellion.

PUNISHMENT CHANGES THE RELATIONSHIP BETWEEN THE PERSON GIVING THE PUNISHMENT AND THE PERSON RECEIVING IT. The person receiving the punishment may try to avoid the punisher. It is natural to try to escape punishment if possible. Or they may become angry with the punishment and aggressive toward the punisher. The strong emotional reaction on the part of the receiver blocks behavioral change. Often, the focus on behavioral change is lost in all of the emotional reactions between the punisher and the receiver. Beth had thought about running away, and once she used *more* drugs in a passive-aggressive attempt to spite her father.

This is probably one of the reasons that churches punish people—not to help people change, but to push them away. The church does not want to be associated with heretics, sinners, and unbelievers. Examples of those exiled include known homosexuals, unwed mothers, adulterers, and divorcees.

IN SOME SITUATIONS, PUNISHMENT MAY INCREASE THE PUNISHED BEHAVIOR. Beth's punishment actually motivated her, in anger, to use more drugs. She did this as a form of rebellion and punishment against her father. Her drug use rapidly increased to the level of addiction.

Our school systems follow the Abusive Christian Model. Teachers, calling attention to the "trouble makers" in an attempt to punish them, frequently cause them to increase their undesirable behavior. This frustrates teachers because punishment actually compounds the problems.

Eventually the errant student may be punished by being expelled. Most of these children dislike school anyway, so that may not be punishment to them. Why not make them go to school longer and help them adjust? As schools follow the Abusive Christian Model, they withdraw love and support, they expel and reject. That is consistent with the model. Punishment does not facilitate change.

PUNISHMENT IS CONTAMINATED. Punishment fails because of the complexities in real life. If pain is used, the removal of that pain actually increases the behavior that occurs when the pain stops. In some experimental situations, rats are placed in cages with electric grids as floors. When the rat is shocked, the shock stops when the rat jumps to a platform. Jumping has been "rewarded" and will likely occur again if there is shock again. Pain (shock) is punishment. The removal of the pain is reward.

Spanking provides a good example of this contamination. When parents punish by spanking, the child is usually yelling and crying when the spanking stops. Therefore, yelling and crying are reward- ed and will likely start again when punishment threatens. Frequently, the child will cry so hard that the parent decides not to spank. The crying and yelling are further reinforced by an avoidance of punishment.

In church members, whatever attitude people have after they have been "punished" by the church will be reinforced. Fear, anger, or rebellion will be the attitude reinforced in that individual. Often, with punishment, the church rewards individual rebellion.

Further contamination occurs when punishment becomes inconsistent. Each instance that is not punished makes the unwant- ed behavior more likely. The absence of punishment becomes a reward. Sneaking around and getting away with "bad behavior" is "exciting," which is another way to say rewarding. In fact, it is more than exciting. It is "winning"; you beat the system. This is similar to gambling. Churches cannot punish consistently because people "sneak around" and sin. This makes the unwanted behavior more likely to occur. In this way churches and Christians contribute to the very sins they seek to condemn.

PUNISHMENT MUST BE SIGNIFICANTLY AND SHARPLY PAINFUL.
If an aversive stimulus is to be effective, it must be painful. A cook touching a "warm" pan will not produce the same results as touching a burning hot pan. According to this rule of "aversive stimulus," for Beth's father to be effective in his use of physical punishment, he would have had to be abusive. Of course, we don't ever recommend that. There are other types of punishment that are not physically painful, such as throwing the child out of the house. There are serious problems with those also.

The most common form of punishment in churches is disapproval. Disapproval does not fall into the category of "sharp and significantly painful." It is more of a nuisance and vaguely annoying. Take dancing and drinking, of which many churches disapprove. The disapproval is not as strong as the reward found in these activities. Anytime the pleasure of the activity outweighs the pain of the potential consequences, punishment—in this case, disapproval—will be ineffective.

AN ALTERNATE SOLUTION SHOULD BE OFFERED. If no alternative solution is offered to the unwanted behavior, confusion, frustration, and anger may force the person to "sin" again. The cook soon learns that a hot pad or towel will prevent the burns. That is a useful alternative method for removing the food from the stove. Beth was not receiving helpful guidance, just hostility and abuse. She needed to learn other, more effective ways of finding relief from her internal pain and finding pleasure, other than using drugs.

An example here is the church's attitude toward sexuality. As an unmarried adolescent, you cannot indulge in sexual relations, you cannot masturbate, there is no acceptable alternative to relieve sexual drives. You simply have to ignore it, to pray, and to wait until marriage. Punishment here is ineffective because there is no effective alternative. For a perpetually aroused adolescent, praying does not work.

Punishment may end in rebellion, anger, resentment, confusion, fear, or a combination of these. No one likes to be punished.

Compliance with rules can sometimes be forced, but at a great and unhealthy cost which rarely produces healthy or effective behavior change. Instead of learning to be better, people who are punished simply learn to avoid getting caught.

DOES CHRISTIANITY PREVENT IMMORALITY?

Will immorality reign supreme if guilt, condemnation, and punishment are not fiercely wielded by the Christian establishment? Not likely. But many traditional Christian groups would have us believe so.

Let's consider one moral issue, sexuality, and look for a moment at what happened in the 1960s when "free love" was the attitude of the day. Religious leaders predicted a general moral decay leading to overall moral disaster. Why didn't the predictions come true? Why are we now seeing a reduction in promiscuity instead? Why weren't most of those people ruined, killed, destroyed, or imprisoned? Why didn't our society collapse?

In fact, it seems the opposite has occurred. These individuals now form the current "Establishment." They are wiser, they know what works and what does not, and most have chosen a more conservative manner of living. Recently, AIDS has been the most powerful motivator for changing sexual behavior. Not punishment. Not Christianity. A natural consequence, AIDS.

People naturally seek structure both in sexual and social morality. They do not have to be forced or punished into it. They will actually create rules that help them understand how to react and behave. Having to make decisions about everyday morality and needing to know what to do in confusing situations is motivating enough for them to desire a rule structure. We know that primitive tribes established rituals and rules of social and sexual behavior. Even the animal kingdom has its mating rules and rituals. Most people do not need punishment and enforcement from external sources such as Christianity to create structure in their moral behavior.

People learn from behavior that is modeled from loving guidance, and from natural consequences. They alter their behavior accordingly. Most of us feel guilt when it's appropriate, when we do hurtful things, without having guilt imposed on us by others. The ones who don't will not feel guilt no matter who tells them they should. As therapists, we know how difficult it is to help people change their habits even when they want desperately to change. For those who don't want to change or control their behavior, the task is usually impossible.

For people who do want to abide by social rules, rejection, punishment, and guilt imposed by Christianity can actually press people into immoral and unhealthy behavior. The emotional stress and anger that results from punishment and guilt can lead them in desperation to alternatives such as alcoholism, adultery, and physical and emotional abuse of others.

When injured by Abusive Christianity, these people may have no place to turn, and feeling desperate, may be unable to make rational choices. We wonder how many times a religious group has condemned a member to a life of pain and anguish because of their punishing beliefs and policies? Oddly enough, though, Christian groups continue to cling to ineffective and damaging methods of control.

As a civilized and sophisticated society, we have learned how to teach and help people with information, reinforcement, and positive training. This is not a new or modern idea. Some American Indian groups controlled their children's behavior by noticing and rewarding appropriate behavior while ignoring inappropriate behavior.

We think most people will, if given a choice, choose to care about others and make good judgments about moral issues. They will learn to make good judgments from several natural methods: by watching others suffer consequences, by listening to others discuss solutions, from loving parents, from individuals who teach them in a positive manner, and, most of all, by suffering the consequences of their behavior themselves.

Individuals subjected to destructive beliefs and practices inherent in Christianity suffer emotional injury. They must learn to survive, to protect their self-image, and to feel good about themselves.

In doing so they often must resort to unhealthy but adaptive behavior which becomes damaging to themselves and to others. In trying to survive, they teach their children the same values and maladaptive patterns. In this way Abusive Christianity becomes a self-perpetuating process.

CHAPTER 4

WOUNDED CHRISTIAN SOLDIERS
Personal Consequences
of Abusive Christianity

Abusive Christianity can hurt people of all ages—children, adults, and geriatrics. They can all be yelled at, slapped, hit, and forced to become a survivor. As a general rule, the adaptation to abuse, when comparing an abused child with an abused adult, will be different. Therefore, the age at which abuse occurs becomes an important point to consider.

IDENTITY VERSUS ROLE

The abused child attempts to find a style of behavior that will either reduce the abuse or lead to an escape of abuse. If abuse occurs at an early age, these attempts to survive will become a part of the child's character. The characteristics will become a part of the child's identity. The abused adult also will attempt to find a style of behavior that will reduce or escape the abuse. However, these characteristics tend to be roles the adult takes on, and not necessarily a part of the adult's identity, unless the abuse is constant and the role dominant and consistent.

It is very important to decide whether the behavior tends toward that of a role, or tends toward the identity or character of the individual. A role the individual has assumed is much easier to change than the character of an individual. "Survival techniques" can be thought of as either roles or identities, and that generally depends upon whether the abuse occurred to a child or to an adult. However, remember the presentation on reification. These concepts of role and character are just that, concepts, and to that extent they are useful.

ADAPTATION TO ABUSIVE CHRISTIANITY

In Chapter 2, we described three categories of abuse within Christianity: Christian Abuse, Abusive Christianity, and the Abusive Christian Model. Briefly, Christian Abuse is the abusive behavior of an individual whose motives for that behavior dwell within Christianity. Frequently, the abusive behavior is an attempt to change the "sinful or bad" thoughts or behavior of another individual. For example, a mother who slaps her child's hand because the child is playing with his or her genitals, or a preacher who terrifies a child, trying to manipulate that child into accepting Christ, is indulging in Christian Abuse. Abusive Christianity encompasses those beliefs, held by most Christians, that are inherently abusive and damaging to people, or that lead to further abuse. The Abusive Christian Model portrays the negative influence that Christianity has had on the family when the family models its behavior on the abusive relationship between God and humanity.

Christianity contributes to the abuse of children and adults when families and social institutions follow the Abusive Christian Model. This type of abuse or punishment is usually linked to Christian beliefs, but does not necessarily need to be linked to those beliefs. The previous example of slapping the child's hands for playing with his or her genitals is not directly linked to Christian belief, but it is certainly influenced by that belief, and it is abusive. It is perfectly natural for children to touch and enjoy their genitals. The family influenced by Abusive Christianity expects children to be "perfect Christian children." That would include not being sexual and having their behavior being interpreted as "right or wrong" (not just childish). And then having "wrong behavior" punished. This same type of abuse also is directed toward adults.

These types of abuse, which have been influenced by Christian doctrine, damage individuals. These individuals, children or adults, must survive. It is these means of survival that we will explore now.

SURVIVORS

Adults who were abused as children develop as survivors. They have learned to survive their environment, even though this survival comes at a cost to them personally. The victims of Abusive Christianity are no different. They are survivors the same as individuals reared in an alcoholic family, a physically or verbally abusive family, or a sexually or psychologically incestuous family. In fact, Abusive Christianity may be the dynamic basis for the dysfunction in all these families. All are survivors. All have paid a high price for their survival, and all suffer from psychological scars that result from abuse.

Abused children suffer their first psychological injuries in the area of trust. All children should be able to trust that their environment will be safe and free from harm. Children should be able to trust that their parents will protect them and be there when the children need them. When a child is abused, the family system has broken down because parents bear the responsibility to do their best to protect their child from harm. Thus, in neglect and abuse, the child's trust has been violated, and children must rely on their own devices and coping skills to survive. These skills can develop into roles or identities and generally fall into certain patterns. These patterns consist of "survival skills" which can be thought of as causing psychological injury or psychological "scars" in the child. Many of these scars are typical of any type of abuse. We will discuss these in relation to Abusive Christianity.

The scars generally include the following:
- Problems with deeply trusting others.
- Problems trusting yourself and your ability to survive rejection.
- A "nurturance deficit," a deep need to be loved, leading to loneliness.

- A tendency to "incorporate" or enmesh with the loved person, to fill this emptiness.
- A lack of self-love or positive self-feeling (poor self-esteem).
- A self-critical nature.
- An awareness that something "is wrong with me."
- Shame and guilt.
- Sexual guilt and problems.

Survivors have problems deeply trusting others. Behind this problem is a lack of trust and confidence in themselves. Before you can deeply trust another human being, you must trust that if anything happens to that person you love, you will be okay, you will survive.

In that irrational part of our mind, the "infant mind" that all of us still possess on the unconscious level, abandonment and rejection equate to death. Indeed, if an infant is abandoned by the caretakers, physically abandoned with no help, the infant faces death. There is a primitive connection between rejection and death, and most of us have that primitive fear that equates rejection with death. How often have you heard someone say, "If he leaves me, it will just kill me," or "I would die without her." To deeply trust another person, you must first trust that you will survive.

To confirm this, one only has to look at the dynamics behind family violence and murder. Murder and family violence may be found in couples trying to separate. As an example, a wife will try to leave her husband. The husband will feel abandoned and will experience an irrational feeling that this is "killing" him. Instead of dealing with his pain, hurt, and fear (of death), the husband will protect himself against this perceived hurt and will act out in a violent manner.

This primitive connection and resulting fear are very powerful in a survivor. If you are a survivor, emotionally your parents were "not there for you" or they abused you. Then, the thought follows that "If I cannot trust my own parents, my own flesh and blood, I certainly cannot trust you (husband, wife, children)." The inner unconscious fear is something along the lines of, "It hurt me so much, not having loving, caring parents, I simply could not survive if I let myself become really close to you and then you rejected me. It would kill me." Survivors cannot deeply trust.

Before you can learn to trust your loved ones, you must learn to trust and love yourself. When you do, the trust in others takes a proper perspective. Any loss will certainly hurt, but you will be confident that "I will be okay." Until you are confident you will be okay, the feeling is "I will die." Learning to trust yourself is learning you *will* survive and do not have to fight for survival. The goal here is to increase your self-acceptance and self-love or to re-parent your damaged inner child.

Generally, this lack of self-love goes hand-in-hand with a self-critical nature. This self-critical nature becomes a voice inside your head that abuses and criticizes you. You carry it daily as it pushes its negative propaganda of how bad you are. This voice is an internalized critical, abusive parent or maybe an abusive minister that constantly berates you, puts you down, and diminishes what little self-love you have.

If you do not respect yourself, and if your internal minister is poisonous, you will feel this compelling need to find someone to love you. You will long for a relationship in which someone would "save" or rescue you from yourself. This compensation for the lack of self-love usually does not work out well. In a way, you use the other person to find the love you cannot give yourself. You love the other person because he or she makes you feel better—saves you from the fear and pain of being a survivor. You use the other persons in an attempt to heal the wounds of a lack of self-love and self-respect.

These internal psychological scars, which originate with our abuse or neglect as children, lead us into needy relationships, and these scars deeply complicate those relationships (see Chapter 5). These scars are common to survivors of all forms of abuse. Our emphasis will be on the scars caused by Abusive Christianity and the types of individual adaptation particular to Christianity.

There are several different styles of adaptation, or maladaptation, if you will, to Abusive Christianity. The different adaptive types are:

- Angry Rebels..
- Christian Perpetrators.
- Self-Punishers.
(a) conscious.
(b) unconscious.
- Sheep; those who commit spiritual suicide.
- Disenchanted.
- The Perfect People or "do-gooders."
- Those who confess and forget it; the religious sociopath.

ANGRY REBELS. Everyone knows the Angry Rebel. These persons feel they have been abused one time too often by Christianity. Now, they have had it and they are angry with God, the Christian church, and religion in general. They return anger for perceived anger and injury for injury. Their philosophy is to abuse the abusers. In many ways, they are similar to the Perpetrators of Christian Abuse. Rebels direct their anger against the religion, while the Perpetrators direct their anger against sinners, vices, social ills, each other, and anything or anyone not conforming to their rigid rule system.

Angry Rebels obtain a perverse enjoyment from starting or entering into religious discussions and telling believers how stupid, irrational, or crazy their beliefs happen to be. They love to wax profane and watch believers squirm, telling them how dirty and vulgar they are. The advantage here goes to the Rebel; the believer cannot cuss back! Thus, the abusive battle wages between the Angry Rebel, who is certainly headed "straight to hell," and the believer, who is "full of shit." There is little or no understanding or acceptance from either. Both are trying to survive.

Jerry was working with one Angry Rebel who considered Christianity a "disease," and had serious plans to burn churches. Obviously, his major means of adaptation and survival was anger. Angry Rebels oppose the Judeo-Christian values in our culture and create art, music, and movies which place an emphasis upon sex, nudity, profanity, the stupidity of the work ethic, and the desecration of Christian values and symbols of our culture. They generally reject any type of spirituality along with rejecting the religion.

The rigidity and the black-and-white views of conservative Christianity form a powerful ethic against which Rebels create their "art of the vulgar." If it were not for the rigidity and the black-and-white nature of this ethic, chances are there would be little rebellion. People do not rebel against flexibility and a reasonable, accepting nature. Therefore, the rigid dysfunctional Christian ethic actually contributes to the creation of the art, music, and language that it finds so distasteful.

Angry Rebels usually bypass guilt, at least on a conscious level. They feel no guilt because they feel justified in their anger. They project their hurt onto the believer and feel that the believer deserves to be attacked because of the pain the religion has inflicted upon the Angry Rebel. The Angry Rebels, like the jealous spouse who attacks his or her mate, are surviving the best way they can. They are covering the hurt and pain caused by Christianity with anger and are attacking the religion.

If Angry Rebels were deeply committed to Christianity prior to rebellion, they may experience a loss of direction in their lives and a loss of meaning and purpose. The anger quickly establishes a direction and adds a meaning to the emptiness left by the abandoned rigid religion. Without the anger, they would feel a loss of meaning, an abandonment, and a powerful loss of purpose and direction. They respond to and survive this loss with anger and rebellion. Such persons are the victims of the Abusive Christianity.

CHRISTIAN PERPETRATORS. Christian Perpetrators are also angry. Like the child from an abused family who grows up to be an abuser, the abused Christian Perpetrators vent anger toward those who disagree with them or stand against them. They see their anger as righteous and they try to make the opposition agree with those views. They do not want understanding and compromise, they want compliance and agreement. They feel that God is "on their side," and they will not compromise "God's will." These individuals can best be described as God's warriors in the battle. They are ministers, evangelists, witnesses for Christ, anti-abortion demonstrators, and anyone who pushes ideas and values on others in the name of Christianity.

They expect compliance. In fact, they demand compliance: "One must bend before the will of God." Right is right and their view is right. Others are wrong. There is no "theory" here. They are dealing with the "Truth." These people will take over an organization and create chaos in that organization (see Chapter 5, Institutional Abuse) to achieve their ends. And ultimately, they will fight among themselves! The problem is inherent in the belief, "I know what God wants."

Christian Perpetrators also share a rigidity of thought, intolerance to different opinions, control with power and anger, a lack of being vulnerable, and a great deal of pro-social anger. These characteristics are not due to addictive personalities, they are due to destructive Christian beliefs, their Bible-based belief system.

Doesn't sound like a victim or a survivor, does it? They do not believe they are victims, either, but they are. They survive by their anger and the rigidity of their beliefs, and to this extent they are similar to their nemesis, the Angry Rebel. These two types of people can start wars together. In fact, the Perpetrators will start wars with each other—or new churches—or different churches. Ever wonder why there are so many different Christian denominations? They were either started by Perpetrators or by people trying to escape from Perpetrators.

People who hand out religious tracts which threaten eternal hell if you do not believe, individuals who insist that you listen to their salvation message, and pro-life advocates that harass people, physically harm people and destroy property are examples of Perpetrators of Christian Abuse. The television evangelist is also a shining example of the Perpetrator. These Perpetrators rationalize that they stand up for God, against all others who disagree and are, of course, wrong. Their anger is usually obvious in the delivery of their sermons. Their greed is thinly disguised as requests for money to "further their ministry and the works of God."

One can find Perpetrators of Christian Abuse anywhere. They can be found in local Christian churches, PTA groups, evangelistic associations, revival meetings, and ringing your doorbell. They gather in front of abortion clinics, at political conventions, and at state and local governing bodies to assert their views and demand compliance.

Yet Christian Perpetrators are survivors and victims. They are victims of an abusive, rigid system of beliefs which places them in conflict with others and with their own feelings and impulses. They have been victimized by the anger, the lack of understanding, and lack of genuine openness and honesty with family members that Christian beliefs can cause. They have experienced exclusion and, at times, rejection and emotional abandonment. They are trying to survive their own human impulses, especially the sexual, which they see as "carnal." They are trying to survive their own fear, hurt, and angry/violent impulses. They survive by covering their hurt with anger. At times, the rigidity of their ethical system will break down and their impulses will surface. They will act out sexually or in greed or anger, in some way which reveals their pain, neediness, and lack of peace. They polarize against their own "evil" impulses in a type of "reaction formation," thus fighting these impulses in themselves and others.

These individuals are wounded by Christianity but are not aware of it. They continue to wound others, some in overt and obvious ways and some in very subtle ways. In many instances they are difficult people to get close to, because they are not "close" to themselves. They have a hard time accepting themselves, especially their impulses and drives. Further, they have difficulty with closeness because they are so angry. They offer shallow platitudes, instead of looking at themselves and revealing themselves to anyone. They will talk of "love," but there is no love unless you agree with them and comply with them. Family behavior is similar to the alcoholic who marries the codependent and rears dysfunctional children.

The Perpetrators distort love. They think that love and anger are opposites. They think that to love is to control people, including their own children, with power and anger. Children are expected to submit to this control. If they do not submit, the Perpetrator parent will withdraw love as a form of punishment (see Chapter 5, Anger and Love). Similarly, if church members violate the rules, other church members will withdraw their love. "Fallen members" are generally expected to leave or may even be excommunicated. In this situation, church members tacitly become Christian Perpetrators.

Perpetrators are narcissistic and their love is narcissistic. Some of these individuals, in fact, would meet the psychiatric criteria necessary for the diagnosis of narcissistic personality disorder. They view their ideas and beliefs as the Truth. They are convinced they are correct and right. As long as your belief is consistent with their belief, you are a "brother" or a "sister" and they will love you. If you disagree or do not comply with their views, you are an "outcast," an infidel or a heretic. Then they do not love you, but look down on you with anger and righteous vengeance.

When you see an evangelist, either on television or in a revival, look at the way they dress and style their hair. They are usually narcissistic in dress, appearance, and the manner in which they speak and interact. Their suits are impeccably tailored and every hair is sprayed in place. They speak with power and bravado, usually with abundant emotion. They use their image effectively.

Power and control are very important to the Perpetrators. The formula is simple: They must have the power and they must be in control. If not, they tend to split the group, leave the group with their following, or overpower those who are in control. They will not give up power because that is not consistent with their belief. They are right. God's word says they are right. They do not believe they "interpret" the Bible, so it is not their interpretation, *it* is God's word. They cannot compromise. There is no room for negotiation. Reason is not effective, either. That is "man's wisdom," not God's word. Needless to say, you can't argue with these folks. It will not work.

Perpetrators, as ministers, are charismatic, persuasive, and have a loyal following. They generally direct their anger to other groups, especially those groups they see as "doing the devil's work." Those groups may be other denominations, women's groups, homosexual groups, any group that does not behave the way they think people should behave. They are *not* tolerant. It is their mission to change these people and win them to the "right way," their way.

Some Perpetrators can be very intrusive. The street preachers have the right, they think, to preach anywhere in the public street. They preach, and they hand out literature, regardless of whether anyone wants to listen to or read their material. It is excellent marketing, but it is intrusive. They feel they have a right to be intrusive and "to win people to Christ."

On August 20, 1991, in Wichita, Kansas, more than 130 anti-abortion demonstrators were arrested after they stormed an abortion clinic. Observers described their actions as "aggressive." The "Christian" demonstrations had been going on for several months and the group had defied several court orders to stop their actions. Such Christian Perpetrators feel justified in being intrusive, in being aggressive, even violent, to make their point. They feel justified in being abusive toward people or a class of people because they are right. They know God's way. The others are simply wrong and *they* need to change.

These Perpetrators of Christian Abuse are "shame based," to use the words of John Bradshaw, who is the host of the PBS series on the family and a well-known writer of self-help psychology books. They are victims of a system of thinking that is rigid and inflexible, that sees the world in black/white, right/wrong terms, and that places values, ideas, and concepts over human beings. These victims cover their feelings with anger, and they project this anger onto others. They are almost always unaware of their shame, their insecurity, and their feelings of inadequacy.

They fear their own thinking and are ashamed of their thinking, so they try not to think. They just "believe," and act on those beliefs. They fear their own impulses and desires and, as such, they are vulnerable. Instead of dealing with these issues, which are internal, they attack these issues in other people. Perpetrators will band together, but only as long as they think alike. They may act close, but only as long as they think you agree with them.

Christian Perpetrators have adopted a "false self," as marriage counselor Harville Hendrix describes in *Getting the Love You Want*. It is a false self even though it is a religious self. This false religious self centers on power, anger, charisma, and control. The Perpetrators remain cut off from a significant part of their human nature. They do not experience understanding and empathy with people who are different. They demand change to their way of thinking. They have learned to survive by protecting themselves with anger and attempting to control others.

SELF-PUNISHERS. If you are a Self-Punisher, your middle name is guilt. One Self-Punisher we know said: "I feel guilty when I drive by a car accident. I wonder what I did wrong!" You are probably familiar with the verse in the Bible "For ALL have sinned and come short of the glory of God." Feeling sinful and feeling short of glory is easy for you. If you have an argument with a friend or lover, you know it is your fault.

The guilt experienced by the Self-Punisher is usually not appropriate to the situation. The guilt is excessive, or the person may feel guilty for really no reason at all. The origin of this guilt is in the psychological scars which result from neglect and abuse in early childhood and continue into adulthood under the system of Abusive Christianity. Low self-esteem and feelings of worthlessness accompany this guilt. These people can feel guilty for being human.

Self-Punishers believe they were born sinners, that they were born bad. This belief influences their development, especially their feelings of self-worth. Consider this, along with all the rules, the do's and don'ts found in conservative Christianity; then place in that formula perfectionism, rigidity, people who point out your wrongdoings in an angry and condemning way, and what do you have? A psychological mess! But a mess that teaches guilt and shame.

Where is the anger in the Self-Punisher? In the Perpetrator, these feelings of shame are projected onto others. In the Self-Punisher, the anger is directed inward. These people mistreat themselves. Their internal self-talk is very negative; that is, they worry. At times, they are unaware that their beliefs and self-talk hurt them.

One client, Austin, was so negative and so self-depreciating that he was amazed when he finally realized how he treated himself. "I don't even treat my enemies that badly," he concluded. He was constantly telling himself, "I can't do that. It's no use." Finally he became aware he would not talk that way to anyone else, so why say it to himself?

These people do angry things to themselves. They do not change jobs or professions even though they know they would be happier. They sabotage success and relationships with their sadness, internalized anger, and guilt. They accept their plight with an attitude of, "That's the way it is."

It is easy to see that depression is common in the Self-Punisher. In fact, one way to conceptualize depression is that it is anger turned inward. The anger expresses itself in negative self-talk and beliefs which end in depression. The low self-esteem only adds to the depression.

Many of the self-help books for depression advocate the combination of changing internal self-talk to more positive self-talk along with exercises to increase self-esteem. You feel what you think (self-talk). It could just as easily be said that you feel what you believe. Destructive Christian Beliefs lead to negative thinking and thus to depression.

Self-Punishers do not have a lot of zest and vitality for life. They will not be a preacher or a "go-getter," as is the Perpetrator. Self-Punishers will not split churches or condemn sinners. They would worry too much about the effects on everyone to do anything that drastic. So they do very little to cause problems. In a way, the Self-Punisher regresses back to an early, childlike stage of development. Self-Punishers are compliant children, guilty children, abused children.

The Self-Punisher may or may not attend church on a regular basis. Those who do not, feel badly about it and worry about it. They make plans to attend on a regular basis "some day soon." Those who attend regularly generally do so to assuage their guilt. They may attend on a regular basis but remain little known to other church members. They are much too caught up in worry and negative thinking to be assertive. Anyway, they would feel guilty about being assertive.

SOMATIC ADAPTERS. Some Self-Punishers manage to escape into illnesses, both mental and physical. They experience guilt, shame, and feelings of powerlessness. They tend to be critical of themselves and thus experience a great deal of internal stress. As a result, these Somatic Adapters are prone to stress-related illnesses along with depression.

If you ask Somatic Adapters about their lives or their feelings, they generally deny having any "problems" other than the physical illness. They focus on the illness as the cause of their bad feelings. To some, the illness seems to be their "cross to bear," or their punishment from God.

The Somatic Adapters may neglect own needs in favor of their families, their friends, or their church. They take care of everyone but themselves. Often, illness becomes a way to escape duties.

The list of stress-related illness is extensive— from cancer, to chronic pain, to the common cold. When people think of stress, they quickly think of jobs, their children, mothers-in-law, the economy, finances, and lost car keys. These issues are certainly important, but one element causes more stress than all of these: *Your mind.* The way you think.

It is not your job that causes stress (unless you work in severe heat or lift heavy weights—physical stress), it is the way you think about your job. It is not your children, not even your mother-in-law. It is how you interpret your environment and how you think about it.

Christianity teaches people to think in terms of good and bad, right and wrong, fair and unfair, sin and virtue. The power of Evil lurks about and may topple the Christian into sin at any moment.

One must be vigilant to avoid the power of Evil. This type of thinking is negative and stressful and is generally rigid and inflexible.

Christianity also teaches us to think in terms of external causes and not internal causes. Spirits guide you. God may "bless" you with good health, happiness and safety. Satan may cause you evil thinking or temptations. You are taught to think of yourself as a type of battlefield between the forces of good, or God, and the forces of evil, or Satan. This very thinking forms a basis for stress.

Ego boundaries are fuzzy. The world is magical. Things outside of you can cause you to think and feel certain ways. So it is quite natural for you to think your stress is found "out there." Of course, you do not feel responsible for this stress, so you feel helpless to do anything about it. Individual responsibility is not emphasized.

As a result, rigid and inflexible thinking, poor ego boundaries, externalization of stress, and magical thinking can combine to produce very unhealthy and stressful worry and thinking—thinking for which the individual does not feel responsible. Some individuals respond with physical or mental illness. Their stressful thinking originates in the beliefs and concepts of Christianity.

SHEEP OR SPIRITUAL SUICIDE. These are the church workers, the churches' "salt-of-the-earth." They, too, can be victims if they give up their identity to comply with their religion. In all fairness, some of these individuals would have no identity without their religion. They would be lost in an identity crisis.

Christianity provides for only two basic identities. You are either a Christian or you are a sinner. To be a good Christian, you must follow. These people follow.

They are usually faithful church members, very dependable and responsible. They make up the largest group of church workers, and they are hard workers. They work as choir members, Sunday School teachers, nuns, deacons, elders, lay workers, and volunteer office workers. They work within the system and they find their identity within the system.

In some instances, psychologically this is a healthy response to a healthy, meaningful, and fulfilling religion. However, some people give up parts of themselves in order to comply with their religion; they give up all or part of their identity. They open up their psychological boundaries and become a part of a system. In order to do this, they actually "kill" their spirit in order to follow their Christianity. Thus the dual label "spiritual suicide" or Sheep.

What do they kill or give up? Frequently, it is their thinking, their rationality, their curiosity, their sexuality and sensuality, their anger—the essence of what makes them unique. They develop a "false self," a "religious self." They are fearful of and ashamed of their human emotions and animal urges. Therefore, they detach themselves from their impulses, which become "ego dystonic." They have internally killed or denied a part of themselves. Generally, these individuals are unaware they have sacrificed a part of their personality. They may have never known their anger or sexuality. Or, they quickly grew to fear their impulses.

These individuals rarely create problems in the church, as do the Rebels and the Perpetrators. They are followers and not leaders. Many Sheep are women, following their traditional role in the church.

There are many examples of Sheep and none of them stand out, which is their very nature. One couple we know had been married 30 years and never had an argument. The family dysfunction was quickly found in the behavior and divorces of their children.

DISENCHANTED DROPOUTS. These are the individuals we often think of when we think about Abusive Christianity. They have generally quit going to church and are hurt or disenchanted with the church minister, membership, or theology. They may have gone through a phase of rebellion. Or they, like the couple we discussed earlier, John and Mary Jane, dropped out as a result of injury and abuse from the religion and their religious leaders.

Another example is this young divorced individual:

At the age of 16 I had started messing up my life. My first error was to get married. My second error was to get a divorce. By this time I was ready to come home and start over. So I went home. However, nothing was the same. Mother had married a really super man. This man offered to help in any way possible, and he was sincere in his offer. Both my sisters were married and gone.

My church wouldn't have me because I was divorced and there really wasn't a place (class) for me anymore. I was 17 just like all my other friends there, but they were single, they hadn't messed up their lives. I hadn't realized being mistake-proof was a prerequisite for being taken back into the fold.

Bottom line, I had lost the support of my religion at a time I needed it most. Don't be mistaken, I was thoroughly and completely shocked. I was puzzled. Disbelief and hurt filled me. Slowly but surely I became very, very angry with what was supposed to be a sanctuary for sinners. A place where all people could worship God. It was evident that the God I had known and believed in as a child was no longer a God who cared for me. I knew I no longer wanted to be part of this horrible farce. It hurt too much. I felt angry, duped, and ashamed.

After one particularly trying experience, I went home to the solace of my pets. It seemed no matter what I did they didn't care. They just loved me. This reality overwhelmed me that day. It dawned on me that these animals had made mistakes. Big mistakes such as getting out of the fence when they weren't supposed to, or chewing up my old stuffed monkey. Never, ever had it entered my mind to forbid them to come back home.

I heard two interesting comments after I left the church. The first was, well, those people just weren't real Christians. A real Christian would never have treated you that way. Of course, no one taught me there was a difference in real Christians and not real Christians. The second comment was from a lady a year or two older than myself who had just experienced the same thing from the same church. Her comment, 'They can have it, there has to be something better.'

Pregnancy of unwed adolescents is another problem which frequently leads to Christian Abuse with the resulting reaction from the victim of abuse. The girl is made to feel dirty and guilty for her sin. You see very few conservative Christian churches with programs for unwed mothers who had unwanted pregnancies. Such a program would be most helpful. However, as long as such pregnancy is seen as a sin and as "evil," there is no help for these people. At least, no help coming from the conservative Christian churches.

Other situations that may lead a person to become disenchanted with conservative Christianity is the reaction to the theological beliefs or to the rule system of the specific church. It is not uncommon for people to react to the rigid rule systems found in these churches. Or they may react to the way members discipline or ignore other members because they have violated the rule system. These Disenchanted see the abuse for what it is, abuse.

Jerry attended a group session of adolescent hospitalized drug abusers which was being run by a "minister" who was also a "Christian counselor." The minister berated and chastised the adolescents for their haircuts and color of their hair, their manner of dress, and the music they listened to. What a display of emphasis upon the trivial while avoiding the real issues of the severe drug abuse!

These kids were angry, and the fight was on. Most had been abused by their parents, so abuse was not new to them. They knew how to fight and how to survive. One young man responded, "If this is Christianity, I want out. I would rather go to hell, than be in heaven with a shit like you." The minister had displayed no love, no compassion, no understanding. The adolescents certainly did not feel understood.

The Disenchanted are sick and tired of all the rules. They are disappointed in the magic that does not work. They are weary of the abuse and the lack of understanding. They want out and they want no part of it. They do not talk about religion. They do not share their views, as does the Angry Rebel, nor do they preach against the religion. They want the religion to leave them alone.

PERFECT PEOPLE AND "DO-GOODERS." These people can literally drive you crazy. Everything is "wonderful" and "a blessing." Similar to Dr. Pangloss in *Candide*, they are addicted to joy and happiness. It is a most wonderful world. They talk about Jesus as if he were the great guy next door who constantly blesses their life. What they lack in reverence, they make up in enthusiasm. The major psychological dynamic in these individuals is denial.

Jerry goes to a local convenience store daily to purchase a soft drink. There is a young woman in the convenience store who is *always* smiling, *always* happy. She is the embodiment of the Bible verse "in all things give thanks." Once she told Jerry that Jesus had blessed her with a flat tire so she could prove how happy life was. Somehow, it's hard to imagine the Savior of mankind going around letting air out of people's tires, but she was convinced and she was happy, happy, happy. This young woman is always saying things such as: "Jesus be with you. God loves you. May Jesus be the light in your life." She uses those words instead of a simple "goodbye." She has probably wanted to "witness" to Jerry but does not feel he is a likely prospect. She wants everyone to know how important God is in her life and she tells everyone, whether they want to know or not. These people tend to be intrusive and they want everyone to believe the way they believe and "share in the joy of Jesus and salvation." They are similar to the Perpetrators, but without any anger or malice. In fact, they deny any anger. God takes care of everything for them and they tell everyone. These people create discomfort in others, because they push their religion on you, and you get the distinct feeling things are not as wonderful as they always seem to be. This overly optimistic view conceals a great deal of buried anger and frustration. But they always give the impression that their lives are "perfect" and everything is wonderful.

Bradshaw, in his book *Homecoming*, refers to these people as "emotion addicts." They are addicted to joy and happiness and, like all addicts, deep in denial, they are partial people, out of touch with their feelings. They attempt to survive those feelings by acting as if they do not exist.

CONFESS-IT-AND-FORGET-IT. These are the religious sociopaths better known as the "hypocrites." These individuals act out, then go to church or mass and "confess it and forget it." They go through the motions of religion, but the religion does not really mean anything to them. They do not live their religion in any way. If they do have shame or guilt, and they may, they are deeply in denial of those feelings. These individuals are survivors in that they deny spirituality in their lives.

Most of the confess-it people still go to church. They are victims of Abusive Christianity; if they respond in any way to the religion, it is socially. The religion means little to their lives, and their "religion" is without spirituality. Their spirituality has been channeled into other areas, such as money, sex, or other addictive processes.

Later in the chapter on sexuality, we will discuss individuals that sexually act out. Their sexual addiction and acting out are based upon being victimized by their religion. Even though they may not act it, they are generally deeply ashamed, but feel trapped and cannot see the alternatives. They are victims of the abusive nature of Christianity, without spirituality or meaning.

Many of the confess-it-and-forget-it individuals victimize others and may even use their religion to abuse others. They are narcissistic and when they want their needs met, nothing stands in the way of meeting their needs, especially not their Christianity. They have detached from their guilt and shame, and those emotions no longer regulate or moderate their behavior. Their control is a desire not to mar their "good" image, and that image is shallow and narcissistic.

James openly admitted that he attended a large local church because, he said, "You can find the hottest women who are usually disease- and drug-free." He was using the church to prey on women, to meet his sexual needs. He saw nothing wrong with this, nor was it inconsistent with his beliefs. "You have to meet them somewhere" was his attitude.

The confess-it-and-forget-it people are not empathetic. Their needs are primary and they do not think of the feelings and plight of others. Almost everyone is aware of the prominent business executive or television evangelist who is very active in church and religion but is unethical in business practice or personal life. They use people and run over people.

These individuals have the same injured and wounded core as the other survivors. Many of their injuries are due to abuses which surround the Christian religion, especially the lack of spirituality found in much Christianity.

RUNNING FROM RELIGION. One way to deal with a stressful situation is simply to leave. If you leave the stressful situation, you can leave the stress. Many who have been abused by their religion, instead of adjusting, adopting, or changing in some manner try to leave. Others have adapted to their religion, but at a personal and psychological cost. They have given up part of their humanity. We would like to pose the question, especially to the Angry Rebel and the Disenchanted: "Can you run from your religion?" We think the answer is no. You may leave your church or your denomination, but you cannot leave your personal religion, your beliefs and values. You can redefine your religion (see Chapters 7, 8, and 9) and seek your own source of spiritual comfort, but you cannot run from yourself. Religion is an important part of who you are—your identity. Spirituality is an important part of being human. We would like to encourage the survivors of Christianity to read the last section of this book and to begin your own spiritual quest.

ADDICTIONS. A word of caution about beginning your own spiritual quest. Bradshaw, in his excellent book *Healing the Shame That Binds You,* states that toxic shame "is the root and fuel of all compulsive/addictive behaviors." (Bradshaw, page 15). We would certainly agree with this, and we would add that many brands of Christianity are perpetrators of neurotic shame. These religions shame people for being human and for what are normal sexual impulses. These religions induce shame by their very belief systems, for example, You were born in sin. Sin which was so bad that only the death of God's Son can save you. This sin is not something you have done, it is the essence of what you are. That is the source of toxic shame. And that is Abusive Christianity.

Since the theory that toxic shame is the basis of compulsive behaviors and addictions seems to make sense, it would follow that Christian religions tend to be addictive in nature and tend to set up other addictive behaviors and compulsive behaviors. Jerry can personally attest to this.

When he left Southwestern Baptist Theological Seminary, where he was studying for the Baptist ministry, he became an Angry Rebel. He was angry with religion and wanted nothing to do with it. He was angry with God. Who could be so stupid as to set up a system of religion which so ignored human needs and human dilemmas and actually contributed to human problems? He was angry with an organization (denomination) that rejected you and did not want you if you disagreed with them. Having been a Perpetrator himself as a preacher, it was natural to become an Angry Rebel.

After leaving the seminary, Jerry became addicted to almost everything. Alcohol, anger, being saved by women, psychology, pocket knives ("my Freudian stage"), and even pieces of paper which he could not throw away. His behavior tended toward the compulsive in almost everything. "I would go to work rain or shine, sickness or health, drunk or sober, hungover or not; I was a work-a-holic!" Jerry recalls. "Although I did not know it at the moment, my life was filled with shame, and I was a mass of compulsive and addictive behaviors."

Personally and in our private practices, we have seen the relationship between compulsive behavior and shame, and further, the relationship between neurotic or toxic shame and early childhood abandonment and trauma. Much of the early trauma is caused by dysfunctional parents, alcoholism, and anger. We believe that the tenets of Christianity have contributed to the basis of that toxic shame. We have seen people addicted to alcohol, drugs, and chemicals in an attempt to fill the spiritual void left by shame rooted in Christianity.

If you were reared with Abusive Christianity or by a family of Christian Abusers, be careful to watch for addictive behavior, and do not be "ashamed" to seek help. Do not forget you are a survivor and do not let the "survivor" attitude stop you from seeking help. The survivor attitude is: "If I cannot do it myself, it cannot be done," and/or "How can they (counselors) help? It's *my* problem." Survivors do not understand relationships well enough to understand help. So, it is difficult to seek and ask for help. Resist that attitude and reach out and trust.

See if you recognize yourself or someone you know in the following lists of Christian identities:

HOW TO KNOW IF YOU ARE A SURVIVOR OF ABUSE

1. There is a feeling of loneliness or aloneness, even when in a crowd.
2. You want very badly to be loved, but usually no one knows.
3. You are not sure what it means "to be loved." And you are not sure what an intimate relationship is.
4. You are very prone to relationships which are enmeshed.
5. You are prone to relationships in which you "save" or take over the person, or they "save" or take over you.
6. You do not deeply trust anyone.
7. You did not really trust your parents. You had secrets.
8. You have a fantasy life far different from your real life.
9. You have difficulty with close relationships.
10. You strongly fear rejection.

THE SHEEP/SPIRITUAL SUICIDE ADAPTERS

1. You do not always agree with your church, but you are loyal to it.
2. You give up your time and yourself for your church, choir, Sunday school, prayer meetings, etc.
3. Your family is proud of you, but often tells you that you do too much.
4. You lose yourself in your church work. You ARE your church work.
5. If you suddenly lost your church work, you would be lost.
6. For all you do, you are a follower and not a leader.
7. If there is something to do in the church, they can always count on you.
8. Frequently your personal life is not as happy as your church life.
9. You may have been hurt by religion but you accepted it along with the punishment/repentance.

THE PERFECT PEOPLE AND DO-GOODERS

1. God has been so wonderful and good for you and to you.
2. You rarely carry on a conversation in which you do not mention Jesus, God, or your religion.
3. You are rarely angry.
4. You have faith that whatever happens, it is for your good and is in God's plan for your life.
5. You believe God answers your personal prayers.
6. You believe God can work miracles, and He does work miracles in your life.
7. God rules the world and has His plan for the world.
8. God is coming again soon.
9. You believe every word in the Bible was inspired by God.

10. You may not be involved in a church, but you are involved in your personal religion.
11. You have no close friends outside of your religion.
12. Your life would have no meaning without your religion.
13. The word fanatic would fit you.

THE SOMATIC ADAPTERS

1. You deny that you have any significant problems or bad feelings.
2. Your doctor tells you that your physical problems are due to stress.
3. You take care of others in your family or your church before meeting your own needs.
4. You feel it is "un-Christian" to complain or be angry with others.
5. You regularly "turn the other cheek."
6. You constantly feel tired or sick.
7. You allow others in your church or family to make decisions for you and you seldom stand up for yourself.
8. You feel guilty when you say "no" or do anything for yourself.
9. You accept the guilt others place on you.

CONFESS-IT-AND-FORGET-IT

1. This book was given to you. You have never bought a book on religion.
2. You believe in God, but you do what you want.
3. You go to church for mainly social reasons. You enjoy the people.
4. What you believe and what the church teaches are not the same, but you have told no one.
5. You have never felt hurt by any belief even though your behavior is not consistent with that belief.

THE DISENCHANTED

1. You feel you have been injured by your religion.
2. You quit going to church and have no interest in going back.
3. You can remember a specific situation or event which hurt you.
4. You do not talk about your religion.
5. You do not talk about that part of your past, when you were hurt.
6. You may have problems with compulsive behavior/addictions.
7. You may have problems with relationships.
8. You tend to withdraw.

THE ANGRY REBELS

1. You are angry with religion.
2. You are angry with God.
3. You quit going to church or when you do go you become angry with the church.
4. When you are not angry you feel depressed.
5. You feel life is pointless and meaningless, but you go on anyway.
6. You have problems trusting people.
7. You have feelings of resentment and bitterness in general and specifically toward God and religion.
8. The words "God," "Christ," and "Christian" are immediate "red flags" to you. You react negatively to the words.
9. You may be happiest when alone, or with nature or animals.
10. You cannot believe what some people will believe.
11. You cannot believe what you used to believe.
12. When upset, you tend to attack, to act out.

THE PERPETRATORS

1. You refuse to think there could be anything wrong with conservative Christian religion.
2. You instinctively or intuitively know, but fear, there is something wrong with conservative Christian religion.
3. You cannot tolerate different views, especially within your own denomination.
4. You feel a strong need to change or control people of different views— or you reject them.
5. Dealing with anger, especially "righteous anger," is easy for you.
6. When you are angry with people, you reject them.
7. At times you hurt those you love because they do not agree with you.
8. You are willing to sacrifice people over your beliefs. (You would "cast the first stone" at the woman caught in adultery, especially if she were in your church!)
9. You hide behind the excuse, "It is the work of the devil" or "That is evil."
10. You probably grow angry and deny all of the above.
11. "If the Bible says it, that's final!" is your attitude. And you know what the Bible says.
12. You externalize your thoughts and feelings.

THE SELF-PUNISHERS

1. You feel guilty all the time or assume guilt in situations which are inappropriate.
2. You fear anger or feel guilty over anger.
3. You think anger/hate and love are opposites.
4. You do not know how to deal with anger in a healthy manner.
5. You don't trust your judgment, your own interpretations of life and the Bible. "If the Bible says it, that is final!"

But you are not really sure of the meaning of what the Bible says.

6. You fear friends and certainly fear your, or your children's, marriage "outside the faith."
7. You fear that without Christian religion, you or your children would go wild.
8. You fear God is not in control of your life.
9. You feel God punishes those that do evil and wrong.
10. As a woman, you have no sexual response, period. No sexual interest.
11. As a man, you feel you are "oversexed." Or you may deny you are sexually addicted but lust after every woman you see.
12. You may confuse psychological intimacy and sexual intimacy.
13. You internalize your feelings and thoughts (worry).
14. You tend to be faithful and dependable.

EMOTIONAL MANIPULATION AND CONSEQUENCES

The emotions used to manipulate in Christianity are the same emotions that end up with people damaged and scarred. In persuading people to make decisions, the persuasion is much more effective if one can involve emotions in that decision making process. Many sales techniques involve excitement, power, and prestige to motivate the customer to decide in favor of the salesperson. When threats to the individual's welfare or life are made, the techniques become abusive.

GUILT, SHAME, AND FEAR. Guilt and shame are the main emotional motivators used in persuading people to become Christians. Lost souls are manipulated by guilt, shame, and fear. These emotions are evoked by messages given to the victim. Examples of these messages are:

- You are born in sin.
- All have sinned and fall short of the glory of God.
- You *must* be saved.

- Christ is the only way.
- Are you ready for the judgment day?
- Christ shed His blood for you.
- You are lost (in sin).
- Eternal life hangs in the balance.

Many churches use an emotional plea for the "lost" to walk down the aisle and "accept" Christ as his or her savior. Pleas to "join the family," or "join the body of Christ," are made to manipulate those to "give up their old sinful ways and become a new person in Christ." The emotions of shame, guilt, and fear are used to manipulate the individual into making a decision. Can one say "no" to eternal life? That is powerful manipulation.

The manipulation in these pleas should be obvious to anyone who has attended a church that gains members by this means. The minister sells the concept to the consumer by using the consumer's guilt, shame, and fear. Granted, the believer thinks that the "sales job" is in the best interest of the consumer, that "eternal life hangs in the balance." However, it is manipulative and abusive to use people's primitive emotions to manipulate them into doing what you want them to do. That is, to come down the aisle and accept Christ and become one of "us."

If you do not do this, you are, of course, excluded. You are an "outcast, a sinner, a reprobate, a heretic, an atheist, an agnostic," and not "one of the fold." You are excluded from the church, from the social interaction and, as far as the church is concerned, you are excluded from heaven. That only leaves one place for you to go. Hell. "*You* are unworthy of heaven." The manipulation by fear and shame does not end.

Sadly, people follow this same type of emotional manipulation in their family affairs, with the resulting dysfunction and scars. Family pressure is consistent and strong so that a child in the family really has no choice but to be of the same religion. The family will then function with the rigid rules, and adherence to the rules brought about by fear and guilt. Then, following the Abusive Christian Model, punishment with anger and lack of intimacy add to the dysfunction inherent in the religion. The emotional and psychological scars from this type of Christianity are well known among therapists and include the following:

- Excessive guilt.
- Excessive fear, especially of the unusual.
- Fear of other religions.
- Fear of different ideas.
- Poor self image.
- Feelings of worthlessness.
- Low self-confidence.
- A shame-based life.
- Sexual dysfunction.
- Compulsive behavior.
- Magical thinking.

To the extent that Christianity promotes shame, it promotes addictions. These addictions may be chemical, emotional, or behavioral. The addiction may be to the religion itself. This type of Christianity captures people. You must do as "they" say. When you do, you feel "a part of" it, you feel good. You feel "high." The price for this good feeling is, as with any addiction, the sacrifice of your individuality, your creativity.

LONELINESS. We would like to venture that people are not born lonely—alone certainly, but lonely, no. Individuals are taught to be lonely. Loneliness is learned right along with shame in the childhood experience. The concepts of original sin contribute greatly to lessons in loneliness and shame. In the concept of original sin, people are born sinners. They *are* sinners. You do not have a problem. You are a problem. You are a sinner. You are unworthy and doomed. This concept reaches the core identity. You are defective. That is a lonely condition. Christian concepts teach loneliness and shame. They create the very need to be "saved," to be lifted out of this miserable condition.

Combine this with the fact that people need to affiliate, and churches of old were almost guaranteed membership. There is really nothing wrong with meeting this need to affiliate in religion. In fact, this is the major reason that people attend meetings, join clubs, social organizations, and business groups.

Church should meet social needs. However, to become a part of the Christian religion, you must believe what that specific religion teaches. And in most conservative Christian religions, you must adhere to certain creeds. If you do not, you are shamed. You are probably doomed, damned, or at least outcast and you end up alone and lonely. Loneliness is a powerful motivator. As a result, church and denominational membership are motivated by powerful emotions in the individual. Emotions which are created, in part, and manipulated by Christian beliefs. This manipulation is in the best interest of the church and church membership and participation.

The scars of Abusive Christianity include loneliness, along with guilt, shame, and fear. These powerful emotions form the bedrock for pathology in individuals and in relationships.

ANGER VS. LOVE. One of the characteristics of the Abusive Christian Model, and one of the typical traits of alcoholic and dysfunctional families, is the confusion of anger and hatred as being the opposite of love. This is a common characteristic of Christian religion, and this Abusive Christian Model may, in fact, be the prototype for the confusion of love versus anger in our culture. This confusion is common in Perpetrators and Angry Rebels. The historical precedent for this behavior was the God of the Old Testament growing angry and either punishing or killing the people for misbehavior.

We have worked with many parents who feel positive about their children. When feeling positive, they say things such as, "I love you. You are very important to me." When those parents become angry, they say things such as, "I hate you. Get out of my sight, I never want to see you again." Or, "Go to your room and stay out of my sight."

The parent is confusing anger as the opposite of love, and it is not. Anger is a part of love or involvement. If you love someone, you will probably become angry with them at some time. When angry, you still love them. The opposite of love is apathy. If you do not love, you have *no* feelings for them. You are apathetic toward them.

In the prototypic Abusive Christian Model, God loves the world, but there is a qualification on that love. You must believe in Him and do what He says. If you do not believe in Him, you will be punished and spend the rest of your life, your eternal life, in hell.

Now, that last part sure sounds like the opposite of love. God doesn't love you any more if you do not obey him, so He withdraws His love and punishes with what certainly sounds like abusive anger. In this manner, in Christian religions, anger and love are displayed as opposites. Either He loves you or He is angry with you.

In the families that have been influenced by this type of thinking, the parent may think as follows: "I love you, but if you do not do what I say, I will no longer love you and will punish you." This is exactly the way the Abusive Christian dysfunctional family operates. They love you, but if you do not obey, they will withdraw love. Then, they may punish you with anger, such as yelling, screaming, and at times slapping and hitting. In these families, anger is the opposite of love. And since anger is not the opposite of love, these families become trapped in a love-anger-punishment-guilt cycle. As individuals, they become confused as to why they treat their loved ones so badly.

People may say, "The reason I punish you is because I love you." This is what they say, anyway. But if really pressed as to why they hurt the people they love, they do not understand it themselves. They are following the Abusive Christian Model.

If by "punishment," you mean setting limits in a firm but caring manner, that is fine. But if punishment is rejection and abusive anger, that is certainly confusing at best and, we believe, misguided. You do not hurt people you love. You guide them, teach them, set limits on them, explain those limits, but you do not hurt them. Anger and limits need not be hurtful or punishing.

We have stated that anger is a part of love. The question now is, how should anger be handled so as not to harm the individual you love? The book *Do I Have to Give Up Me to Be Loved by You?*, by Jordan and Margaret Paul, is an excellent manual on how to deal with anger without hurting the person you care about. Anger must be addressed within intimacy. Intimacy is defined as "dealing with real feelings and issues." In order to do this, first we must examine anger more closely.

Much of what looks like anger in an individual is not really anger at all. Anger is what we call the "cover emotion." The real emotions below the surface of the protective anger are usually hurt and fear. Why are these feelings of hurt and fear not directly expressed? Why are they covered with anger? If people feels hurt and do not trust people not to hurt them, they certainly do not want to be vulnerable by exposing their hurt. If you express hurt, you are vulnerable to being hurt more. If you cover the hurt with anger, you do not feel vulnerable, but you also are not dealing with the real feelings or the real issue.

Anger can also be a cover emotion for fear. Jerry recalls an episode in which he used anger to cover his fear.

> Once when my son was younger he was playing in our front yard and not paying attention to his surroundings. During his play, he ran into the street directly in front of a fast-moving car. The driver swerved and narrowly missed him. I found myself yelling in an angry manner at him to pay attention to the traffic and watch what he was doing. I slowly became aware I was not angry. I was afraid that I would see my son injured and have to deal with his and my trauma. The real issue is a message of fear because of love. I was able to stop the anger and share my fear and comfort my son.

The anger is a way to avoid being vulnerable and avoid facing fear.

Anger can also be narcissistic. Narcissistic anger is based on the attitude that "The world is not working the way I want it to work, so

I am going to get angry with it." Or, "You are not behaving like I want you to behave, so I will become angry with you—to manipulate you to behave the way I (the narcissist) want you to behave."

This anger is self-centered. This is precisely the type of anger God seems to display as conceptualized by conservative Christianity. "If you do not believe in my Son and follow the way I want, I will punish you forever." That is narcissistic anger. This type of narcissistic anger in the Christian belief system is the opposite of love. "God will punish you forever." That is not love. You help people that you love.

Anger is much more complicated. It is connected to our values. It can be a projection of those characteristics that we hate in ourselves onto other people, so we become angry with them (when, really, we are angry with ourselves).

So, the goal in dealing with anger is to realize that it is a part of love. That is a difficult personal discovery, and it entails being vulnerable. You learn to trust those you love and to become vulnerable with them so you can deal with the real emotion and the real issue involved.

DEPRESSION/SUICIDE AND PUNISHMENT. Jack had a wife and three kids. He was a devout Christian and conservative family man until he experienced an emotional crisis which caused him to face his homosexual feelings. Having shoved back those "unacceptable, un-Christianlike" impulses for years, they seemed to envelop him and take control. He admitted himself to a psychiatric hospital with symptoms of depression and suicidal ideas.

The conflict between his religious beliefs, which completely rejected homosexuality as sinful and wrong, and his physical needs became clear during therapy. He saw himself as condemned with no way to reduce the conflict and no way to escape the conflict between his marriage, his religion, and his homosexual orientation. He could not resolve his inner conflict and pain. Three days after he was dismissed from the hospital, he killed himself with a .45-caliber semi-automatic pistol.

Depression and suicide are many times symptoms of suppressed emotions, including anger, deep shame, frustration, hurt, grief, and fear. The attitude in Jack's church was that homosexuality was a sin. He realized that leaving his family and acting on his homosexual impulses would bring shame on him and his entire family. He could not abandon his religion and family, and he could not abandon his homosexuality. He was indeed in a "double bind situation" (damned if you do and damned if you don't). He resolved his shame and his conflict by committing suicide.

Christianity generates the negative emotions that can cause depression. The rigid and inhuman ethics can lead to frustration and hopelessness. Christianity rejects sexual impulses except within marriage. It condemns homosexuality completely and thus rejects an entire class of people.

Jack couldn't discuss his homosexuality with any church members. He was too ashamed. So his religion removed his only access to health, which was to verbally deal with the issue and attempt to resolve the issues or vent and learn to accept his feelings. His feelings of shame gained power and eventually control of his behavior. Even though his religion condemned suicide, evidently he felt it was his best alternative to spare his family shame.

Jack is not an isolated example. We have worked with suicidal teenagers who were pregnant, involved in drugs, and afraid to talk to anyone because of their religion. People have been pushed to the brink of suicide because of the punishing and perfectionistic ethics found in Christianity.

The point here is that the Christian religion can kill you, literally (see the "salvation myth" discussed below). Christianity is a very angry and violent religion, with rigid ethics and punishment prominent. People can and will be sacrificed to these ethics. They can be "removed" from the "Body of Christ" by excommunication, social shunning, or by their own hand.

PSYCHOLOGICAL DYNAMICS AND ISSUES

People operate by emotions and by a system of rules or maps, which are generally unconscious but nonetheless control their behavior. These rules and beliefs contribute to personality "dynamics" which influence and guide aperson's thinking, feelings, and everyday decisions.

We have already discussed the Abusive Christian Model and how that system of beliefs can influence the behavior of an individual. Frequently, these beliefs serve as models for everyday behavior, mapping the way we act and react in certain situations. There is a strong relationship between these everyday behaviors and the concepts taught and preached in Christian religion. Let's examine these issues and these behaviors.

THE SALVATION MYTH AND ORIGINAL SIN: INTRAPSYCHIC INJURY. If you believe in salvation, then you believe that people were born in sin and that humanity was evil and destined for hell. Part of the psychological price one pays for belief in salvation is that people should be "ashamed." We all are evil and vile sinners, destined for eternal punishment in hell. There is nothing we can do. We are helpless and our only hope is for salvation.

Now, what type of self-image will develop in persons who are reared with this type of thinking? Consider their self-confidence and self-worth. Will they person develop feelings of deep shame? Is punishment appropriate? They certainly need to change their birthright. What about initiative? Do you wait—for salvation? Or do you become assertive and control things yourself?

We believe the psychological cost, or "intrapsychic injury," is very high for this type of belief system and causes the following psychological problems:

- Toxic shame.
- Low self-worth.
- Poor self-image.
- Low self-confidence.
- Worry and "internal punishment."
- Low expectation of success.
- Passivity.
- Low self-initiative.
- Lack of assertiveness.

This type of thinking is destructive and negative and can cause an abusive attitude toward people, especially toward children. Children then internalize a "punishing" aspect to their personality and end up with a great deal of negative and abusive self-talk. They can berate and punish themselves internally, becoming depressed or even suicidal.

We often see people in counseling who treat themselves as if they are really awful people (born in sin). They internally talk to themselves in ways that they would *never* talk to anyone else. (Shouldn't you at least treat yourself as well as you treat a friend?) Their internal self-talk is truly negative and abusive. This type of thinking logically follows given the religious belief about the basic nature of man.

The ultimate end to this line of thought is suicide. In suicide, feelings toward the self are so negative and the internal punishment is so great that to kill one's self becomes an option. All too frequently, this option is chosen. It is the ultimate in self-punishment for an individual who feels unworthy of living—death at one's own hand.

Frequently the salvation myth plays directly into suicidal behavior as a "plea for help." In this situation, the "suicide" is intended to end with the victim being saved by some person. By being saved, the suicidal person gains love and proves self-worth, at least in the eyes of the other person. Suicidal individuals act out an internal "salvation myth," salvation at the hands of a loved one. They are really wanting to be "saved" from an internal process of anger, shame, self-hate, and self-abuse/punishment. That, of course, cannot be accomplished with an external rescue by another individual. Sadly, the spiritual aspect of the suicidal individual's life has generally been badly damaged by Abusive Christianity. No spiritual alternative for living exists.

BOUNDARY ISSUES AND CODEPENDENCY. The basis of codependency is, in a large part, seated in the psychological boundaries of an individual. These boundaries are probably part biological, as they can be seen in many animals but are influenced in humans by our language and beliefs. All tend to lose boundaries with loved ones. We confuse their behavior with our feelings, frequently blaming them for the way we feel. The question we must ask now is, do our beliefs help clarify our boundaries, or do they make things worse? Abusive Christian beliefs, we believe, contribute to codependency. These beliefs are: original sin, discrimination against women, salvation, and the belief in spirits.

In the Old Testament, God gives the example of confused boundaries by not separating His feelings with the actions of sinners. Sinners "made" Him angry, and as a result, He would destroy them—entire cities of them. In those situations, God "models" poor boundaries. The sinners seem to control God's feelings and behavior. The attitude seems to be, "Do good, make God happy. Do bad, make God mad." That attitude, along with other beliefs, contributes to the development of psychological boundaries without clear distinction.

A poor self-image forms the cognitive basis for the problems with psychological boundaries. The concept of original sin sets the stage for this problem in that it contributes to the development of poor self-concept and a lack of self-confidence. People lose respect in their abilities with the influence of the belief in original sin. People are born sinners. That belief leads to a poor self-concept.

This belief in original sin, along with the feeling of a lack of self-worth, is followed by the belief in salvation. Something outside ourselves must save us. God must save us and we must believe in Him for this salvation. We cannot do this ourselves. The power is "outside" of us. The responsibility is outside of us. We are responsible to believe, but the power of salvation is outside our boundaries. We have no power. The power is God—and God is out there.

Following closely is the belief in salvation by the Holy Spirit. In Christianity, boundaries are vulnerable to invasion by spirits and demons. It is believed to live a good life, "the Spirit" must lead you. Evil spirits can lead you astray. It is easy to see how psychological boundaries are blurred and fuzzy based upon this belief system. Since these spirits lead people, a confusion of responsibility exists; hence the statement, "The devil made me do it." These beliefs contribute to poor psychological boundaries and codependency.

Codependency is usually found in women more frequently than in men. Indeed, women are still seen and still treated as second class by Christian denominations. They are to follow and to obey. It is little surprise that many women are codependent upon men.

If spirits have control and God has control, the next step is to believe that other people have control of, or are responsible for, your feelings and actions. The common phrase "you made me mad" reflects our deep belief that others are responsible for our feelings. This is modeled by the behavior of God described above, when He grew angry because of the wicked ways of sinners and killed them.

Many of us, who have been subjected to this type thinking and belief, must learn to develop a healthy self-concept and psychological boundaries. These Christian beliefs confuse that development as children. Even as adults we often confuse the origin of our feelings and suffer emotional pain. A good example of this is the failure to separate "my" emotions/behavior from "your" emotions/behavior. "She makes me feel so happy." "He makes me so angry." How do they do that?

Other people cannot actually "make us feel" any more than spirits can invade our boundaries. They cannot enter our nervous system and control our feelings. This perception of external control indicates "weak" boundaries or enmeshment with another person.

Weak boundaries are also indicated when we lose our objectivity and lose "ourselves" in our beliefs and religion. There are many individuals who have lost their boundaries to Christianity, Alcoholics Anonymous, codependent groups, and other belief systems. Their identity and that of their group merges. They lose their personal identity and objectivity. Criticism of that belief system then "makes them angry." To criticize the belief system is to criticize the individual. Objectively, what difference does it make if someone does not agree with what you believe? Why should that change your feelings? Unless, of course, you confuse your identity with your beliefs.

Loving ourselves as individuals and feeling secure, separate from and different from any other individual or system of belief is what is important. Another individual or belief system, regardless of religious perspective or influence, cannot control our emotions unless our boundaries are weak and we are vulnerable.

The beliefs of original sin, salvation and the Holy Spirit, along with the behavior modeled by God, form the basis for blurred boundaries and codependency—so common in our culture. If codependency and poor boundaries are to change, our beliefs must change. Codependency is as common as our Christian background.

PASSIVITY AND WOMEN. The prejudice against women is deeply rooted in conservative Christian history and belief (see "Sexism and Racism" in Chapter 5 for a more extensive treatise on women). In Christian religion, God is seen as male, the Heavenly Father. The first person God created was a man. Woman was made from a rib bone of man, Adam. It was the woman who gave Adam the forbidden fruit of the tree that expelled them from the Garden of Eden. For centuries women were seen as second-class creatures to man, and this belief is still held in Christian churches. Just look at the lack of women ministers, priests, church leaders, and top church administrators.

The most harmful consequence of this belief is that both men and women in our culture internalize these beliefs and form "internal maps" with expectations of how women should behave and of their value in our society. Sadly, we still see many women whose internalized belief system leads them to accept their role as "second-class" citizens.

These women are passive and accepting. They remain in marriages and relationships that are abusive and demeaning. They "obey" their husbands and follow their husbands to new jobs. They remain in jobs that are abusive, with less chance of promotion and, frequently, lower salary. They have accepted the Abusive Christian belief about women. Discrimination against women is an excellent example of Abusive Christianity in action. What you believe can hurt you.

SPIRITUAL POVERTY, THE DEATH OF CREATIVE THINKING. As we have mentioned, there is an almost unspoken ethic in Christianity not to ask questions about the religion, not to doubt the religion, and not to think rationally about the beliefs. The ethic is constrictive and rigid and can lead to an internal rule system which denies creative thinking and creative impulses. Judgment, rigid thinking, punishment, and creativity simply do not go together.

Historically, Christianity has reacted and attempted to abolish concepts which are not consistent with the way Christians believe and see things. When scientists first suggested that the earth was not flat, but round, this was considered heresy. The Bible clearly stated the earth had four corners and that heaven was "above" and hell was "below." So, there was no way the earth could be round. Probably very few Christians believe in a "flat earth" now. However, there is still a Flat Earth Society, for those of you who care to join.

The next creative idea was that the earth was not the center of the universe, but that the sun was the center and several planets revolved around the sun. The Christian leaders of the day were deeply disturbed by such a sinful idea and wanted it abolished.

The concept of evolution is still not accepted by some Christians. The fight over whether evolution should be included in school textbooks is alive and well. If it is included, the "science" of creationism should be included too, say the conservative Christians. Creationism is not a science but a concept in Christian religion. In fact, it is a concept in several religions. So should we also include the creation concept from Buddhism? Or, how about some of the beautiful American Indian myths of creation? Shouldn't all be represented? Some states could end up with some of the most unusual "science" textbooks in the world if they do!

In 1991, Oliver North addressed the Southern Baptist Convention. He made a statement to the effect that religious freedom was intended to protect God-fearing people from government and not protect government from God-fearing people. If you really understand conservative Christianity, you realize that the government, as well as other religious views, needs protection!

Historically, Christian leaders have wanted to control, control, control. The concepts of science, such as the freedom to ask questions, to search, and to interpret observations with theory, is not consistent with the Christian concept that the Bible is Truth and everything you need is found therein. These types of Perpetrators of Christian Abuse are indeed dangerous to science and to government. Everything must be consistent with their beliefs and the concept of religious freedom is not consistent with their religious beliefs. "There is but one way, the Christ." "Narrow is the path." Other religions would not flourish in a government controlled by conservative Christians. Books like this one would not be printed.

The psychological effect of this type of thinking is a vague paranoia with guilt, problems with trust, excessive caution, and a block toward creative thinking. You have to be careful what you think or whom you listen to. You could be led astray by your own thinking. This is why people who marry or even date from different Christian religions or, God forbid, a different religion entirely such as Judaism, have such problems. They do not think alike. They do not believe alike. The families of each will think that the other is "wrong" or "bad." The relationship is not off to a wonderful start. This type of Abusive Christianity promotes fear, a paranoid attitude, and a distrust in people who are different. Creative thinking is not compatible with this belief, unless it conforms to the belief.

RIGID MORALITY AND PROFANITY. When we were younger, one of the first things we learned was that Christians do not use certain types of words. Needless to say, we almost fainted when we heard George Carlin's "ten words you never hear on television"!

This poses an interesting psychological question: Why are some words "dirty" and some words not dirty? Think about that for a minute. Why is one four-letter word "dirty" and another four-letter word "clean"? Another way to ask this question is, how do words become emotionally loaded? It is really a question of censoring.

Christian opinions of certain activities and behaviors is what makes some words "bad." So some words associated with sex, bodily functions (especially excrement) are considered "dirty." Why? Why are sexual functions and bodily functions, which are normal to everyone and every animal, dirty? Because certain people say they are. No one is born thinking certain words are profane.

One could make a case that the very attitude of censor and prohibition gives these words power. And the people who censure are very often "Christian." So it seems that the roots of profanity will probably be found in Christian religion. They give power to a language they find repulsive.

This is an interesting psychological position. The ethical rigidity and punishment orientation of Christianity gives more power to the very words it finds offensive. In those who believe, it can create a double bind. When emotionally upset, you may use the very language that you hate. However, that language would not be so powerful if your belief system were more relaxed. You suffer guilt or you are certainly upset and offended by a lot of what is called "entertainment" today (because of "the language").

Granted, this language is not reflective of an eloquent, educated word choice, but it is a large part of our culture and at this point it is probably entrenched. The best way, albeit a very slow way, to reduce the language's power is to reduce the reaction to it. In that way, eventually, its power will erode.

The language will not kill you. It only has the power that you grant it.

CHAPTER 5

THE SLINGS AND ARROWS OF GOD
Relationship Consequences of Abusive Christianity

A busive Christianity can hurt not only individuals, but also their relationships with others. Of course, the "real" effects of any abuse are dynamically involved in both individuals and relationships at the same time: They're intricately intertwined. So it's no surprise that some of the emotions and patterns of behavior we discussed in Chapter 4 pertaining to individuals can also be seen in the relationships these individuals have with others.

The seven major individual maladaptive patterns to Abusive Christianity tend to cluster into three categories, which are characterized by the emotions of guilt, anger, and denial. They are as follows:

THE ANGRY
Rebels
Christian Perpetrators/Warriors
Disenchanted - angry/hurt
THE GUILTY
Self-punishers
Sheep
THE DETACHED OR DENIAL
The Perfect
Confess-it-and-forget-it

Each of these three types is a survivor. They share this similar characteristic, but they differ in the style or pattern with which they adapt to their survival. Some survive with anger, some with guilt, and some by detachment and denial, but they do survive and adapt to the abusive problems presented by Christianity.

As you might imagine, living with and relating to these different types can present different problems in relationships. The Angry relate from a very powerful position, the Guilty seem to be powerless, and the Detached are emotionally missing from the relationship.

THE ANGRY

The Angry people include the Angry Rebel, the Christian Perpetrator, and the Disenchanted, which we discussed in the previous chapter. These individuals survive using anger, especially the Angry Rebel and the Christian Perpetrator. They generally use anger, although at times in subtle ways, to dominate people. Of course, there are times when they are not so subtle and will give people close to them literal "hell."

They appear powerful, and in relationships they come from a position of power. They project blame on others, especially the guilty, who usually are willing to assume it. You will not find these people shy and retiring. Get in their way and they will let you know. If it happens to be your fault, they will let you know that, too.

They may lack empathy for others, and they especially lack empathy for the suffering they may cause. Both the Christian Perpetrator and the Angry Rebel place beliefs and rules above people, and as such they are willing to attack, hurt, and sacrifice people because of their belief system. When they become aware that they have psychically or psychologically hurt someone, they feel justified because they were fighting for what God wanted (Christian Perpetrators) or fighting against those "deluded religious fanatics" (Angry Rebels). Both feel justified. Both are suffering from the damage of Abusive Christianity.

This abuse can also be found in their families and relationships with loved ones. In fact, intimacy frequently brings out this anger.

These angry people tend to be the abusers in our society. They abuse those that do not believe like they do. They can be found in the angry Christian minister who preaches adherence to abusive and unrealistic ethics, or the cult leader who abuses his followers, or the angry atheist who abuses Christians for their beliefs.

They may abuse their husbands, wives, and children—abuse them because they "love them and want them to do right." If the children and spouses do not "do right," punishment follows. The abusers become caught up in the Abusive Christian Model.

Probably the best way to understand these people is to look at the unhappy relationship between Randy and Jane. Randy was a college professor and a religious rebel. He hated all "Christians," yet their influence dominated his life and actions. He was rigid, abusive, powerful, and intelligent. His wife Jane would fall into the guilty category. When Randy would rage and yell at her, she would yell back in defense of herself and then feel horribly guilty about it. She accepted his explanation that he "would not yell if it had not been for her." In fact, Jane was so guilty that even her children abused and took advantage of her. In one family session, her nine-year-old son said, "Mom, you are so stupid!" She responded, "I know." She would escape into her work as a bookkeeper at a major accounting firm. They displayed the classic relationship cycle of the abuser and the abused, and their children also were learning the roles.

The relationship between Randy and Jane had started by salvation (see Salvation Myth, relationships) and enmeshment. Randy had "saved" Jane from a horrible alcoholic family of origin (a history which he would later use to abuse her). The salvation was completed by the fact that Randy felt wonderful about saving her. Needless to say, they "fell from grace" as the relationship developed.

Randy's parents were conservative Christians, attended church regularly, and prayed at "every damn meal." Randy had been severely abused by his father, who wanted him to "do right." Randy was "scared" into accepting Christ at a very young age. He still remembers the experience as terrifying because of his fear of "going to hell." "I believed that shit," he said.

He quit attending church during his college years and grew to hate the church and its beliefs. Jane still went to church, but Randy would not let her take the children. It is interesting to note that Randy did not directly abuse his children until they were 12 or 13. In fact, he would allow no discipline and no limits to be placed on the younger children. These children were developing into abusers, too.

We have seen this type of developmental history in abusers. It is well known that abusers of children were generally abused as children. We have observed that some children whose parents were abused may receive no discipline. The parents are afraid that they will abuse, so they give no discipline at all. These children have received no direct verbal or physical abuse, but have been abused by the lack of limits and consequences in their development.

It is very important to understand that setting *no* limits on children is abusive because they will not be able to adapt to a world that, indeed, has limits. Randy, as a reaction to his abuse as a small child, vowed to NEVER abuse his children. So he would set no limits and give no discipline. As a result, the children grew up very selfish and wanted everything to go their way. As teenagers they became uncontrollable. At that point Randy tried to control his children according to the typical Abusive Christian Model. Of course, it did not work.

Randy is angry with Christianity for what it did to him. However, he follows the same Abusive Christian Model. He punishes his wife and now his children. He will sacrifice his family for his rules.

Randy has frequently shared fantasies of being rescued (saved) by a beautiful woman, which is how his relationship with his wife started. Consistent with the influence of the Abusive Christian Model, Randy confuses anger as the opposite of love and punishes with his anger. His wife has enough guilt for the entire family, and she magically believes God will change things "some day." So she stays with her abusive husband. The family did not change while in psychotherapy and is still together.

The angry type is not always a male. Sheila is a nurse and is very aggressive. James is her "perfect" husband. Both were reared in a very conservative Christian environment. James never gets angry and is always calm and relaxed. His wife thinks he is forgetful (about birthdays, anniversaries, and important events) and he is always late. He is a deacon in their local Baptist church, but he is not overly involved in church activities.

Sheila runs their life and does a good job of it, but she is sick and tired of taking care of James. "He is like having another child," she complains. She is verbally abusive toward James, while he generally sits and smiles—which "drives me nuts," she says. Sheila is a Christian Perpetrator and James is the Perfect One. Socially, everyone thinks James is the "perfect" husband and "perfect" father and that they have the "perfect family," but Sheila is seriously thinking about divorce.

Sheila is aggressive, angry, powerful, and projects all her anger on James. She becomes angry when things do not go her way. She thinks in terms of punishment and the withdrawal of love instead of understanding. She feels she is "right" and will not compromise or look at herself.

In relationships, these angry people are difficult to deal with. They do not handle disagreement well and, in psychotherapy, they tend to "take over." "Doc, you gotta do something with James here. The guy ain't real!" If James doesn't do better, we certainly know who's fault *that* will be!

We are not saying that the Abusive Christian Model and Abusive Christianity caused ALL of these individuals' problems. But they most certainly contributed. The way we approach life and the way we think have been profoundly influenced by Christian beliefs. With its long history, Christianity set in motion dynamic problems in our culture which exist in marriages and relationships—withdrawal of love when angry, expectation of perfection, the tendency to see all things in terms of right and wrong, rigidity, the tendency toward punishment, and the tendency to sacrifice people for beliefs. Christianity has served as the prototype of these dynamic problems.

We placed the Disenchanted under the label of the Angry. With Rebels and Perpetrators, the anger is usually a cover to hide insecurity, hurt, and fear. With the Disenchanted, the hurt is very close to the surface and they tend to back away from religion. Many Angry Rebels become Disenchanted when they mellow with time. The initial injury and the survival modality still exist.

In relationships, you will not experience the anger with the Disenchanted, unless you begin to push them as to their beliefs and ideas about religion. They usually have a "live and let live" attitude about religions; they do not want to participate, however. They will let their children and their spouse participate, but they will not. They have given up religion because of their spiritual injury at the hands of Christians.

They also tend to be somewhat closed and uncommunicative about religion. They do not talk about religion and they neglect the spiritual aspect to their lives. Often, they do not even believe their lives have spiritual elements. As a result, their spouses frequently feel there are parts of them that they do not know or understand, or that there are aspects of their relationship that are missing. So, in the areas of religion and spirituality, the Disenchanted are difficult to get to know intimately. They will resist and pull away. Disenchanted couples will try to live both their lives without any reference to religion or spirituality.

THE GUILTY

In relationships, the Guilty are more than willing to assume the blame for anything within remote reason. They are the ones that end up being abused in a relationship and feel they deserve it or it was somehow their fault. They are generally unable to get out of relationships because when they try to, they feel guilty about what they are doing. So it is not unusual that they end up abused in "intimate" relationships. Even when verbally and physically abused, they frequently feel they drove the other person to anger or it is some sort of punishment or trial from God. Many think God will take care of it, so they do not have to worry or do anything. God will somehow magically rescue and save them, so they tend to be passive.

They are the powerless, the punished, sometimes referred to as a "doormat" personality. The Martyr. They escape the reality of their abuse into their suffering, their depression, and their guilt. They feel there must be some purpose to their suffering, "or God would not do this to me." They are trapped by their beliefs.

In less dramatic situations, these are the people who do all the work in churches and businesses and then feel depressed and abused, but too guilty to say anything about it. They are followers and not leaders. They *are* generally good workers. In fact, they work a great deal of the time. As a result, they can be neglectful in intimate relationships while they do church work or work for everyone else.

The guilty, especially the Sheep, try to take care of everything and everyone. They are "codependent." They tend to be women. They lose their boundaries, try to do too much, feel guilty about that, then cut back, and feel guilty about that, too. You can drive them crazy if you tell them to take time off, or relax and do nothing. They feel especially guilty when they do nothing.

Alexi was the wife of a music director in a church. She did all of the work at home, while her husband did the "spiritual" work. He would visit people in hospitals and nursing homes, and he had late night choir practice. She did all the cleaning, cooking, laundry, lawn work, washed the cars, and took care of four small children. Chris, her husband, was the Perfect One and she was the guilty one. After six years, she was wanting some help, but he was always so busy with the church work.

She wanted to confront him about his lack of helping her and his helping everyone else, but she said she "just couldn't do it." He worked much too hard and she did not want to add to his burden. He was as addicted to his church work as she was addicted to her housework. Intimacy was obviously lacking. They could not talk to each other and deal with these issues. She could not share her feelings with him. They were, in effect, cut off from each other, isolated, yet living together.

This is the typical picture of the guilty Sheep. They will work and work and work and then try to protect the person close to them from their feelings. They would feel "too guilty" to say anything.

They would not want to hurt anyone's feelings, even if the work was killing them. They take care of others, even others they do not know well. They "suffer for Christ." The suffering is needless and in vain.

THE DENIAL PEOPLE

Alexi's husband, Chris, is an excellent example of the denial "perfect" people. Chris would not deal with issues of work addiction. He would typically deny that he was addicted in any way. He was simply doing the work "the Lord had called him to do." He felt very good about his work, and in our family sessions, the vague feeling that he was somewhat superior, somewhat better than us came across very clearly. He knew what he was to do and it was God's work and not a matter of discussion. His denial was pervasive, his aloofness, impenetrable.

He would ignore his wife and her rather passive pleas for help. There was no psychological intimacy in the relationship. They could not talk about the issues of his overworking, her overworking, his perfection and perfectionistic attitudes, or her guilt.

On the surface, these relationships appear wonderful—a devoted mother and a father who works so hard for his church (business, whatever) and his beliefs. Chris said he was happy. He loved his work and he loved his family. He was unaware that anything could be wrong. His wife came to counseling, and when his wife finally did talk with him, he still could not believe anything was wrong. He was very happy she was in counseling, because something must be wrong with her. Being the guilty one, she willingly assumed the role of the identified patient in early sessions.

Relating to "perfect" people is very interesting. One gets the feeling they really are perfect, they simply have not died and gone to heaven yet. However, nothing much will change when they do. God might have to "shape up" heaven for them, though. Relating to these people is an exercise in denial. They have no problems. Their life is wonderful and all is well. These are the kind of people that live together for 50 years and "never had an argument." They also say, "The Lord has been wonderful to us," a lot. These types of people are fairly commonly found in ministers and the religiously devoted. They, too, are difficult to get to know, because they do not know themselves—or their anger and their hurt. They are living the image of "the good Christian." They may well be out of touch with their lives and their families.

The confess-it-and-forget-it people are also in denial, but they present a very different picture. Their behavior is far from perfect. They are out to enjoy life and get everything they can out of life. Religion simply does not have a practical impact on their lives.

In relationships, they tend to be unpredictable and it is often difficult to trust them. It is not at all uncommon for them to be the children of very rigid, moralistic preachers. The old adage that the "preacher's kids" are the worst is all too often true. Many conservative Christian Perpetrators/preachers lack emotional availability in the family. The resulting injury in the children may well lead to the confess-it-and-forget-it, survival style. They attempt to find love and acceptance in their behavior.

The need for love and, in females, the resulting early pregnancies are common. Addictive processes are common and if their lives really fall apart, it is a toss-up what will happen. They may fall back on the conservative ethical base of their religion. They may become rebels or perpetrators, or they may maintain their destructive, self-centered lifestyle. Those that love them and are close to them usually end up on an emotional roller coaster ride.

They tend to be difficult to help, because they have heard it all before and they turn off lectures as if they had a switch inside their heads. They know how to nod and say "yes sir" and "yes ma'am." Then when they leave, they do as they please. As they become older, they tend to mellow, but they leave in their wake numerous damaged relationships with friends, lovers, and family.

They, too, are difficult to get close to. They are escape artists in relationships. They can keep you at bay with humor, comedy, fun, excitement, and drama. But they are hard to hold down, and establishing psychological intimacy is not easy and takes time. It is difficult for them to deeply trust others.

Under the superficial exterior lies a rigid ethic that they simply cannot live up to; they have given up and tend to escape into sex, drugs, and "fun." Their fear of psychological intimacy instills a fear they will be hurt even more by those that want to help them. Trust takes time. Punishment and lectures make matters worse.

THE ABUSIVE CHRISTIAN LOVE/PUNISHMENT CYCLE

THE LOVE/PUNISHMENT CYCLE

Father God	Church	Parent	Conscience
\	\	\	\
Man	Members	Child	Impulses

The idea behind this graphic is to display that the Abusive Christian Model we discussed in Chapter 2 is actually a cycle. The same cycle is found between God and man, the Abusive Christian church and the members, parents and children, and then an internalized cycle between our conscience and our impulses.

The first part of this cycle is the action displayed by God, the churches, parents, and our conscience. This will be called the parent part of the model. The "parents" show the following characteristics: Love—Expectation of Perfectionism—Discovery of Sins—Withdrawal of love—Anger—Punishment.

The second part of this model is the response displayed by Man, church members, children, and our impulsive nature. This will be called the "child" part of the model. The "child" shows the following characteristics: Obedience to toxic and rigid rules—transgression, inadequacy—response to withdrawal, abandonment, isolation, fear, shame—survival, with an internalization of the love object-parent values. That is, the child takes on the characteristics of the abusive parent. Thus the cycle never ends.

This cycle, the Abusive Christian Love/Punishment Cycle, is not a static model, but an interaction between the parental god-type figures and the child figures. As if this Abusive Christian Model had been some "Great Template," it is repeated over and over in our culture. It repeats itself in the way Christian churches interact with their members, the way parents interact with their children, and, the way that we, on an internal level, interact with ourselves.

It is taught that God created man, and God placed man in a place of perfection, the Garden of Eden. There was only one rule, not to eat of the forbidden fruit. Man broke the rule and God cast Man out of the Garden. There is no record of any divine explanation as to why not eat of the fruit. There appears to be no attempt to train, teach, instruct or explain—simply, "Do not do this." Man, curious as he was created, was unable to comply.

Thus the beginnings of the model are revealed. God loves Man. God sets the rules. God expects compliance and obedience. God expects no questions. If the rules are broken, God will withdraw His love and punish. If compliance is not obtained, God will kill.

Man broke the rule and Man was punished. Man was cast out, again with no recorded explanation or reason—simply, that is the way it is. There was no negotiation. The rule was rigid. Man's role in the interaction was revealed. Man was to be obedient. Man was to follow the rules without question. Man was unable, so Man is shamed and sinful. Punishment is due.

As the history of the Judeo-Christian religion was "revealed" to man, or as it developed, God seemed to be even more angry with transgression. If cities erred, God could and would destroy them. The concepts of heaven and hell further added to the rigid, angry nature of this God, in that God will punish people forever if they do not comply.

This concept, the Abusive Christian Love/Punishment Cycle, has been internalized by people in our culture. As a result, this model is found in our churches, our legal systems, our families, and in the way we deal with ourselves. Abusive parents commonly act this way with their children.

It is frequently the model we adhere to even when dealing with ourselves. Freud talked about the constant inner struggle between the Superego and the Id; between what we call conscience and our inner "base" impulses. Many people we work with have powerful punitive inner voices with which they chastise and punish themselves. They do not treat themselves in a loving and caring manner.

In the Abusive Church, people are invited and welcomed with initial love and acceptance. These churches want to grow and welcome potential new members. If you decide to join the church, there are things you must believe and rules of behavior that you must follow. Different churches have different rules, but to be a "good church member," you must attend, believe specific doctrine, and follow their rules for behavior.

If a church member breaks the rules, the Abusive Church as a body (that is the other members) will react to the behavior of that individual. If the behavior is bad enough, such as open adultery or unwed pregnancy, the Abusive Church will withdraw its love and fellowship for that member. Usually, the member is socially aware and simply drops out of the church.

If the member happens to be a church minister or leader, that individual will generally be asked to leave the church or give up the ministry. Love is withdrawn and punishment is set. They are not helped; they are not loved. They are punished.

In trying to correct and deal with their children, many abusive parents follow the very same model or map. The parents' motives are excellent. They love their child and they want "the best" for him or her. Frequently those expectations are rigid and perfectionistic. Many children, in an attempt to live up to this ethic, become perfectionists and demand of themselves and others nothing short of perfection.

Those children that transgress find their parents upset and angry with them. Typical to the model, the parent becomes aloof and emotionally distant from the child. Some parents yell at their child, as if volume of voice were some sort of punishment in itself. These parents follow the dynamic of love, expected perfectionism, transgression, rejection and punishment—the Abusive Christian Model.

Initially the child wants to please the parent. They want and need the love and acceptance of the parent. The same could be said about the individual's response to God. The new Christian wants to please God. The new church member wants to please the church. The individual wants to please and feel good about himself or herself. For the sake of simplicity we will talk about parent and child, but in most instances the same could be said about the other relationships.

The children are subjected to rules from the parents. Since these rules are "from God," there is no discussion and no compromise. They are absolute. The parent feels little need to explain the rules or listen to the reaction of the child or negotiate.

The children simply cannot measure up to these rigid and unrealistic rules. The child responds with fear and anxiety, especially as the parent grows angry and frustrated with the child. The rules have an urgent and compelling air about them, because they are associated with authority. If there is a problem, by process of elimination, the child is seen as the source of the problem.

This message comes through loud and clear as the child learns to see himself or herself as "a problem" or defective. So the child begins to grow in shame and self-doubt in this system. The child is left with feelings of inadequacy and isolation from being unable to measure up. In effect, the child becomes a survivor.

The child needs and wants power to survive, as is typical with victims of hostage situations, many of the children "identify with the aggressor." When individuals are held hostage for long periods of time, they eventually may identify with those holding them hostage. This is a way to gain feelings of control, because the loss of control is so fearful. To identify with the aggressor is to also gain a feeling of power and so to further escape the fear.

The cycle is made complete by the response of the child. Children will identify with their parents, even though those parents abuse them. As a result, when they grow to adults, they will treat their children in the same way. They become just like their parents. If the Abusive Christian Model is followed, they will expect obedience to a rigid and unrealistic system of rules, and they will punish transgressions.

This identity with the aggressor fully completes the "abusive Christian love\punishment cycle." The model will be carried on, as it has generation after generation for 2000 years.

POVERTY OF COMMINICATION: THE RULES

Psychological fallout from the Abusive Christian Model is pervasive. Claudia Black, in her book about children of alcoholics, *It Will Never Happen to Me,* says the four rules for dysfunctional (alcoholic is one type of being dysfunctional) families are:

Don't Trust.
Don't Talk.
Don't Feel.
Act like everything is okay.

Those same rules are consistently found in families that suffer from Christian Abuse and that follow the Abusive Christian Model. There are so many things that you "should not" or will not talk about in a family that has been influenced by Abusive Christian values. You will not talk about:

sins you do commit.
sins you commit and enjoy (except around the "right" people).
fantasy sins, your fantasies
sins, period, except to condemn.
areas of sex, personal habits.
doubts about God.
aspects of Christ's life (sexual, illness, disease).
alcohol consumption or tobacco consumption.
your disbelief of the church's rules or beliefs.

Jerry remembers a group of hospitalized adolescents who were talking about problems with their girlfriends and boyfriends. It was the consensus that they would not discuss this with their parents. They did not want to be discredited, for example, with some statement like "you're too young to *really* be in love." Or they were afraid their problems would be seen as trivial. They did not want to endure the mocking, the "advice," the humiliation, and the humor at their expense. So they simply did not talk to their parents.

The level of trust in these families is not high. Children cannot talk to parents. Husbands cannot talk to wives. Given an Abusive Christian background, there are too many rules which are too easy to break. If these adolescents tell their parents, they will not only have to deal with their own anger, guilt, and shame, but they will also have to endure a "lecture" and advice about how bad and wrong their transgression happens to be. Therefore, it is much safer to not talk and not trust. On issues of vital importance and urgent need, communication breaks down because of the internal guilt and fear of chastisement from the parent.

The same holds true for couples, not just for parent-child communication. We frequently see individuals involved in affairs because they were "unable to communicate" with their spouses. The classic example is the husband that has ceased to communicate with his wife over time. He finds himself attracted to another woman, and he certainly cannot talk to his wife about that! That is a sin. That is against the rules. So the husband does not stop the behavior. He stops communication.

Thus, communication dies and along with that dies the psychological intimacy. He and his newfound friend can talk about "anything." As psychological intimacy with the spouse dies, psychological intimacy (probably enmeshment) with the "friend" grows. The set-up for the affair is complete.

If you are married and find yourself attracted to another person, that is a very important issue. It should be discussed with one's spouse. "What does this mean?" "Are we cutting off communication with each other?" "Are we not giving needed attention to each other?" Psychological intimacy is based upon open communication.

The problem goes beyond parents and couples. Research has indicated that very few church members believe everything within the rule system and belief system of the specific church. That is to say, a significant number of members will not believe specific church tenets. However, this is almost never discussed. Try going into the local Southern Baptist conservative church and saying you are a loyal member, but you do not believe in miracles or the virgin birth and you would like to discuss this in Sunday School. You will not last long. You are simply wrong—period. There will be no discussion.

If you cannot trust and you cannot talk about important issues, you certainly will not reveal how you feel, especially if you feel guilty, fearful, and vulnerable. In Abusive Christian churches, anger is not acceptable—except, of course, righteous anger, which is generally given in punishment. Sexual feelings are not acceptable and are rarely discussed in most Christian churches. The rules are often very subtle, but they are powerful. Individual church members will not feel safe to open up and psychologically expose themselves if their thoughts, behavior, and feelings run contrary to the stated beliefs and rules of the church.

Example: A client had suicidal thoughts and feelings, which he shared in a Sunday School class. He was lectured that suicide was the ultimate sin, and he clearly got the message, "Do not bring this up again!"

Jerry and his wife were once asked to teach sexuality to a group of 13-year-old children in the local Unitarian Church. He didn't know who had more trauma in dealing with their feelings about open discussions of all aspects of sexuality and birth control—Jerry, because of his Southern Baptist background, or the children. Even as they discussed many important issues dealing with sexuality—the fears, the expectations, the hopes, and the delusions—it was obvious the rule was that this subject should not be discussed.

The rules found in Abusive Christian thinking breed an environment that is not psychologically conducive to openness and honesty. Trusting each other with vital but vulnerable feelings and issues is discouraged by the environment of rules, sins, and punishment. However, most people are not aware of this lack of communication. They have learned to "act like everything is okay." And they believe they are okay, until these areas are exposed and opened. Then the rigid thinking and the condemning attitudes attempt to stop communication. This environment leads to a poverty of communication and to emotional isolation as well.

EMOTIONAL ISOLATION

People reared with Abusive Christianity are survivors. They are survivors because their religious beliefs make unacceptable many of their human feelings, thoughts, and impulses. They are people at war internally between their Christian beliefs and their humanity. They have learned to survive by keeping quiet and not communicating about important feelings and issues. They hide behind a "Christian mask," a mask they may not be aware of.

In relationships, this lack of honest self-revelation can lead into emotional isolation. It can be very difficult to establish emotionally close relationships with these individuals, and that is a key to their recovery. They have to allow people, therapists, counselors, and friends to get emotionally close to them. Sadly, they do not find this acceptance in Abusive Christian (usually conservative Christian) Churches.

There are obvious problems. Most survivors of Abusive Christianity are afraid to open up and be accepting. The Perpetrators and Rebels are too angry. The Self-Punishers are involved in their guilt and fear opening up, and the Detached *are* emotionally detached. They do not know they have a problem.

A Perpetrator or a Rebel will convert other emotions into anger. If they are afraid of intimacy, they will tend to become angry. If you hurt their feelings, they will convert hurt into anger. When confronted with the fear of abandonment, they will become angry. The Self-Punishers, Disenchanted, and Sheep will tend to convert these emotions into guilt or depression. They are equally difficult to get close to, but the picture is different because the dominant emotion is different. The same, of course, holds true for the Detached. They will tend to ignore or deny their emotions and remain emotionally distant.

One interesting aspect to this emotional isolation is that the individual will frequently be aware of it while others are not. Socially, the individual appears very open and giving. They have learned to "act okay." They think all others are "open and giving." But beneath the facade, the mask, they sense their isolation and loneliness.

ANGER, FEAR, AND GUILT: SOCIAL MANIPULATION AND CONTROL

Abusive Christianity tells you how to live and what to do (The Rules) and then sets about using emotions to manipulate and control you to conform to these rules. The most common emotions used to manipulate and control are anger, fear, and guilt. The concept of God as an angry God is common in the Old Testament. God seems willing to punish those that do not obey Him. Thus, the fear of God's wrath motivates people to behave and conform. The anger of God induces fear in the follower. Thus the old saying, "The fear of God is the beginning of wisdom." In essence the follower feels threatened by the possibility of punishment. Therefore, the follower will change behavior, follow the rules, in order to avoid the fear of punishment. That is motivation by abuse.

As a child, Jerry frequently heard, "Is God trying to teach you a lesson?" This was most often said when something "bad" happened to a person or when a person had been caught doing something wrong and was about to be punished. Jerry assumed you were supposed to believe that you had somehow made God angry and now He was getting even with you, taking out His anger on you. Since this destructive belief includes that God controls what happens in your life, the potential for retaliation is truly fearsome. God can do anything to you He wants. He is God, after all. He can kill you and send you to hell. Just look at what happened to the cities of Sodom and Gomorrah (Gen. 18: 20-21; 19: 24-28), Ai, and poor old Job.

This is another Destructive Christian Belief or, at least, Judeo-Christian belief. The fear is intended to control the behavior of the individual to "motivate" that person via fear to do "right." Control by fear of the anger of God. Manipulation using fear and Destructive Christian Beliefs. (The Destructive Christian Belief is that God controls events in your life.) This belief reduces God to something of a self-centered adolescent that vows to get revenge if you don't do things His way.

Guilt is also frequently used to control behavior in the Christian belief system. Carol, a male client, constantly heard the phrase, "The Lord will not be pleased." Carol's father was a Pentecostal minister and felt it was his responsibility to make God happy by his behavior. Carol strongly believed he had to "do the right thing" or God would be upset with him. If he erred, he felt very guilty.

Carol's father was a very calm and serene man who did not control his son or his congregation with fear and anger. He controlled with guilt. His son learned quickly that pleasing the Lord was the same as pleasing his minister father. Father seemed to have a "direct hotline to God." Father's word was law, or "The Lord will not be pleased." We assume the "earthly father" would not be too happy, either. This is an example of using guilt to manipulate belief and behavior to what the "Lord," minister, or church wants. This form of manipulation is abusive in that it does not respect the individual's ability to think and decide on his or her own.

One of Jerry's pet peeves is the way his childhood church and all Southern Baptist churches "save people" and encourage them to become members. At the end of the sermon, they give an "invitation" for people to come forward and publicly profess their belief in Christ and join the church. Usually, there is a very emotional appeal intended to manipulate people by using guilt, fear, and the individual's need to affiliate. They will plead and sing more verses to get the person to come forward. Legal contracts signed under this kind of emotional coercion would not be valid. It is blatant emotional manipulation via guilt and neediness.

These means of emotional control are commonly found in Christian churches and are also commonly found in families influenced by the Christian ethic. Throughout the Old and New Testament God used these means to control people and churches. Guilt and fear as manipulation are commonly used in churches today. So it stands to reason that families would use these emotionally manipulative means to control family behavior and the behavior of children. Carol had to behave in a certain way to please his father, both heavenly and earthly. This is, of course, enmeshment between father and son; it makes the son responsible for the father's emotions. The abuse here takes a further twist in that it is also very close to what is called emotional incest.

Dr. Pat Love, in her book *The Emotional Incest Syndrome*, does an excellent job describing this pathological relationship between a parent (or adult) and a child. In emotional incest, it is the responsibility of the child to please the parent, to make the parent happy. When the pleasure takes on a sexual connotation, then it is sexual incest. When the pleasure or happiness is only emotional, then it is emotional incest. If one feels it is the responsibility of the child to please them emotionally, then that represents emotional incest. This aspect of enmeshment is toxic, manipulative, and abusive, whether it is with the Heavenly Father or earthly parent or any adult. Needless to say, it is not the job of the Christian to "make" God happy. That is simply another form of manipulation and abuse.

One point needs clarification: It is certainly normal and healthy for parents to take pleasure in the skills and accomplishments of their children. If children fail or have difficulty, you love them and help them. The children do not control your emotions. If they fail and you become sad and depressed and chide the child for "hurting" your feelings in a way that makes the child responsible for your feelings, that is very close to emotional incest. It is also an attempt to control by making the child responsible for your emotions.

LOVE AND ANGER AS OPPOSITES

OPPOSITES

Abusive Christian Model

Love_____Anger

Healthier Psychological Model

Love _____Indifference

\

Anger

In the Abusive Christian Model, love and anger are seen as opposites. If you love someone, you love them. If you are angry with them, you no longer love them. Not only do you no longer love them, but you are angry with them. If you no longer love them, and you are angry with them (or they "made" you angry), it is appropriate that you punish them. When you punish them, if you do not love them, it does not matter if you hurt them. It does not matter if they are sent to hell in the Abusive Christian Model.

This unhealthy, first-century model is still in practice today. Notice the statistics on wife beating and abused children. When angry, we tend to punish or hurt people. We stop loving them.

The healthier model sees love and indifference as opposites. Anger is seen as a part of love. When you are angry with someone, you still love them. As a result, you do not hurt them, even if you are angry with them.

In Chapter 4 we discussed how individuals cover hurt and fear with anger and how much of that anger can be narcissistic. How does this anger affect relationships, especially marriage and families? That will be the focus of this section.

When anger is viewed as the opposite of love, values change. Since you feel the opposite of love, it is okay to attack and hurt the individual, even if only psychologically. As we have noted, this is how God dealt with his anger. In this first-century model, God withdrew love and punished, hurt, or even killed those with whom he was angry.

In the book, *Do I Have to Give Up Me to Be Loved by You?*, Jordan and Margaret Paul construct a model with a "flow chart," of how to deal with love without hurting. Their book can be used as a handbook to train people in dealing with anger in a constructive manner, and in recovery from the Abusive Christian Model.

Briefly, the first point the Pauls make is that if you love someone you intend to protect that person. The rule is: "You do not hurt those you love." You do not hit them, yell at them, or insult them. Even if angry, you DO NOT HURT those you love. You protect them from hurt and harm. If you love them, you want to know them at deeper and deeper levels, how they think and feel, separate from how you think and feel. Furthermore, you want them to grow to know you at ever deeper levels.

Next, if you are angry, it is your anger. It was not created by your spouse or your children. You are a sealed unit. No one can create or directly cause anger in you. No one "made" you angry. Your anger is the result of your fears, your hurt, your narcissism, your internal battles, and your values. Dealing with anger within intimacy means you share yourself. You try to understand the real cause of your anger. The *real* cause of your anger is inside of you. It has to do with your perceptions (whether accurate or inaccurate), your values, your beliefs, fears, and hurts. The issues "causing" your anger are yours! You then share that understanding with your loved one. You do not use the feelings as an excuse to "give the other hell" or to manipulate. You share yourself—anger and all.

Let us look at the behavior of a family as an example. As a child, Jerry once left a tool outside for several days. It rained and the tool rusted. His father dealt with his anger in the only way he knew. He withdrew his love and punished with his rage. He yelled, "You do not care about me. You don't give a damn about me or my tools, or that I have worked my butt off to buy them. Don't you ever even think about using ANYTHING of mine, ever again, you understand? Now get out of here, I don't want to see your face!"

Jerry's father understood verbal punishment. He was both an alcoholic and a deacon in the local Baptist Church, so which came first, the dysfunction caused by the Abusive Christianity, or the dysfunction caused by alcoholism? This style of interaction is consistent with abusive Christian doctrine.

Let's look at options. Using another style of interaction, one in which each individual is responsible for his or her behavior and feelings, Jerry's father could have said, "Jerry, I love you, and we need to talk. You left one of my tools out and it rusted. I was reared in a very poor family and my tools are very important to me. Because they are important, it hurts me when they are abused and I really become angry when they are abused. Would you please be more careful next time."

There! Jerry would not have felt hurt and rejected and would have understood his father at a deeper level, and it could have touched him that his father was being honest and vulnerable. His father would have been dealing with the *"real"* issues causing his feelings, and not covering the real feelings with anger and blaming the anger on his son.

This behavior is not enmeshed. The father would be responsible for his feelings and for sharing his feelings. Dealing with anger this way really works.

But do not underestimate the power of the enmeshed belief that "you made me angry" and the power of the Abusive Christian Model. This type of enmeshed behavior is modeled by God in both the Old and New Testaments. The behavior of sinful people "made" God angry, so he destroyed them, as recorded in the Old Testament. In the New Testament, sin and sinners offend God to the extent that he punishes them with eternal damnation.

We can suppose that, in some way, this behavior must make Him feel better. Those against Him suffer. At least, He must feel justified. This type of enmeshed thinking does not make sense when attributed to a deity. It sounds much more similar to an enmeshed, petty earthly father. As counselors, we sadly know that many earthly fathers follow this model.

THE SALVATION MYTH: INTERPSYCHIC INJURY

In the Christian concept of salvation, people must believe in and trust God, through Jesus, to lift them from sin and despair into a new life, "salvation," and the hope of heaven. You cannot do this alone, by yourself, you must have faith in Jesus. The message is simple—you cannot save yourself. You cannot do it alone. This dynamic is commonly followed in individual fantasies (Chapter 4) and in romantic relationships in our culture.

We have postulated that Abusive Christianity leads to individuals' becoming survivors, and survivors are emotionally isolated and lonely. The Christian concept that people are born into sin, along with the fact that there are so many feelings and issues perceived as evil or forbidden, leads to shame and thus to survival. These deep psychological injuries of loneliness, shame, and emotional isolation form the basis of needs, from which an individual wants to be "saved," and salvation comes from outside of yourself.

Inside the individual's mind, this salvation attitude leads to hopes and fantasies of being "saved" usually by money, drugs, power, possessions, position, etc. On the social level, this shame, loneliness, and emptiness drives individuals to relationships in order to fill that emptiness. You need someone to love you, to "save" you from your loneliness.

People do not see this process as a problem and seek help via counseling and psychotherapy. They view the problem as external. "I need to find that special person for me." When they "save" you, everything will be fine, you think.

Actually this *is* an individual problem, an internal process, which reflects shame and a lack of self-worth. Shame and a lack of self-worth follow Destructive Christian Beliefs and being reared under the Abusive Christian Model.

The problem cannot be solved by simply finding "Mr. Right" or "the Right Woman." The "right" individual for you does not exist. This type of thinking reflects the projection of an internal problem as external. The statement, "I need someone to make me feel good, the right person for me," reflects inner feelings of incompleteness and loneliness. This thinking is a "hang over" from the salvation fantasy, that a "special" person (external) is going to save you. *Healthy love is not a function of another individual. It is a function of your capacity and ability to love.*

There is a dynamic similarity between how the sinner thinks and behaves when he is being "saved," and how the abused individual thinks and behaves when they find Mr. or Ms. "Right." Both of these experiences include individuals who are lonely, isolated, in sin and despair, and who are waiting and expecting to be saved. One is saved by God. The others are saved by another individual. The process is the same.

We refer to this relationship experience as being "emotionally saved" by another person. A person experiencing this type of relationship salvation thinks the other person is "making me feel wonderful." This rescuer has banished despair and loneliness. They say things such as: "I have found Mr. Right"; "Linda is for me. She makes me feel wonderful"; "She is my life"; "God intended us to be together"; "I couldn't live without him/her"; "She is the light of my life"; "Without him, life would not be complete." These descriptions of "relationship salvation" sound more like one has found a religion than a relationship.

Actually, this is a form of relationship enmeshment. The Christian concept of salvation and this experience of relationship salvation, via another person, have very similar dynamic aspects. You are lost and lonely. Your condition is not your responsibility. You must find another individual (or Being) to save you or rescue you. There is nothing you can do to help yourself. You are condemned to sadness and despair until you find this other person. And when you find this other person, that person makes you feel wonderful, "saved." This type of thinking is magical, unhealthy, and it leads to unrealistic, destructive expectations in relationships that will not last.

We believe the Christian concept of salvation is the prototype for enmeshment, this relationship problem of "salvation" by another person. Further, this prototype models passivity, lack of assuming responsibility for your own welfare, and seeking external solutions for internal problems.

MARRIAGE

The authors met for lunch one week day to discuss this chapter. During the discussion, we decided to include a short section on the influence of Christian thought upon marriage. We wanted to find a copy of the marriage vows, as read in Christian churches.

While walking to his car, Jerry spotted a small black-leather bound book on the ground in the parking lot. It was *The Book of*

Common Prayer of the Protestant Episcopal Church in the U.S.A., published by the Seabury Press, New York. The book had been dropped (we later called and returned it to the owner) and in the book was a reading for the Christian marriage vows. Although we do not believe that "God provides"—in fact we believe that belief is abusive—we were then sure we should include a section about marriage. The manual had been "provided" for us! We found a certain amount of humor in what Carl Jung called the synchronicity of events.

Until recently, marriage vows included that the wife should honor and obey her husband. Thankfully, this was omitted in the Episcopal vows. Women should not be reduced to children by the marriage vows, nor should they be relegated to second-class citizens. However, it is still a common tradition for women to give up their last name and take their husband's name. The children of the marriage always carry the husband's last name. Why? In our Christian tradition, women are still secondary to men.

The marriage vows seem to emphasize that if the couple follows God, He will bless them with a happy marriage. It also implies that God may choose to bless the union with children. Does that mean an unhappy marriage is punishment from God or that the couple is somehow not following God? What about the couple that loses a child during pregnancy? Is that the punishment of God? Did they do something wrong? Of course not. To think so makes God brutal, a characteristic more common to people.

Marriage problems generally have their roots in each individual's family of origin and in survival issues. What men or women learn from their families, they carry with them into their marriage. It has been our experience that some conservative Christian couples are difficult to engage in individual or marriage counseling, mostly because of their belief system. Some of the reasons we have heard for avoiding counseling are:

My life is in God's hands, not mine or a counselor's.

Whatever is God's will, will be done.

God can work a miracle.

I don't need help, God directs my life.

I just wait and pray.

I have faith that all things work for good for those that are in God's will.

Not my will, but His will be done.

Basically all of these reasons mitigate against seeking help from professional counselors for marriage problems. Many of these reasons are consistent with Christian marriage vows and beliefs. Any belief that would lead a couple to avoid professional help with marital problems would most certaintly qualify as a destructive and dysfunctional belief.

If you have marital problems, you probably could benefit from marriage counseling. However, many individuals believe that God will take care of them and they do not need help. That attitude certainly sounds similar to a dysfunctional survivor. Yet, it is consistent with many Christian marriage vows. If you have marital problems, seek professional help, do not wait on magic from God. That is not a healthy belief.

Next, does God bless marriages with children? We found this belief in many marriage vows. With our limited knowledge of biology, we do not believe God causes children; sexual relationships do. Those couples without children have a medical or genetic problem and not a religious one. They are not bad people. They are not cursed people. They are simply unable to have children—or they may not want children.

Yet Christian marriage vows seem to imply that God decides whether or not He will bless a couple with children. That thinking or belief system could certainly be harmful and damaging to a couple unable to have children.

We once worked with a couple who badly wanted a child. The wife had difficulty becoming pregnant and lost a child in the beginning of the second trimester. Their minister told them God was punishing them for something they had done, something bad. That is an excellent example of Abusive Christianity at work.

Marriage is a complex relationship which is not doing well in our present culture. We do not believe it is up to God to correct this situation. We do not believe it is a functional or helpful belief to wait for a miracle from God. We must understand the complex dynamics of relationships and help people adjust to each other's dynamics and style. Churches could help by providing counseling centers with well-trained, competent counselors to help their members. Instead, we have heard some of our clients tell us that the church "counselor" told them to pray a lot and "get your lives right with God."

Not only is that not "counseling," it is in no way even helpful. It is another example of what we call Christian Abuse. Marriage and pregnancy are complex issues which do not lend themselves to simple solutions and preachments, such as "pray a lot" or "get right with God."

These ideas and concepts which are frequently found in Christian marriage vows are examples of Destructive Christian Beliefs. People believing and teaching these vows as valid directly or indirectly abuse or hurt people. It leads people to expect that God will make everything okay and wonderful in their lives and marriage, if they will only follow his will. It keeps people from seeking the help they need while waiting on magic.

The family is in trouble in our culture. We think Christianity has contributed to that problem. We certainly believe it must assert leadership to correct that problem. The first step is to admit that many of the beliefs are destructive and people have been spiritually injured. They fight about good and bad, right and wrong, and they do not know how to spiritually unite and transcend these deep-seated problems.

FRIENDSHIP

In order to establish and maintain friendships, it is essential that people accept other people with different ideas, beliefs, and concepts. Either that, or they can only befriend individuals similar to themselves in belief. The beliefs found in most Abusive Christian churches lead people to believe that they are right and other denominations or other belief systems are wrong. Thus, it is their desire to convert these "other" people from their sinful and evil beliefs and not accept them as they are.

This "conversion" ends up as an attempt to convince these "other" people to think the way you think and behave the way you want them to behave or the way your religious values say they should behave. If they do not agree, they are not accepted. If they do not change, they are not accepted. Usually anger, rejection, and punishment are dispensed to these individuals that refuse to convert. This religious xenophobia blocks friendship, and it promotes prejudice and fear of anyone who is different than you.

If it does lead to xenophobia and prejudice to those outside your religion, it also lends itself to strong bonds within the specific religious subculture. These individuals bond together in their faith. This is usually a healthy bonding even if it is prejudicial and exclusive. However, at times it can become an unhealthy, an "us against the world" attitude. This attitude can reach psychotic proportions, such as Jim Jones and his religious cult in Guyana. Groups of people can be persuaded to believe this "us against them" attitude and form strong bonds and fears of others.

Jerry recalls that being raised in a Southern Baptist church, he was wary of Catholics. He was taught they were dangerous people who were trying to take over the world. When John Kennedy was elected president, he was afraid of what might happen. Kennedy, a Catholic, was very different than a Baptist.

The rule was that Baptists should date Baptists, marry Baptists, and befriend Baptists. Catholics should be kept away and certainly out of control of our affairs. Christian religions are exclusive.

This idea of bonding together and fearing and hating others may be a human trait, but it is certainly found and promoted in Abusive Christianity. In fact, this concept is, to a certain extent, inherent in all Christian religions. The very question "Are you a Christian?" implies "Are you like me or different from me?" A lack of tolerance for difference and a need for people to change their beliefs to "belong" to the group is indeed a part of Christian theology.

SEXISM AND RACISM

Martin Luther King said that the 11 o'clock hour on Sunday morning is the most segregated time in our nation and his statement is still true. The same could be said about churches' discrimination against women. Sexism and racism permeate both Protestant and Catholic churches. When one looks into the leadership in these organizations, one finds few, if any, women. There are no women who serve as priests, and very few women who serve as conservative Christian ministers or preachers. Both Catholic and Protestant leaders, mostly all male, have begun "to study" the role of women in the church.

The current struggle among Catholics and Protestants centers on whether women should be allowed in leadership roles and be allowed to serve as priests, ministers, and preachers and teach in conservative theological seminaries. The Southern Baptists appointed a committee in 1992 to study whether women should be allowed to preach and be granted faculty status in the theology department at Southwestern Baptist Theological Seminary. As of this printing, there were no women with faculty status in theology at Southwestern Baptist Theological Seminary.

Most of our businesses and governmental institutions have made advances in granting equality as to race and sex. Not so in churches and not so in church leadership. Churches are exempt from federal equality laws, due to the separation of church and state. So the federal government has no power in the regulation of equality among races and sex in the churches. Until recently, there was little pressure on the churches to grant equality.

Catholic bishops commonly proclaim that women are equal, but one only has to examine the structure of the organization and the leadership to see very few blacks and no women. It seems what the bishops say and what the church leadership does are two different things. The lack of women and blacks in leadership roles is a further example of Abusive Christianity. Because it hides in the cloak of Christianity does not make it any less abusive.

It is interesting to note that the "Southern" Baptists were named "Southern" because of their support of slavery of the blacks. So there are no blacks in the Southern Baptist Convention and, so far, no black or female Southern Baptist ministers. Likewise, there are very few blacks and no women represented in leadership roles in the Catholic church.

Racism and sexism have existed in the Christian churches for centuries. In fact, there are few female Jewish Rabbis. From the onset of our culture, we have incorporated these beliefs and practices of segregation and sexism. Christianity is the origin of this type of discrimination. It is little wonder, then, that American businesses were dominantly white male until recently.

Thankfully, some progress has been made in government and in business. However, racism and sexism are still alive and well in all of our Judeo-Christian institutions. *We will not have triumphed over racism and sexism until we have eradicated these issues in our religious institutions.* The churches are not part of the solution. They are part of the problem, and a large part at that.

As individuals, we have incorporated these beliefs and practices into our perceptions to the extent that few people see the discrimination which exists in our churches. Because of these beliefs, which in subtle ways preserve and promote racism and sexism, most individuals and groups are hesitant to suggest change in our Christian and Jewish organizations which would end these prejudice practices.

In 1992, when the police officers were acquitted for the beating of Rodney King, riots erupted in Los Angeles and several cities across the nations. Where were the churches? Black churches responded. White churches responded. Separately. Segregated.

Most Christian denominations are for the most part segregated. How can the churches claim moral leadership when their own house is not in order? The answer is simple. They have no moral leadership! If they try, it is much like the parent who, while smoking and drinking alcohol, lectures his children on the evil of drugs.

MIRACLES: THE ABUSE OF THE CHOSEN

Those individuals who feel chosen by God may not intend to depreciate or harm others, but that is frequently the result. They make statements that are probably not well thought out and based on an emotional reaction. For example, consider the statement, "God punishes the wicked." If someone has just harmed you, that can be a comforting thought.

Why does God not rehabilitate the wicked or simply change them? Why punish them? Punishment would certainly satisfy the sadistic needs of the individual who was wronged, but overall it does not help or facilitate change. But our belief, "God will punish the wicked," remains strong, and it influences our judgment and behavior. We think and act in terms of punishment only and gear our social institutions with punishment in mind (schools and prisons). As a "Christian belief," we are not supposed to question or think about the implications of that belief. Simply believe. As a result, many beliefs are not well developed and end up making matters worse, or hurting people.

People often feel "chosen" when they survive an experience that could have killed them, or they survived while others did not. For example, after a severe tornado at Wichita Falls, Texas, several people commented to the media that they were so glad God had spared their lives and that God had seen fit to rescue them from this great disaster. After airline crashes, it is common for survivors to say that God had seen fit to save them, or God had brought them through this with minimal injury. When a child is kidnapped and returned alive, it is common for the parents to say that God protected and brought their child back to them.

Such incidences do appear to be miraculous. However, what about the victims who did not survive? Will God kill 130 passengers on an airliner so He can display how special nine or ten individuals are? Is this the way God displays His mercy?

This kind of information is absolutely devastating for the families of individuals who did not survive. As a culture we attempt to be very sensitive to the needs of minorities and to the pain of prejudicial statements which would further hurt those minority groups, but we will allow, through the media, families of disaster victims to be brutalized with this kind of statement without even thinking about it.

Jerry works with families of murder victims, and has seen the pain and injury inflicted when another parent states in the media, "God brought my child through this." Of course, families of murder victims question, "Why did God not protect my child?" "What have we done that is so bad that God would not protect and deliver our child?" They painfully wonder why their loved one had to suffer and die in such a cruel manner. This suffering is complicated when someone says, "God saved my child."

Regardless of one's theological beliefs, it is outrageous to traumatize families of murder victims and disaster victims further. These statements increase the already deep trauma for these family members. Those who feel chosen by the grace and mercy of God increase the trauma to those who were not.

This belief unintentionally inflicts pain and agony on an already abused minority, the minority being the loved ones and friends of disaster and murder victims. This prejudicial Christian abuse is sought and played by the media in an innocent, but brutal fashion. Someone needs to speak out for this abused minority.

ADVERTISEMENT: ABUSE OF ENTITLEMENT

We have looked through the local yellow pages and newspaper and so far have found a:

> Christian day care center
> Christian lawyer
> Christian counselor
> Christian schools
> Christian financial planners
> Christian beauty shop
> Christian shoe repair
> Christian plumber

Our research was far from extensive, but we would like to ask what is the message here? Are these businesses better than or significantly different from other businesses? Should you trust these people to be more honest or fair than other businesses? What is it they want to communicate? Do they not want business from Jewish clients or other religions?

One of our clients who went to a Christian counseling center said she felt shamed by the staff at the center. They told her, "If your faith were stronger you would feel better," and "Just trust the Lord." She told us she felt even more inadequate and depressed after her "counseling" and she decided to quit going. She was pleased to learn that we classified the activity at the "Christian counseling" center as "Christian abuse." She agreed, she felt abused.

This is not to say that all Christian counseling centers are abusive. They are not. But any business that says "Christian" really tells you very little about the business, unless of course, it is associated with a denomination or a religious institution or activity.

CHILD ABUSE

Children can potentially be abused by any number of people. Parents, teachers, schoolmates, other children, ministers, and almost any adult can abuse a child. The type of abuse can be emotional neglect, emotional abuse, verbal, physical, and sexual abuse. Psychotherapists and researchers are quickly becoming aware of areas of abuse that were ignored or unknown in the recent past.

Families function by complex and generally unconscious systems of rules and systems of thought that we are defining and perceiving for the first time—for example, codependence, enmeshment, emotional incest. These are recent terms in our culture. The family system of rules and thinking can lead to neglect and abuse in children.

For example, the belief that a child should be perfect can lead to the abuse of that child, simply because children cannot be perfect. It is our contention that certain Christian belief systems are conducive to abuse and neglect of children. We have presented the Abusive Christian Model in Chapter 1, punishment in Chapter 3, and anger versus love in Chapter 4.

These Christian ideas and concepts work together to promote an atmosphere that encourages child abuse by well-meaning parents. When we look at the belief system and the manner in which God interacted with man, follow the rules or face hell, we evolve a family rule system that provides the basis for interacting with children in an abusive manner. The rules from an Abusive Christian model, which facilitate child abuse in families are:

- Parents or God have the power. Children have none.
- Parents love/control the child.
- Children must obey the rules.
- There are no alternatives (rigidity).
- Perfectionism ("children of God") is the standard.
- Disobedience will be punished.
- Parental love will be withdrawn.
- The parent will be angry.
- Children will suffer physical and mental pain (hell).

If that model and those rules are followed in families in our culture (and we believe this is the dominant model) they will lead to child abuse. It is frankly that simple. However, families and family rules are varied and complex. One element of these rules may be dominant, such as perfectionism, and others may be absent. We believe these rules are behind parenting behavior in our culture today. When these rules are translated into dynamic behavior, the typical scenario goes something like this:

The parent loves the child and has high expectations, probably perfectionstic expectations, for that child. The parent wants the child to achieve and obey. If the child does not obey, the parent becomes angry. The rules and the standards are rigid. The child must obey. The child may be given a second chance. If the child fails to obey, the child will be punished. The more rigid, perfectionistic and angry the parent, the more dramatic the angry punishment.

Punishment may include children being hit, beaten, sent to bed without food, or even starved. But the principle, the rule, must be rigidly adhered to. "This is for your own good," the parents frequently say to the child. But in the end, the children suffer. These parents actually love their children. They have high expectations for their children. These are not bad, mean, and/or evil parents. They are following the model they were taught. They may be addicted to or locked into the model and unable to see any alternatives for their behavior. But they are not bad people, even though their acts may be abusive and violent. Punishment will not help them. They are masters at punishment, and they punish themselves. They must release their shame and anger and learn a new model of love and respect. They need moral leadership from churches, not more punishment.

The goal of family therapy is to change this model. To bring in more understanding, more flexibility, a willingness to examine the system of rules, to question the rules, and to bring in the concept of discipline within love. As with sexism and racism, must culture change and the religions follow? That is what is happening now.

EXCLUSION FROM THE GROUP

In most Christian groups, especially conservative Christian groups, inclusion is based on conformity. If you do not believe as the group believes, and behave within the guidelines of the group, you may well be excluded. It is very interesting that in Christian groups, exclusion frequently takes precedence over help. People will be sacrificed if they do not adhere to the belief.

In the first chapter, both writers told of how they were excluded from groups because their beliefs and behavior did not measure up to the Abusive Christian Beliefs and rigid rules. By their very nature, the different denominations are exclusive. Baptists associate, go to church, date, marry, and rear other Baptists. They exclude other religions.

To be included in the religious group, you have to conform in belief, dress, and behavior. Or you have to keep your difference very quiet. Christian religions, as they now exist, will never pull our nation together.

INSTITUTIONAL CONTROL

Nowhere is the term "hostile takeover" more appropriate and accurate than when conservative Christian members fight over control of their institutions. Their behavior often and appropriately fits our term, "Christian Abuse," and their behavior fits the Abusive Christian Model of withdrawal of love and punish with anger. In the May 4, 1991, edition of the local newspaper was an article headlined "Baylor University regents reject Baptist plan, make own offer." The problem, as outlined in this article, had revolved around the election of the board of trustees for Baylor. The board members are responsible for making policy and in essence overseeing the management of the university. A significant number of board members were appointed by conservative Baptists in the state organization. Recently, the board voted to make a majority of the board "self-perpetuating," thus bypassing the majority control of the conservative Baptists. The reason for the self-perpetuating board was "to protect the 12,000 student school from the threat of a fundamentalist takeover."

The Baptist fundamentalists believe in a very strict and literal interpretation of the Bible. They have been in control of the national organization of the Southern Baptists for several years now. The article noted that "fundamentalists also want to take over the Texas Baptist Convention and control Baylor."

By the very nature of their conservative beliefs, if you disagree, you are "going against God's will." Their will, or God's will as they see it, must prevail! Since they truly believe they KNOW God's will, to give up control would be to go against God. They will fight with "righteous anger," and they will fight for all beliefs within "God's will."

The belief system of the conservative Baptist is contrary to and against the "academic freedom" concept of a liberal arts program in a university. So the idea of trying to be reasonable and allowing them to teach their courses in the way they wish will not work. They want control. They want the power to control ideas that "they think" are contrary to a literal interpretation of the Bible. We emphasize the term "they think" because over the history of Christianity, "they" have espoused several scientific opinions which have not held up well. Early Christians thought the earth was flat because the Bible says earth has four corners. They also thought the earth was the center of the universe and they were less than kind to the idea that the sun was the center of the solar system. They are convinced that they KNOW what GOD wants, therefore they cannot compromise on issues.

The regents at Baylor know the teaching of evolution, the teaching of certain philosophy classes, art classes, certain types of literature, and academic freedom in general would be gone if the fundamentalists took over the university. It appears the Board of Regents thought this issue serious enough to remove the power to control the institution from the fundamentalists. Academic freedom does demand that the fundamental Baptist view be taught, along with other conflicting views.

A very similar control battle is brewing at Southwestern Baptist Theological Seminary. In the same local paper on March 12, 1991, an article stated that the Baptists are trying to create "an agency to accredit Southern Baptist seminaries and schools." The next paragraph is revealing:

While Southwestern is having no trouble with accreditation, two of the six Southern Baptist seminaries have had accrediting troubles recently because of changes in hiring procedures and doctrine requirements imposed by fundamentalist trustees.

The fundamentalist Baptists want to control the institutions to "weed out" any view or any person which does not agree with their conservative doctrine. There are two recognized and established accrediting agencies for seminaries, the Association of Theological Schools and the Southern Association of Colleges and Schools.

If a school loses accreditation, several undesirable consequences follow. The students at those seminaries could not transfer to another accredited institution, because the accredited institution would not accept their course credits. The students in the unaccredited seminary would not have their degrees recognized. Thus they could not teach and could not continue to do graduate work at an accredited institution. The seminary and its students would lose recognition.

Neither the plight of the seminary, nor the students, is an issue to the fundamentalist. The fundamentalist Baptists want control and they do not allow divergent views. It is part of their philosophy. You are either right or wrong. They are positive that they know the will and plan of God. If you disagree you are wrong. If you are wrong you must be punished or banished. The dysfunctional aspects of excessive control, rigidity, black and white thinking and the use of anger, intolerance, and punishment are alive and well in the denominations of the Southern Baptist and in other denominations as well.

In the same local paper on March 13, 1991, there appeared an article "Gay, premarital sex, issues divide Presbyterian church." The issue was ordination of ministers into the church and whether their sex lives should be revealed and/or examined. If the behavior is "sinful," such as premarital sex or homosexuality, should these individuals be excluded? The conservative elements of the Presbyterian church want control, and they tend to be exclusive, intolerant, rigid, and they see these issues in terms of black and white doctrine and not in terms of people being discriminated against.

This is not to say that the liberal element cannot follow the Abusive Christian Model; they indeed may. They also may be rigid, intolerant, see issues in terms of black and white, intolerant of conservative views, and so on. This rigid position is not as consistent with liberal views and belief systems, but it still can be found. The issue is, when you strongly think you know the view of God, as conservative Christians think, then you can treat the opposition with disdain and abuse because you are right and they are wrong.

Doctrine can create problems in any Christian denomination. Should women be allowed to be priests? Should Catholic priests be allowed to marry? On and on. The point is, when conservative Christians know they are "right," they will fight for their views. Because of their views, they can classify opposing views as sinful and evil. The debate then becomes rigid. Variation is not allowed. People can be sacrificed if their beliefs differ.

Institutional control then becomes symptomatic of the conservative Christian belief and practice. That practice includes excessive control, rigidity, black and white thinking, intolerance of other views, anger, and punish or banish. They become the "Christian Abuser" to people with divergent views.

CHRISTIAN CHURCHES: A LACK OF MORAL LEADERSHIP

Christian churches have no positive moral leadership in:

> sexism
> racism
> homosexuality
> family violence
> unity of peoples
> sexual education
> sexual dysfunctions
> sexual perversions
> sexual acting out
> child abuse

Christian churches are in need of "conversion." Christian churches discriminate against people because of their sex, their race, their different creeds, and their sexual preferences. They are divisive, separating Baptist, Catholic, and Jew. They frequently preach the Abusive Christian Model, which if followed in families, promotes child abuse. Their rigid sexual ethics and fear of sexual issues and differences promote secrecy, in which many perversions hide. They generally avoid sexual education which is realistic, honest, and open. They turn their backs on those who "transgress" and need help, unwed pregnancies, couples in affairs, sinners all.

Our families and culture are in a crisis. Christian churches do not help. They are part of the problem. Punishing churches will not help, either. There has been enough punishment.

ONLY GOOD FOLK GO TO CHURCH

Jerry recently spoke at a Christian church and noticed several things. Everyone there was white. Everyone there was properly dressed, clean cut, and neat. There were no people of color, no people that looked different, no prostitutes, no obvious "druggies," no unwed mothers.

That is one of the major problems with churches. Only good people go. The people that really need help and need churches, *do not go*. In fact, generally, they are not welcome. If your church is "white," can you imagine the welcome a group of, say, ten black prostitutes would receive? What about ten well dressed black people?! If your church is "black" can you imagine the welcome a group of white pimps and drug dealers would receive? "Bad" people, especially if they are of different races than our segregated churches, are simply not welcome. Churches want good people, ONLY. We do not want people on drugs, unwed mothers, adulterers, prostitutes, or people of questionable moral virtue.

The church wants to preserve the status quo. They do not want to be an instrument of change. Or, they set up shelters for the homeless usually at a safe distance from their homes and churches. Or they will send out missionaries to foreign lands, when we need counselors and helpers in our own communities. Christian churches have become clean, almost antiseptic. They do not want to get their hands dirty.

In order to help our nation, our people, all people, "good folk" in churches need to get their hands "dirty."

CHAPTER 6

BEWARE: BE FRUITFUL AND MULTIPLY
Christianity Causes Sexual Dysfunction

The concepts of Christianity have inflicted extensive damage in the area of sexuality and sexual behavior. The scars run deep. Few people in our culture have gone unscathed.

Abusive values and attitudes, which have their roots in Christian sexual ethics, form an integral part of our culture. Christian sexual values have pervaded our history and development for centuries, and affect our current sexual development, regardless of religious affiliation, race, creed, or color. Damage ranges from sexual suppression and severe shame, to sexual addiction, sexual dysfunctions, and sexual acting out.

The story of Danny is a common one, relating many of the sexual maladaptations set up by the Judeo-Christian ethic. Danny, a construction worker, received no sexual training in his rigid Christian rearing.

> Dad told me two things about sex. The first was "If you sleep with a girl and she gets pregnant, you're gonna marry her." He never said sex or intercourse, he said "sleep with," so that threw me. I thought that sleeping with a girl would make her pregnant. The

other thing Dad told me about sex is, "A girl who will do it with you, will do it with everyone else." Therefore, when I got in a relationship with a girl and we had sex, I lost respect for her and that ruined the relationship, and I dumped her. You spend your life with all these sexual feelings and try to explore them in the relationship with someone you really like and are really attracted to, but then when you finally do it, you lose respect and it's all over and you start over with the next girl.

In my family, sex was something you didn't even talk about until you got married. If you asked a question, it was irrelevant because unless you're getting married, you don't need to know. The one piece of information you do get is "wait until marriage." Sex becomes the great mystery.

I got my education from a pornographic magazine that showed nude women with little stars to cover up their nipples. Nipples became the most appealing part to me because that's what I couldn't see. They became the evil part of a woman and that's the part I wanted. After that I found some really explicit sex cards from Mexico that showed group sex and were real disgusting, but they showed everything.

I got the message even masturbation is taboo. We read in the Bible about that guy that lost his seed on the ground and God punished him. Therefore masturbation is a sin. That throws kids for a loop. They're told all sex is wrong, so they are not able to differentiate between abuse and healthy sex.

Puberty hit me before anyone else my age. One day an older man walked up and propositioned me. He told me how to masturbate, and I tried it. Once you cross the line by masturbating, you've done something bad. So you are bad. Once you cross that line, you might as well do anything. Even if a boy is approached by a man, well, he's already done bad so what difference does it make. The only sex education I got as a child was sexual abuse by several different men, some of them in my own family.

The total lack of positive information about sex, or *any* information, is common. Danny went through what many people in Christian society experience:

- The fantasy and secret allure of pornography, with the resulting guilt.
- The guilt over masturbation, a normal human behavior.
- The feeling that "sex is wrong" and the resulting guilt, confusion, and hopelessness..
- The history of family sexual abuse in a rigidly Christian family.
- The vulnerability to homosexual child abuse, simply because he had no clear understanding of sexual limits.
- The lack of understanding of sex.
- The intense need for love.
- The confusion of love with sexuality.

All of these aspects of Danny's unguided sexual behavior directly relate to problems precipitated by Christian sexual ethics.

CHRISTIAN SEXUAL TRAINING

When we first considered the question of Christian sexual training, our response was "there is none." But after much thought and countless sessions with our clients, we got a different answer. It is *negative*—worse than no education. The descriptions we heard of Christian sexual training range from the openly hostile to the very subtle, but all were harmful and abusive. As with most aspects of family dysfunction, the effects ripple through generations. What are the ideas, concepts, and beliefs that contribute to this negative aspect of Christian Sexual training?

THE SEXUAL RULES IN CHRISTIANITY

Rules concerning Christian sexuality are taught via sermons, Sunday school lessons, discussion groups, and parent/child discussions/confrontations. These dicta pass by word of mouth from adults to children, generation to generation:

- Don't act sexual—except as humor.
- Sex is sinful and dirty.
- Sexual intercourse before marriage is wrong.
- Any type of sexual outlet before marriage is wrong. Masturbation is wrong. Pornography is wrong. Touching yourself "down there" is wrong.
- Wearing revealing clothing, showing your body is wrong.
- Talking openly about sexual intercourse is wrong.
- Thinking about sex, fantasy sex, or "lusting after women in your heart" is wrong.
- Good children, with good parents, are not sexual.
- Sex magically becomes okay with two words, " I do."
- Sex is for married procreation.
- Adultery—sexual intercourse with someone other than your spouse—is wrong.
- Don't talk nasty, don't use sexual language.
- Terrible things happen to people who have sex.
- Pregnancy, before or outside marriage, is at best a sin and often a catastrophe.
- Homosexuality is wrong and "unacceptable to God."
- Certain "unnatural acts," such as fellatio and sodomy, even between married couples, is wrong.
- Sex is a mystery.

- If you ignore sex, you won't have to deal with it.
- If you know too much about sex, you can "lose your values" and act out on your knowledge. Sexual knowledge is dangerous!

Most of these rules are negative. Sex, even information about sex, is perceived as sinful, wrong, and dangerous. Christianity is obviously replete with prohibitions about sexual behavior and sexual information. Sexuality is perceived in terms of good and bad, right and wrong, and discussion concerning sexuality should not last too long and certainly not be explicit.

Powerful values, along with powerful emotions, are assigned to sexual terms, sexual words, sexual attitudes, and sexual behavior. The emotional significance given these sexual terms and subjects has a dramatic impact on people, especially children. They elicit anxiety, fear, and anger about sexuality.

One colleague related an incident that happened while he was in graduate school for social work. At dinner one evening at his parents' home, he asked his mother and father why they never told him about sex. They looked at each other, then at their plates. The father literally dropped his fork. The father finally said, "You never asked." Needless to say, the son never asked again.

NONVERBAL MESSAGES ABOUT SEX

Sex education is more than a parent sitting down with a child and telling what goes where, or what not to do. It is an accumulation of verbal and nonverbal messages which include words, or the lack of words, gasps, facial expressions, gestures, laughter, approving or disapproving glances, threats, styles, habits, and behaviors. Sex education begins when a child discovers that boys are different from girls, and it proceeds from there, whether or not a parent or any other adult ever says a word to that child about sex. Many of the rules are never openly taught to a child. When a child touches his or her genitals, and the "offending" hand is slapped, the message is clear. "That is wrong!"

Nonverbal messages emotionally charge sexual terms, subjects, and behaviors. A wonderful example of nonverbal messages at work is seen in the film comedy Pretty Woman. An executive takes a prostitute into a swank hotel, where he is staying in the penthouse suite. At the lobby elevator, they encounter a snobbish matron and her wealthy husband who display surprise and disapproval toward the hooker (who is, by her outlandish outfit, obviously a hooker). They turn their heads away. At this the hooker props up her leg and lifts up her mini-skirt saying, "Oh, honey, you know what's happened? I've got a runner in my pantyhose!...I'm not wearing pantyhose." The matron gasps. The husband's jaw drops as they stare in shock at her behavior. The matron says, "Close your mouth, dear."

No one would have had to say a word. The older couple's attitude was clear from their nonverbal communications. These nonverbal messages of disgust and disapproval are the result of a collective negative attitude toward sexuality inherent in Christianity and its historical predecessor.

Most of what is taught about sexual attitudes is taught without words. These nonverbal communications, the glances to the side, the hesitation in speaking, the lack of direct eye contact, teach children how to think, behave, and feel about sexual matters.

In a structured group encounter, individuals shared those moments when parents, or a significant individual, relayed a message about sexual information or values. Joe told the following story:

> When I was about 16 years old, I really wanted a girl-friend, and I desperately wanted to have a sexual experience with a girl. I knew that I needed a condom, but I was too afraid to walk into the local drug store and buy one. I was too embarrassed.
>
> Several of my buddies and myself set out on a quest to buy condoms. We could never get the courage to go into a store and buy one. One of my buddies had a friend that delivered drug store supplies, to the local stores. We went to ask if he could

help us. Much to our delight, he was more than willing to help us, however, we had to buy in bulk, which amounted to about 120 condoms. We only really needed three! But we decided to go for it. We pooled lunch money, allowances and finally came up with the money. We made our purchase of 120 condoms. Each of us took one for our billfold, but that left 117, and we had no idea what to do with that many condoms.

Anyway, I was elected to take home the extra condoms, all 117. After looking for a good hiding place in my room, I decided to line them up on a partition between the drawers in my dresser. It was perfect. At least, I thought so.

One day, when my mom was putting up clothes, my sister heard mom scream. I was not at home, so my sister ran into my room. She found mom sitting on the floor surrounded by condoms, holding a drawer. Evidently, one of the drawers had become stuck, mom had pulled on it and out popped the drawer and all 117 condoms.

When I came home, all the condoms were gone. Mom and Dad never said a word and never asked me where all of these things came from. They must have thought I was into some really "heavy" sex!

The nonverbal attitude communicated about most sexual situations is disapproval. The feelings communicated are generally anxiety, fear, disgust, embarrassment, and guilt. The association between anxiety and sexuality alone can cause a great deal of damage to sexual functioning. Fear and anxiety block sexual arousal and lead to sexual dysfunction. Combine these feelings with guilt, shame, and embarrassment, along with the message that sex is dirty, bad, and sinful, and it is truly a marvel that anyone in our culture is sexually functional. Looking at all the new books on sexual addictions and sexual dysfunctions, we see that many individuals, indeed, are not sexually functional.

Another nonverbal attitude originating from Abusive Christianity is that sex is powerful and dangerous. It can save you or it can kill you. The forbidden mystique serves only to increase the power of sexual messages. It is little wonder advertisers use sex to sell everything from ball bearings to cold drinks. Sexual messages grab our attention and make a memorable impact.

These visual advertisements, most of which are reactions against conservative Christian ethics, still associate sexuality and sexual behavior with a plethora of confusing and contradictory messages. Sex is forbidden, powerful, dangerous, evil, fearful, dirty, bad, and can induce and cause shame, guilt, anxiety, embarrassment, panic, rage, and murder. Given this attitudinal and emotional miasma, there is fertile ground for sexual dysfunction. This is the groundwork by which Christian sexual ethics contribute to sexual dysfunction.

Did your family openly and comfortably discuss sexuality and the values and implications of sexuality? Or was the attitude, "Here, let me tell you about this, but then, keep your mouth shut." When it comes to sexual function, you are what you were reared with, both verbally and nonverbally.

DIRTY WORDS/SEXUAL WORDS

For a live demonstration of the nonverbal messages about sexuality, gather your family together and try the following exercise. See how many different names or synonyms you can think of for the list of words below. You could also try this at Sunday school or as a party icebreaker, or with any other group for that matter. We would love to do this exercise with a group of television evangelists!

Each person must say the word out loud and a list of synonyms must be recorded. You should easily come up with 10 to 15 different words for each category. A warning: the list will be "dirty and vulgar."

- male sexual organ
- female sexual organ
- the sexual experience

- oral sexual experiences
- orgasm
- erection

Carefully watch the people in the room as the words are uttered. The wide eyes, the hands over the mouth, red faces, hands covering faces, the anxious laughter, the lack of eye contact, all will signal that rules are being broken.

The rules are: We should not talk like this; you don't say these words in public and especially, you don't say these words in front of adults or parents. These words can get you in trouble. These words are dirty. Some people may refuse to take part in this exercise. They may be unable to speak these words. Most people have certain words that they find especially offensive.

Once, while Jerry was teaching an introductory psychology class, he had the class come up with their list of "dirty words" while he wrote the words on a blackboard in front of the class. At the end of class, he forgot to erase the blackboard. The next class, an English class, was taught by a rather puritanical professor, who must have had some difficulty understanding the purpose of the list of words found on the blackboard. The dean was called in to observe the list. In the end, academic freedom prevailed, but these words do upset some people.

In counseling, we often find ourselves trying to help married couples overcome their discomfort with sexual words. We use this exercise to initially impress people with their fear of sexual words, but ultimately to help the couple feel more comfortable with their sexual communications. At times, the exercise demonstrates just how uncomfortable the couple can be with any type of sexual subject.

Many families will not even consider trying this exercise. They will be honestly unable to come up with any list, because they perceive these words as so wrong and sinful. The families and individuals who perceive these words as "bad" also generally view people who use them as bad, crude, and vulgar. These perceptions extend to the acts and body parts themselves. Thus, sexual organs and acts, natural acts of procreation, become perceived as bad. When normal sexual body parts and acts are seen as vulgar, this contributes to sexual dysfunction. Thus the beginning of training in sexual dysfunction is both caused by and reflected in the negative attitudes toward these "dirty words."

Why are these words perceived as "dirty" and "vulgar?" Is there anything inherently dirty about these words? Is there something dirty or bad about the body parts and acts they stand for? A great deal of emotion and censure are associated with these words. They are perceived as wrong, powerful, and dangerous, but we cannot explicitly define why. These words are bad because we have been taught they are bad. We have learned to associate these words with powerful, fearful, and "dirty" emotions of guilt and shame. By their very censure, these words gain power.

How did we learn these sexual words were vulgar and dirty? Now we know your local conservative Christian minister did not stand up in the pulpit and read a list of these words and say "These are dirty and vulgar so please do not repeat any of them." Even though most ministers do not read a "dirty word list" and proclaim it "dirty," the source of this negative attitude is the stance that conservative Christian religion takes against sexual expression of any kind. Sex is rarely discussed or taught. It is still forbidden. This negative attitude gives sex its power and mystique. It is the fuel behind the power of the "dirty words."

Why is it so difficult for people to talk about an act they do so frequently? People are ashamed to use certain sexual words, or talk about certain topics. These attitudes reflect the massive scarring from the wounds of Christian Sexual Abuse.

We do not condemn or encourage the use of this "vulgar" language. The words, in and of themselves, are not bad, but their use is still emotionally loaded in many circles. If you wish to maintain an "acceptable" image in our culture, it is probably best to avoid using these words. However, acceptance of this language will remove the power of this language. The first step in achieving effective communication about sexuality is being comfortable with vocabulary.

SEX EDUCATION IN SCHOOLS

The lack of an acceptable sexual vocabulary contributes to the difficulty in educating children about sexuality. Discomfort with sexual issues leads to the neglect of sexual education of any kind. Resistance to sexual education in public schools persists, even today, especially in the southern states. Often there seems to be no understandable rationale for that resistance. The source of this resistance, seated in the abusive Christian sexual attitude, maintains that sex is dirty and bad and should not be taught in any school. There are several issues involved in Christian discomfort with sex education.

The first issue is fear, along with a considerable amount of revulsion. The belief is that children have no need to know about sex. In fact, in many conservative Christian belief systems there is no need to know about sex until marriage, if then. The fear behind this is that, if we tell children and adolescents too much about sex, it will remove the prohibition against sex and the fear of sex.

The next issue is based on the assumption that talking or teaching about sex condones sexually acting out. This same logic has not been applied to excessive drinking and reckless driving, thank heavens. Information about sex, alcohol, and drugs does not make it more likely that people will act out in these areas.

Christian thinking stresses that sexual knowledge is dangerous. We strongly believe that a lack of sexual knowledge is dangerous. Poorly informed children make poor decisions, and they interpret the secrecy as, "sex is dangerous, bad, and sinful."

Another issue, sexual ethics, is neglected. Christians fear schools only teach the hydraulics, not the meaning of "sexuality." In some educational situations, this is accurate. As a culture, when we focus on sex, we focus on little else. We rarely focus on emotional intimacy, closeness, openness, and bonding. When we examine the sexual, we ignore the relationship, at least the psychological aspects of the relationship.

Relationship training could easily be included in sexual education. The different lifestyles and values surrounding sexual expression, the importance of developing intimate, open, close relationships all could be included. However, Christians react against this because they want only their own restrictive moral values taught. The negative attitudes of anger and fear on the part of many Christians, close the door on discussions about curriculum in sex education.

Conservative Christians will not negotiate when they think they are right. Why should they—after all, God is on their side. Thus, they will sacrifice people because of their belief system. We once observed a group whose goal was to plan content for a class in sexual education. There was a conservative Christian minister in the group. He was preaching loudly, sounding angry, insisting how important marriage is to sexual expression. We had the distinct feeling he would verbally abuse anyone who disagreed.

Open discussions about subject matter for sexual education classes are often difficult. A great deal of fear and anger is exacerbated by the discussion of sexuality. Often, conservative Christians are so confused and fearful about sexuality, because of its identification with "sin," that they will attempt to ban the teaching of sexual material entirely. Or they will attempt to ban the inclusion of homosexuality. The attitude seems to be, "Don't look and don't talk and maybe it will go away."

The fact is, sex will not go away. Sex education should be openly taught in every middle school and every high school in the country. These classes should be mandatory! These classes should emphasize the fears and prohibitions associated with sexuality and the responsibilities involved in sexual relationships. We would even encourage the teaching of sexual education in churches, by knowledgeable professionals.

TYPICAL WAYS CHILDREN LEARN ABOUT SEX

Where do children and adolescents learn about sexuality? Adolescent and adult clients tell us of their sources:

- From a friend who heard it from a friend who really had no idea.

- In the closet.
- In the streets like everyone else.
- From adolescents who pressured me and then engaged me in various group sexual activities.
- From pornographic materials which often offer an unpleasant, unrealistic view of sex.
- From watching animals.
- From scavenging through dictionaries and encyclopedias looking up body parts and suggestive words.
- From a parent who would rather be in Cincinnati.
- From the walls in public restrooms.
- I didn't. I never did, no one ever told me.
- From a book, left in my drawer under my underwear.
- I had to figure it out myself, on my honeymoon.
- I was just told, "Don't do it."

No wonder kids and adults are so confused about sexuality today. With sources like these, most people have no choice but to deal with sex in an instinctual way, just going with their feelings, or in a rigid, controlled fashion dictated by the Christian belief system. There is no acceptable source of healthy sexual education available. Many times well-meaning but poorly informed parents add to the problem rather than to the solution.

HEALTHY ALTERNATIVES FOR TEACHING SEXUALITY

Much better options exist than children learning about sex from the streets or from other children. To achieve these options, we must take action. How should children learn about sex? The teaching sources should be well informed, knowledgeable, and comfortable with sexual information. They should be aware that others, especially adolescents, will not be comfortable, but will be tense and anxious about sexual information. This discomfort usually is expressed in anxious laughter and crude comments and jokes.

The following represent appropriate optional sources for teaching sexual information:

1. From churches where well-informed teachers teach healthy values.
2. From spiritual leaders, ministers who have been well trained.
3. From loving and understanding parents, who have been trained in formal courses at their churches or colleges, and who are comfortable with their sexuality and capable of explaining the values of the family.
4. From schools and community programs, which reinforce and explain healthy values and provide accurate information.

The information needs to be presented in an open and relaxed way. Questions should be dealt with in an understanding and kind manner. Values should be presented in a nonauthoritarian fashion. Alternate lifestyles should be discussed in a way that's not judgmental. Relationships, communication, loving, caring, and expressing anger in a healthy manner would be included in the curriculum.

HEALTHY SEXUAL VALUES

Removing the Abusive Christian influence from sexuality will take more than a change in educational style. Our nonverbal reactions to the topic must change. For nonverbal reactions to change, we must become more and more comfortable with sex as a topic, and more and more secure in our own personal values and life style. However, we must start somewhere. So what follows is a list of ideas about sexuality, which are healthier and less abusive than those currently espoused by conservative Christian values.

- Sexual functioning in humans is natural and normal.
- Sexual exploration and sexual behavior is normal in children and should not be punished. If limits are

needed, they should be explained and established in a loving and caring manner.

■ Discussing and talking about sex is an appropriate means of learning about both sexual functioning and sexual relationships.

■ Thinking about sex and having sexual fantasies is normal.

■ Masturbation is normal and natural in both men and women.

■ Sexual words are not really harmful in any way. The harm lies in the perception and values of the listener.

■ Sex is not a mystery. There is a lot of good information which is rather easy to obtain.

■ There is nothing dirty, bad, or sinful about the human body. Our bodies should be a matter of pride and care.

■ To ignore sex and sexual information is to remain ignorant and ill-informed. Adequate information helps people use good judgment in making sexual decisions.

■ People who decide to have a sexual relationship will have to accept the consequences of their behavior. In our culture, at this time, they, especially women, may be seen as bad and sinful.

■ People who decide to have a sexual relationship are not bad people.

■ Married people who have sex outside their marriage are not bad people.

■ Affairs reflect individual problems or relationship problems and it is okay to seek help from well trained professionals.

■ We should help people with sexual problems, not condemn them.

- Careless sexual relationships can have disastrous consequences, psychologically and/or medically.
- Sexuality at its best is an expression of psychological closeness and commitment.
- Recreational sex, although an exciting concept, can reduce people to objects of gratification. At its best, sex is "I thou," not an "I it," relationship.
- Adequate information about sexuality and sexual relationships is essential to healthy sexual relationships and blends well with healthy sexual values.
- Men and women cannot expect to automatically become comfortable with sexual behavior just because they have committed to a relationship through a ceremony.
- Homosexuality is not a sin. It is not "bad."
- Oral sex and anal sex are not aberrations; they are options.
- Sexual diseases do exist. Knowledge is vital to making an informed choice.
- Sexual abstinence is not an aberration; it is an option.

The Abusive Christian Sexual Ethic wields power in a subtle manner. A stand against this dysfunctional system must be powerful and convincing. The values offered here make good sense in terms of today's reality. Christian sexual ethics lost touch with reality long ago and, in doing so, lost power over many people in our culture. Today, we want our values to make sense to us.

CHRISTIAN SEXUAL ABUSE: IMPACT ON MARRIAGE AND FAMILY

Abuse includes telling children they are worthless, stupid, and unlovable. Certainly abuse would include telling children that certain parts of their body are evil or certain bodily functions are dirty.

Christian Sexual Abuse encompasses all those sexual rules and messages, both verbal and nonverbal, having their roots in Christianity which damage an individual's sexual identity and development. Damage from Christian Sexual Abuse comes as much from what is not said as from what *is* said. By definition, Christian Sexual Abuse is abuse. It is negative and damaging, either by acts of commission or omission. By contrast, positive, healthy messages are not abusive.

When parents are so embarrassed or ashamed because of the "wrongness" or sinfulness attached to sex, they may avoid discussing it with their children. This gives the child a message that sex is something shameful and dangerous; you should not talk about it at all.

Many adults are ashamed and fearful to talk about sex, the genitals, and the sex act. We find couples married for years who avoid talking about sexual experiences within their own marriage. They are ashamed to talk about sex and they lack a common, comfortable vocabulary to deal with sexual information.

These covert, nonverbal attitudes are passed down from parent to child; then, in turn, when that child matures, they are passed down to the next generation of children. Most parents teach their children these attitudes, not because they are sadistic and intent upon doing damage to their children, but because they are in conflict themselves. The parents feel a powerful need to control these fearful sexual impulses in their children because they fear the same impulses in themselves.

Thus the fear, and the nonverbal perception of danger and shame, can be transmitted generation to generation, from fearful parent to soon-to-be fearful child.

The message? Sexuality is dangerous, shameful, dirty, and bad. The parent attempts to repress and control in their children those same fearful sexual impulses they repress and control in themselves.

Individuals with conventional Christian backgrounds complain that their parents never gave them any positive input on or about sex, but provided plenty of negative feedback. When Christian parents do talk about sex to children, their feelings about this forbidden subject are all too evident. One young woman, Mary, described her "talk" with her mother, a devout Catholic.

> Mom never looked me in the eye. She fidgeted and squirmed and was obviously very uncomfortable. Instead of using proper terms for genitalia, she talked about "down there." We were to be asexual. Good Catholic girls don't do this. Only bad girls have sex. Later on, when as a college student I began seeing a man separated from his wife for two years, it was made clear to me that I was a terrible person. I had to move out of my house because they couldn't accept the relationship. The messages about sex were, it was bad, wrong, and sinful.

Communication about sexual matters was never very good between Mary and her mother. But Mary was clear that sex and sin were closely associated. Mother feared even talking about sex. When her mother found out Mary was seeing a married man, even though he was separated, Mary was forced to move. Her mother had no choice. Her rigid, punitive Christian sexual ethic led her to reject her daughter. Rejection rather than helping is common in Christian sexual abuse. Another example of Christian Sexual Abuse can be seen in Susan's story.

Susan was the perfect child. She always did the "right thing" and was "very close" to her mother, perhaps too close. Her mother told her all about her father's affair with Lou Anne. Susan knew all the details and "somehow this seemed wrong. I knew too much." The message communicated by Susan's mother was that the father was "nasty and vulgar." Susan did not want to be around him. Susan's family was not particularly religious although her mother "had a shoebox full of evangelism tapes" which she listened to. With few words and subtle nonverbals, mom imparted the attitude that sex was disgusting and immoral, and reinforced the rule that "men cannot be trusted."

In her early sexual exploration while lying in bed, Susan remembers pleasurable feelings, but she also remembers powerful feelings of guilt. As a result, she stopped touching herself sexually. Even though she had sexual relationships with boys, she never had an orgasm. She decided since she was 16 and sexually active, she should go see her gynecologist for a "checkup" and birth control pills. She felt so nervous and so guilty, "I drove down an alley so no one would see me and parked a block away so no one would see my car."

Mom found out anyway, but instead of asking Susan or even talking to her daughter, she wrote her a letter! She told Susan there was no reason for her to go to the gynecologist unless she was sexually active.

Mom had the you-will-rot-in-hell tone in her voice when she finally asked Susan, "Are you sexually active?" The perfect child lied. She said "No," out of fear. "What would the neighbors think?" Mom asked. "How would the neighbors know if I am on the pill," Susan quietly wondered. Susan was acutely aware that she could not be open and honest with her mother. Communication had broken down between mother and daughter. The mother, due to her rigid views and fears, was unable to be helpful. At this point, the closeness between mother and daughter ended.

Susan had internalized the nonverbal messages that sexual relations were dirty, bad, dangerous, and shameful. She also learned to shut out family members when sexual issues arose. As an adult, Susan still feels sex is dirty, even with her husband. She has negative feelings when her husband "pats me on the fanny," but she is unable to tell him. Susan does not want these feelings and does not like feeling offended and dirty. She feels hostage to the negative feelings and messages she nonverbally learned as a child.

People tend to "normalize" their family experience. That is, they perceive the rules and nonverbal messages in their family as "normal." When they grow up and have children, as parents, they may be unaware they are passing the same negative sexual messages to their children. As parents, they, too, are just acting "normal." Even if the parents are aware of the negative nature of the messages, those messages still may seem normal or "right" to them. Negative attitudes toward sexuality are so prevalent in our culture that we tend to perceive the negative as right and correct. Only in situations of extreme abuse, such as sexual abuse and physical abuse, do parents recognize they are abusing their children, and often not even then. When people think their experiences are "normal," the denial that those experiences are abusive is massive. In this way, they protect themselves from self-blame and bad feelings.

Several clients described abusive upbringing by Catholic nuns. The nuns hit them with rulers and scolded them when there was any sexual overtone to their behavior, such as sexual jokes, language, and crude, adolescent comments. Initially, these clients did not see the nun's behavior as unusual or abusive. It was "normal." The clients saw no connection between their current sexual problems and this childhood sexual abuse.

Bill was reared by Catholic nuns. He vividly remembers being rapped on the knuckles with rulers. Even though his memory for specific details is poor, he does remember the punishment was frequently for "inappropriate" sexual behavior. Once, he received a particularly severe punishment for having another student's artistic rendition of a nude female in his possession.

Bill came for help because he no longer felt sexual excitement in his 30-year marriage. He only found stimulation in "dirty sex" such as affairs and prostitutes. However, even those experiences were unfulfilling because of the extreme guilt and depression he suffered afterwards.

His sex life now consisted of pornographic material and fantasy. He had become deeply disturbed when his sexual fantasies began to focus on his youngest daughter. He was locked in a secret world of sexual fear, pain, and anguish.

Bill required lengthy psychotherapy in order to trust us enough to talk about his secret life. Because of his rigid Catholic upbringing, his choices at first were limited even to the point of talking about sexual issues. Therapy progressed rapidly after that. In fact, the entire family became involved in therapy. Especially noteworthy was the fact that the oldest son had developed very similar problems in his own marriage.

Anything that affects one member of the family affects the entire family. If the parent is unhealthy, undoubtedly the child will pick up and carry on the dysfunction in some manner.

We are amazed at the directions that these dysfunctions take. While Bill was unwilling to end his unhappy marriage or to even be honest about the sexual issues because of their "wrongness," he was willing to go outside of the marriage for sex, also wrong. We can only believe that rigid Christian rearing creates such sexual conflict in people that they, like scared animals, run toward the path of least resistance. However, this path is often the most pathological and ends up creating more problems than it solves.

In our culture, marriages are in trouble, and marriages are the foundation of the family. Many, if not a majority, of marriages end up either unhappy or in divorce. The message is confusing and bizarre: The only relationship in which Christianity says sex is acceptable does not work!

As the foundation of the family breaks down, we must ask what rules and nonverbal messages are our children being taught about marriage and sexuality? Could Abusive Christianity and Christian Sexual Abuse have a hand in this lack of stability in marriage? We certainly think so.

THE SEXUAL REVOLUTION VERSUS THE MORAL MAJORITY, 1960-1990

The "Sexual Revolution" of the 1960s was a reaction to the toxic, stifling sexual ethics of conservative Christianity. The revolution was quite similar to what professionals term an adolescent rebellion. As the rebels grew older and as the social environment changed, the pendulum slowly returned to a conservative sexual ethic. At this time "The Moral Majority" and the "P.T.L." came into their political power.

Currently, our culture seems to lack a sexual identity. Marriages are breaking up. There are more single-parent families now than in 1950 and more couples living together without benefit of marriage.

Sadly, morals are dictated more by disease than by principle. Those who claim leadership have little effect. Conservative Christian churches, refusing to enter the 20th century, espouse the old Victorian sexual ethic in a condescending and authoritarian manner.

Monogamous relationships do not seem to work. Couples grow disenchanted with marriage without knowing why. They often divorce because it is the easiest option. Their anger toward each other makes them "feel" they are not in love any more. They are oblivious to their own narcissism, and do not know how to reach out to a separate human being, to share their feelings. They are psychologically trapped between the Sexual Revolution and The Moral Majority, not knowing whether to rebel or conform. There is a search for some middle ground, and that has to fall between the very conservative attitudes and the very liberal attitudes. No one has mapped out this middle ground. A family therapy adage truly fits here: "You can't do what you don't know." Because this middle ground is such a mystery, people give up; they divorce.

After divorce, the individuals decide to remarry or to "live together." But they vacilitate between the old Abusive Christian Model of withdrawing love and punishing with anger, or a liberal model of hedonism, "do whatever makes you happy." Future relationships are in trouble before they begin. Sexual freedom rarely seems deeply fulfilling, so the individuals feel "lost." They are vulnerable to "relationship salvation" or "sexual salvation," relationship styles which will not ultimately work. Our culture seems in evolution, without end or goal. More alarming, no rational moral leadership establishes or advocates any direction that is currently effective.

The emergence of phenomena such as the "Sexual Revolution," and "The Moral Majority" polarize the issues further and reflect the lack of direction of our culture. Neither approach is working very well. The issues are polarized into good versus bad and sin versus virtue. Our culture is losing ground in an attempt to establish a sexual and marital code of ethics.

Dialogue about sexual and marital relationships is dominating television talk shows. Excellent books are being published on relationships and marriage. This dialogue is badly needed. If only our churches were as open and honest about the issues as the rest of our culture, meaningful direction might be established.

THE 1990S' MORAL DIRECTION

In the rearing of children, the most important environment is the family. Family is the primary unit, and the most important part of that unit is the marriage. Even at its best, divorce is abandonment for children, who will be spending time with one parent or the other. As the parents begin to date and eventually remarry, the children have to deal with more confusing issues and conflicting values.

Our current cultural relationship practice is serial monogamy. Divorce. Remarry. Divorce. Live together. In terms of percentage, serial monogamy is probably the current "norm." Where are we headed? What happens to children in serial monogamy? What values do they learn? Why do marriages break up? Churches should have the courage to face and deal with these questions. We know some churches discuss these subjects, but they avoid dealing with volatile and "untouchable" issues. They use these dialogues not to search, but to preach.

Many marriages break up because of sexual affairs, or because someone outside the marriage is more caring, understanding, and accepting than the partner in the marriage. We believe the breakdown of psychological intimacy and sexual intimacy is the direct result of the Abusive Christian model and rigid sexual ethics.

Affairs—why do they happen? Could affairs be acceptable in our culture? Could husbands or wives have an affair, but still maintain the family? We have never or rarely seen an affair where the couple talked about the affair openly and honestly prior to the beginning of the affair. Healthy marriage demands psychological intimacy and trust. Yet couples generally cannot talk about potential affairs before those relationships become sexual. Christian values present adultery as "so bad," most couples can't discuss it. Thus, intimacy is lost due to Christian values.

What does the affair represent? Does it represent some sort of "relationship salvation" or "sexual salvation"? Do people seek to save themselves from their own "bad" feelings, which they blame on the marriage? If couples could openly and honestly discuss this, would there be a need for an affair? Sarah can speak to this point.

Sarah came to us seeking help with her husband. He was aloof and distant from her. She had been talking to a male friend at work and they were growing closer and closer. In fact, they had kissed each other while alone in an elevator at work.

We had seen Sarah's husband. Although he knew nothing about the other person, he knew "something" was wrong with the marriage. He had not expressed his concern and worry to his wife. He was a reasonable, caring husband.

Sarah was appalled when we recommended she tell her husband about the "other man." Luckily, we saw the couple prior to the sexualization of the "other" relationship. Sarah agreed to tell him. Initially he was angry, but his anger quickly abated. He had not been open or honest with her, either. They began to talk and share their fears and feelings. The interest in the "other man" diminished. The husband was mature and secure enough to deal with this information without over reaction. The marriage grew closer and more secure. They made an agreement to always talk about attraction to any other people. They felt it could reflect some problem in the marriage, such as taking the marriage for granted, and they called this openness "insurance against an affair."

What if the interest did not abate? What then?

Would group marriages work? Might an open marriage work? What about jealousy? Is jealousy based upon ownership? What would happen to children in a group marriage? Would everyone love them and take care of them? Would there be "affairs" outside the group or would the group be sexually exclusive? Are we headed this way with our serial monogamy? Or is serial monogamy a way to "ride the rail" between The Moral Majority and liberal hedonism?

What about polygamy—it has a good Biblical heritage. Would jealousy intrude? Is jealousy an illness? What about polyandry? Are males too possessive? What would the values be here? What about the extended family? What about children and their fathers? Is the issue of fatherhood important, or simply the result of our male-dominated culture?

Is it wise in our culture to live together before marriage? Will this help marriage or hurt marriage? Is marriage really necessary? What is your goal in an intimate relationship?

These issues and many more need to be discussed and thought about by people in our culture. Not from the bipolar point of view of good and bad, but honest, open discussion as to what will work and where we are headed. We need to be open and honest, and not afraid of the answers we may hear. We need to avoid "pre-packaged" values that do not seem to be working.

Our experience is that monogamy works best. With that position, we have to ask why marriages are faring so poorly in our culture? Why are divorce rates so high? We must face the idea that we may be wrong. Monogamy may be doomed in our culture. We must have dialogue about options and solutions. Preachments about what a sinner you are if you differ from our rapidly failing cultural norm simply do more harm than help.

We frequently hear the plea, "We need to return to the basic Christian values and the family." But as long as those ethics are embedded in an abusive model, such as the Abusive Christian Model, they will not work. They are not working today. What needs to be substituted is an attitude of openness, caring, love, and trust that people have within them the power to reason and discover what is right and just.

Gone are the days when authorities can dictate morality and threaten with hell or censure if everyone does not comply. That means of dealing with people should be abolished. The abusive, rigid, authoritarian system of Christian values is a narcissistic attitude of "this is what God (or "I" in reality) wants." These attitudes are destructive to creative personal growth and often lead to more serious problems.

CHRISTIAN CONCEPTS THAT CONTRIBUTE TO SEXUAL DYSFUNCTION

Christian values about sexuality provide an environment in which unhealthy sexuality flourishes. Some Christian concepts and practices actually contribute to forms of sexual dysfunction and sexual perversions. Granted, there are other processes and contributing factors to these sexual problems. However, the influence of Christianity has been an extremely powerful force in the creation of sexual dysfunction.

Human sexual behavior is a function of one's biological processes, learning experiences (beliefs and concepts), and feelings. Common wisdom today advocates that feelings directly result from what one has learned, or how one thinks. That is, feelings result from thought or accumulated learning.

When individuals are immersed in conservative Christian thinking, the way they perceive the world, the way they structure their thinking, and the content of what they think are all influenced by the belief system.

The following psychological dynamics contribute to sexual dysfunction and have their origins in conservative Christian belief and practice.

BLACK-AND-WHITE THINKING AND ETHICS. In Christianity, extremes become the rules. There is little gray. Almost everything is divided into good or bad, black or white, heaven or hell, God or Satan, right or wrong. Ideas, behaviors, people, and groups are usually classified according to these polar concepts. If something is not good then it must be evil, if it is not right then it must be wrong. Few qualifiers are used.

Christians are often uncomfortable with saying, "Well, sometimes this might be wrong or under some circumstances this might be wrong, but given different circumstances it could be neutral or even good." Christian ethics are absolute, right and wrong, from God. They do not believe in situational ethics and they resist letting any situation influence the ethical belief. So, this type of belief sets up rigid rules which rarely, if ever, allow for circumstances.

Examples of this rigid black-and-white Christian thinking are: sex before marriage is wrong, homosexuality is wrong, public displays of affection are wrong, lusting in your heart is wrong. The statements are absolute.

In the Christian ethical system, people do not need to think; they must accept the ethic which is given from "on high." The job of the Christian believer is to follow the absolute ethic and not to question or doubt. Doubt is seen as sinful and bad. One must not doubt. One must believe. The ethic is absolute, godly, and right.

The rules are so rigid and so unrealistic that people have no option but to perceive themselves as bad, sinners, and shameful for having normal human impulses and urges. For example, the messages that sex is dirty, that it is wrong to touch yourself "down there," that lusting in your heart is wrong, and that masturbation is wrong leaves most people perceiving themselves as sinful and bad. The situation is hopeless and circular. You will sin again and again and again, or you go in the opposite direction and become asexual. Either way, the black-and-white ethic injures people. This style of thinking nurtures sexual dysfunction.

DIMINISHED INTIMACY, INCREASED ANXIETY. Christian sexual ethics lowers the ability to talk openly and honestly about sexuality. This diminishes intimacy and as such is destructive. Families do not deal with the complex issues of sexuality, self-esteem, fear, and shame. The disapproving nonverbals teach that sex is a fearful and forbidden subject. This creates anxiety, and the subject is passed off with some sort of creed such as, "Sex is wonderful if you are in love," or "Sex before marriage is wrong—period." Thus ends the discussion.

This lack of ability to talk openly carries with it several nonverbal messages. The clear message is, "We should not talk about this," thus the diminished intimacy. Further messages convey that this topic is fearful and dangerous. When parents give this emotionally loaded message to their children or adolescents, the children believe them. Sex is fearful and dangerous. At this point, the parent is not emotionally available to the child for questioning and talking about this issue. If the family cannot talk about this, it means sex is a very powerful thing—something so dangerous and powerful as to not even be mentioned.

Inability to openly and emotionally deal with the powerful, fearful topic of sex has an impact upon the child. The child does not feel nurtured. In fact, children may realize they have transgressed into an area which is alluring but dangerous. Usually, the child quickly learns to keep quiet—a tense, anxious quietness.

These children are emotionally abandoned. They must survive on their own, with minimal information and support from their families about complex sexual issues. There is a lack of positive information as well as a lack of support and nurturance. Adolescents can feel the powerful "don't talk" injunction about sex. They perceive the tension within their parents when the topic is sexual.

Since intimacy is dealing with issues in an open and emotionally appropriate manner, the power of the sexual issue destroys psychological intimacy. Adolescents quickly learn to talk to their friends and not to their parents. Many parents cannot openly deal with sexual issues, because their own feelings of fear, anxiety, and their thoughts of sin and evil are simply too powerfully dominant. The final result is intimacy is diminished and anxiety is increased.

These two dynamics—secrecy, along with anxiety—form a basis for sexual problems and dysfunctions.

SEXUALIZATION OF INTIMACY

Sexualization of intimacy occurs when sexuality becomes the focal point of the relationship, or when sex becomes the major means of establishing closeness. Here the rule is: To be close is to be sexual. What are the different types of intimacy and why do people often avoid these other means of intimacy? Why do they rapidly run toward sexuality?

People need intimacy and closeness. They need to be physically touched, which we will refer to as physical intimacy or sensuality.

They need emotional sharing, which is emotional intimacy, such as crying with or laughing with others. They need to be open and honest verbally, to deal with important issues, which we define as psychological intimacy, such as sharing secrets and talking. Finally, people need sexual intimacy.

Often, physical intimacy, along with psychological intimacy, naturally leads into sexual intimacy, but sensuality and emotional closeness are separate from sexual intimacy. Children need touch, sensuality, but not sexuality. Healthy marriages need as much sensuality as sexuality. So we will define the different areas of intimacy as physical, verbal, emotional, and sexual.

DEFINITIONS OF THE DIFFERENT TYPES OF INTIMACY

- Physical Intimacy is physical touch, at times called sensuality.
- Verbal Intimacy is also called psychological intimacy. That is when people talk about important issues.
- Emotional Intimacy is when people share feelings, when they share their feelings about important issues.
- Sexual Intimacy is physical intimacy with the intent to sexually arouse, including sexual intercourse.

Does Christianity "shut down" different areas of intimacy? This can occur when family systems act out the Abusive Christian Model. First, let's look at the parent/child relationship. Parents may grow upset with the child because the child does not obey. Consistent with the Abusive Christian Model, the parents then withdraw love and punish with anger. Because of the withdrawal of love, they lose physical, verbal, and emotional intimacy with the child. Nurturance, touch, openness, and closeness are lost to the child. At this point, the child becomes a survivor in the family.

This dynamic is the same or very similar to any dysfunctional family. For one reason or another, love is withdrawn or abuse takes place, and the child becomes a survivor. Child survivors usually have difficulty with emotional intimacy, and they are prone to sexualize intimacy. The neglect and abuse found in most families may find its origin in the Abusive Christian Model.

When a child is reared with this model, trust is diminished; the child cannot trust that the parents will be emotionally available. As a result, as an adult, the individual fears most types of intimacy. The individual fears loss of love, nurturance, and closeness. When another adult, of the opposite sex, shows attention, closeness naturally results. The question now becomes what type of intimacy results.

Childhood fears surround emotional intimacy, so the couple bypasses the work required for emotional and verbal intimacy and rapidly "sexualizes" the intimacy. These adults are afraid to share their feelings and talk about their secrets, so they follow the path of least resistance, which is sensuality and sexuality. Fuzzy ego boundaries can bring on a perception that the other person is making you "feel good." This further reinforces the sexualization of intimacy.

When the sexual passion diminishes, the intimacy begins to break down. The relationship may terminate, or it may psychologically limp along. The male will feel there is not enough sex. The female will feel there is not enough touch, tenderness, or understanding.

Thus, the Abusive Christian Model can produce adults who quickly sexualize relationships, because they have difficulty with verbal and emotional intimacy. These individuals may lack the ability to invest the time, the energy, the trust, and the courage required to establish a fully intimate relationship.

In our culture, having sex is easier than really, honestly talking about sex and the resulting relationship. The Abusive Christian Model, along with Christian ethics, set the stage for sexualization of intimacy. In fact, sexualization of intimacy could be considered "normal," it is so prevalent.

People need intimacy. In their search for love, they find sex. When sex breaks down, the relationship breaks down. The search for love starts again. They find sex again. When other forms of intimacy are inhibited, sexuality is intensified. Thus the Abusive Christian

Model and Sexually Abusive Christianity leads to sexualization of intimacy and sexually acting out.

SEXUAL SALVATION. Christians are taught they cannot save themselves. A power or force outside of themselves is necessary for salvation; that power, of course, is the Christ. This model, or archetype, forms the basis for other behaviors. The model incorporates the thinking that something outside ourselves controls and influences us. This is the central idea in codependency. We would like to examine this from the Christian perspective, where this type of thinking originated.

When we feel "lost," lonely, or ashamed, we may seek "salvation" in relationships or in sexual relationships. In Sexual Salvation, sex becomes a powerful force involving another person. Because of our Christian history, this "sexuality" often feels outside of us, as if it were in the other person. This person "pulls" us with sexuality. This sexuality can "save" us from ourselves, our shame, and our self-doubt. In this manner, sexual relationships can become powerful in their pull. We must have sex or relationships in order to feel okay or whole.

We generally see Sexual Salvation in men more often than women. Women are more prone to Relationship Salvation (see Chapter 5). Often men must engage in a sexual relationship to feel okay. They may use romantic language and feign love and intimacy in order to establish a sexual relationship. The major goal, however, is the sexual relationship.

One client described his need for a sexual relationship: "It keeps me out of that river of hell, or oblivion. I can't feel good unless I am engaged in sex." He described the sexual aspect of the "salvation" as "concrete linking with heaven," and the loss of the sexual relationship as "hell." Most of his relationships were what he termed one-night stands.

In a married couple that sought help for marital problems, the wife's complaint was, "All he wants me for is sex. Sex all of the time."

His major complaint was that when she became angry and upset, she would terminate the sexual relationship and he "had to have it." For him, sex had reached salvation proportions. His focus was on sex, and there was little psychological or emotional intimacy. We had a strange feeling this man did not really know his wife. She provided the sexual road to his salvation. She was an object in the relationship.

In Sexual Salvation, sex itself becomes a god as it reaches religious proportions in the individual. Sexual addictions may result. At that point, sex becomes more important than the relationship with the person involved.

WOMEN AS SUBMISSIVE. In Christian theology, in the beginning, God made woman from man's rib. Women have been treated as property and as second-class citizens ever since. Many churches still treat women as inferior to men. Churches are immune from prosecution by civil rights laws, so discrimination goes unchecked. Rarely are women given administrative or ministerial duties. There is certainly a message there.

Sexually, in traditional Christian views, women were the property of their husbands. Women were required to be obedient to their husbands and to please their husbands. Pleasing husbands, of course, included sexual pleasure whenever the husband wanted. The man reigned as head of the household and dominant over his wife.

This abusive ethic and first-century view of women still exists today. The abuse of women in marriage and the problems of domestic violence, battered women, and marital rape are issues that won't go away. In fact, they seem to be growing.

Before we can teach women to value themselves, we must teach the churches to value women. Women must teach in seminaries, preach, and be able to serve as priests. Women need to be on an equal basis with men in all of our religious organizations. The churches cannot claim moral leadership in this sensitive area until they rid themselves of prejudice. Our interest in this section of the book is to call attention to this attitude toward women as a source of sexual dysfunction in both women and men.

SOMETHING FORBIDDEN IS A POWERFUL MOTIVATOR.
Christianity allocates sexual behavior to the ranks of the forbidden, and that which is not allowed can be all the more alluring, exciting, and difficult to resist. When dealing with a powerful biological drive, such as sexuality, the forbidden becomes even more compelling.

We cannot openly talk about sexual relationships. Sexuality is controlled by a rigid set of rules stemming from Christianity. The nature of sexuality is that of "forbidden fruit." By its very nature, a sexual affair must be furtive and secret. People "sneak around" to have affairs. Why? They are forbidden. They are wrong. They are bad. This is not only true about affairs, it is true about all aspects of sexuality, except possibly, sexually oriented advertisements.

It is our nature as humans to seek out, to be curious about, and to be attracted to, that which is denied us or which seems different or exotic. To hide, deny, or conceal an experience is to make that experience more provocative, more appealing, and more stimulating. This forbidden nature contributes to sexual behavior becoming powerful and compulsive.

SUPPRESSED SEXUAL DRIVE. Christianity allows few options for satisfaction of sexual needs. When few options for release or satiation are available for a physical need, anxiety and pressure may build to the point that control is difficult or even impossible. For example, if animals are deprived of food or water, eventually they will go to dramatic lengths to satisfy their needs. Sex is a physiological need, very similar to the drives for food and water. Christian sexual ethics limit the options for meeting human sexual needs to one specific circumstance. That is, sexual expression is only allowed between husband and wife.

Since sex is a biological drive, suppression of sexuality creates anxiety which increases the intensity of the sexual drive. In other words, when sexuality is frustrated and denied, it creates pressure within us that can result in uncomfortable emotions and abnormal behaviors. It is something like depriving someone of sleep for a long period of time. We would expect that within a short period of time they would be able to think of little else except satisfying that need for sleep. So suppression of one's sexual drive can result in preoccupation with sex, and possibly, uncontrollable sexual urges. Or, those who can more successfully enter denial will experience a sexlessness.

GUILT, FEAR, SHAME, AND IGNORANCE ABOUT SEXUAL NEEDS. As previously noted, Christian sexual ethics allow very little to be taught about sexuality. As a result, most people lack awareness of what is normal when it comes to sexuality. Ethics ban thinking or feeling sexual; sin can be found in lusting after a woman in your heart. Masturbation is a sin.

It comes as no surprise that strong emotions, such as fear, guilt or, shame, become associated with normal sexual desires. This sexual fear, guilt, and shame results from ignorance. Ignorance, combined with Christianity leads to negative feelings, and all of these negative feelings about sexuality lead to anxiety, which, in turn, will adversely affect sexual behavior.

The effects range from sexual repression to sexual addictions and aberrations. At best, the individual's ability to relax and enjoy a natural sexual expression, even within marriage, may be blocked. Anxiety, resulting from Christian ethics and ignorance, actually blocks the individual's ability to relax and enjoy sex, even in an "appropriate situation."

ABUSIVE CHRISTIAN MODEL

Briefly, in the Abusive Christian Model, God tells us to believe the way He wants or He will withdraw His love and punish—in some belief systems, punish with hell. Frequently, family systems act out this model and sexual relationships can certainly follow it as well. Withdrawal of affection and withdrawal of sex are found in many marriages as a form of punishment. Withdrawal of sex or affection can be used to control and manipulate to achieve one's own ends and goals. Such sexuality is abusive in nature, as the model is abusive in nature. Inappropriate sexual behavior results when couples follow this model.

We have to laugh at the crazy messages about sexuality. In one television program about the use of condoms, the host had to use a banana to demonstrate putting on a condom, because he could not use an anatomical model of a penis. Now at least, we are confident people in our area can practice "safe sex" with bananas. Needless, to say, these messages, which are highly influenced by Abusive Christianity, are unhealthy and at times downright stupid.

CHAPTER 7

SEXUAL DYSFUNCTIONS RELATED TO CHRISTIANITY

What happens when people learn wrong information and values about sex? They become sick sexually. Remember, what you believe and how you think will determine how you function sexually. Each of the following sexual dysfunctions results from some combination of the dynamics we discussed in Chapter 6. As such, these sexual dysfunctions have their roots in Christianity.

Causes of Sexual Dysfunction:
- Black-and-white thinking/Black-and-white ethics.
- Diminished intimacy and increased anxiety.
- Sexualization of intimacy.
- Sexual salvation.
- "Forbidden fruit."
- Suppressed sexual drive.
- Negative emotions and ignorance about sexual needs.
- Abusive Christian Model.
- Women as submissive.

These dynamics contribute to the following sexual dysfunctions:
- Nun/whore syndrome.
- Premature ejaculation.

- Marital rape.
- Sexual inhibition, frigidity, and impotence.
- Loss of passion.
- Sexual perversions.
- Sexual acting out: promiscuity/infidelity.
- Homophobia/ego dystonic homosexuality.

THE NUN/WHORE SYNDROME

The term "nun/whore" has been around for years. As far as we know, the term is a takeoff from the Freudian theory of the "Madonna/Whore Complex." The duality of the label is striking. It brings into mind those images of wonderful saint-like women and in contrast, images of deceitful, vulgar women who use people.

This duality is "real." It starts at puberty when "bad girls" have sex and "good girls" do not. This duality of identities impacts the behavior of both males and females. It affects self-concept in females. It affects the way males chose companions and how they treat them sexually and socially. This evaluation of females as good or bad is based on the values found in Christianity.

The psychological issues that contribute to the "nun/whore" syndrome—and which have their origins in Christian beliefs and practices—are black-and-white thinking, "forbidden fruit," sexualization of intimacy, sexual salvation, and guilt and ignorance.

In high school, most of the males want to date and be seen with the "good girls." And the girls who are both attractive and good are especially pursued and valued by the young males. But, most young males have lurid fantasies about the "bad girls," and envy the boys who "score" with them. This creates the dichotomy of the nun/whore, the good girl versus the bad girl—the epitome of black-and-white thinking. In our culture, this duality influences the relationships, identity, and sexual adjustment of both men and women in several ways.

One variation is "hit-and-run artist." This pattern usually begins with "relationship salvation" or "sexual salvation." Initially the male sees the female as the "nun," with the power to save him and make his life complete. The romance can be wonderful. As the romance turns sexual, problems arise. After the first sexual encounter, the feelings of the male abruptly change or begin to die away. Eventually the male leaves the relationship and looks for another female "savior." The process is repeated.

The most dramatic manifestation of this variation is the "one-night stand." The male tells the female how wonderful she is and, after a sexual encounter, he never calls her again. The nun quickly becomes the whore. The whore is abandoned after being used. Once she has taken on the "bad girl" image, the male is not attracted to her any more. It is interesting to note that the sexual pursuit is by the male, but the label of bad girl or whore is given to the female. The female is defined by how she responds to the male pursuit. No female can become a "whore" without the participation of the male. The male gets off scot-free.

Often, men place a great deal of pressure on the female to have sexual intercourse. In other cases, the couple date quite a while before the relationship turns sexual. At this point, the entire relationship revolves around the forbidden fruit. The tension in the couple is palpable. After the female finally consents, the man drops her. This can be devastating to the female. The pressure, the sex, and the abandonment take their toll. One female client remarked, "I felt suicidal. I thought I was crazy, totally inadequate sexually."

If the female blames herself for the loss, the experience can have a powerful impact on her sexual adjustment and her identity. She may feel she is "bad" or think she is sexually inadequate. In some situations, "bad" females will then sexually act out with numerous males in an attempt to find love and sexual adequacy. This confirms their sexual identity as "the whore," and increases their shame.

Stewart brought his sister, Sheila, to counseling because she was sexually acting out. He loved her and was very worried about her. Sheila was nineteen and a freshman in college. Her family was very emotionally cold and she wanted to be loved. Initially, she was tearful and upset that she was "so bad." The shame exacerbated her need for love. She was sexualizing intimacy and increasing her shame and did not know or understand emotional or psychological intimacy.

In counseling, she quickly learned, "THERE ARE NO BAD GIRLS." Sex had simply been the best way to find the love she wanted. The whole concept of "bad girls" is based upon black-and-white thinking, guilt, and ignorance of normal sexual needs. She took control of her life rapidly and currently feels very good about herself.

The dichotomy of the nun/whore in this variation can entrap both the male and female. The female is entrapped in that she is shamed and abandoned. The male is entrapped to love and leave, and to never establish long-term intimacy.

The process of this variation is the initial encounter, the romance, the sexualization of the relationship, and then the abandonment. There is no psychological intimacy. The couple does not deal verbally with the issues that the encounter precipitates, such as the black-and-white thinking, the guilt and ignorance of sexual needs, and the salvation aspect of sexuality. There is an avoidance of emotional intimacy and there is abandonment.

Obviously, sex is seen as "bad" by the male, although he may not be aware of that. Usually men in this situation are in denial and project the "bad" upon the female. The male fears emotional intimacy and will not talk about his fear of closeness, fear of loss of control, and his growing coldness. Instead, he runs from the "bad girl" he has created.

For the male, the sexual encounter is both "bad" and his ultimate desire. He very badly wants a fully intimate relationship, but to achieve it he must talk about his powerful ambivalence about the sexual relationship. The fear and the feelings of guilt and shame which surround the sexual act prevent him from being able to communicate his needs. The male is generally not conscious of this and simply leaves the relationship.

Take the example of Vince, who sought treatment to help resolve his fear of commitment. He had been living with a young woman for two years. He described her as a wonderful woman, just the type of person that any man would want. She was his best friend and extremely compatible with him. They had similar goals and a lot of fun together. But for some reason, he had an almost irrestible urge to run, to take a job in another state, and leave her behind.

His only complaint about the relationship was that after their initial sexual encounter, he felt no more sexual desire for her. At first, he was passionate. But, similar to other relationships he had in the past, once he began to respect the woman as a friend and a partner, he lost all interest sexually and felt the urge to pull away.

We began to look at his past history and his dysfunctional family life. The family was strict and Catholic, and he received his early education in parochial schools. "The nuns beat it into my head that sex was dirty and nasty and only to be used for procreation, and then only by people who wanted to raise little Catholics," Vince recalled. "And every time you masturbate, you kill 60,000 to 80,000 potential Catholics."

Vince couldn't possibly relate sex to "love-making." Sex was something you did to women you didn't care about, not to someone who you felt was your best friend or that you loved. But then, why should you stay with a woman you felt no passion for? As feelings of commitment began to intrude, the conflict, anxiety, and fear rose and he wanted to run.

Vince learned that his "lack of passion" was a cover for his fear of a fully intimate relationship with a woman. When the relationship turned sexual, or "bad," he would emotionally abandon "the whore." Because of a conflict in his sexual values, he could not "make love" to a woman he loved. If he did, the "love" was destroyed. His conflict was between his own internal values, which created the nun and the whore.

A second variation on this theme is what we call the "nomad." Here, the dichotomy manifests itself after the couple is married. The process evolves over a long period of time, rather than being an abrupt reaction to sexualization of the relationship. The couple may have been married for several years and may have several children. However, this variation can show up in short-term marriages with no children.

The male begins to see his wife as the "nun." She is the mother of his children, and he has a great deal of caring and respect for her and her role in the family. Yet the male feels that "something is missing." The sexual relationship is not as passionate and as compelling as it once was. The male generally projects the blame for this on his wife. "She doesn't turn me on like she once did." At this point, the male is set up for his search for the "whore," for a woman who does turn him on. This process can be acted out via affairs, pornography, or even fantasy.

Joe had been married two years and stated that he deeply loved his wife. Six months ago, he started to purchase pornographic magazines and recently he had called the "phone sex" lines. His wife had found the 1-900 phone calls on their phone bill and had confronted her husband. It was that confrontation that led to them to marriage counseling.

In the initial interview, Joe's wife assumed the identity of the indignant nun! She was angry, condescending, and shaming toward her husband. Carrying her unconscious role further, she had refused to have sex with him. The husband was deeply ashamed of his behavior, saying, "I feel terrible. I am really sick, but I can't stop myself." His wife reinforced those feelings, calling him weak and a pervert, then stating in tears, "You don't love me."

She was righteous and sexless. He was sinful, evil, and mired in sex. Their roles, she being the "good girl," he being the "bad husband," had been pushed to the extremes. Their perceptions were so laden with "good/bad" evaluation that they were not able to see each other, at least in realistic terms.

The issue was much more complex than simply "good or bad." And as long as they remained stuck in their roles, no progress would occur in therapy. Joe's wife's belief system simply had no flexibility. It was black and white. Her husband was wrong and a pervert, and she wanted no part of him. She left counseling while Joe remained. She eventually left the relationship and divorced.

Many men, who are caught in this nun/whore dichotomy, will resort to affairs. They generally sexualize intimacy with the new lover and romanticize the marriage. "Sexual salvation" may play a part; the man feels "saved" and alive in the affair. He becomes the nomad. His wife is the nun. He wanders, seeking "whores." Of course, none of this is ever talked about. This whole process is kept in motion by a lack of psychological intimacy.

Several things can happen if there is an affair. The man may have a brief affair and then drop the lover. Or, he may feel "saved" and unable to let go of the psuedo-intimacy and the vitality of the affair. Then he can become trapped between the "nun" and the "whore." He must chose his family or his lover. Finally, the man can unconsciously set up being caught, and then be forced out of the marriage or punished. The choice is made for him when the wife discovers the affair.

Let us quickly point out that the labels "nun" and "whore" are set up by the "black-and-white" nature of conservative Christian thinking. The male may or may not think of the women as good or bad. However, the conservative Christian community will see them, and the affair, in these black-and-white terms.

The third variation is the confused. The confusion occurs prior to marriage or outside of marriage. In this variation, the male may be confused, the female may be confused, or both may be confused. This can be the final stage of the nomad variation or can be a variation in and of itself. The individual experiences conflict between biological impulses and Christian values. Biological sexual impulses are the "whore" of the personality. Our Christian values call for us to be the "nun." Thus, the conflict and the confusion of what to do with sexuality outside of marriage.

Consider the trite cliche we were told in Sunday school. "If you really love each other, you will not have sex until after marriage." That type of black-and-white thinking is very simple and very clear. But it is not all that simple when one considers the power of the biological sexual impulses. Would the logical opposite of the Sunday school statement be valid? If you do have a sexual relationship, you do not love each other?

If you "lust in your heart," does that mean you do not love each other? Because that is forbidden, too. With values such as these, love and sexuality become confusing. It is certainly easy to become confused as to love and sexuality and, as the sexual relationship is forbidden, the power of the sexual impulses increases. This adds urgency and pressure to the situation. To "do it" or not to "do it," that is the question. And it can be a torturous question.

Should we have a sexual relationship or not? Should we wait until we are married? Where does sex fit in with love? Where does sex fit in before marriage? Where do you draw the line? Masturbation? Heavy petting? Nudity? Doing the right thing can become very confusing. The simplistic ethic of "Do not have sex until after marriage" doesn't seem to work any more. It certainly does not tell us where to stop. The issue is much more complex than the black-and-white statement.

"Do not have sex outside of marriage." That ethic leads people to lie and into bizarre behavior that includes everything except vaginal sex. If you are a "good person," you can be deep in passion with tongues darting, hands roaming everywhere, orgasms, but as least you "didn't do it." The relationship can become confusing, and compromised. You feel alive and sexual with your lover. You do not feel alive and sexual with your spouse.

In relationships outside of marriage, the confusion takes the expression, "I love my spouse, but I can really talk to my lover, and we have really great sex." Thus, the wanderer ends up confused, having to choose between the "nun" and the "whore," with no realistic basis for decision-making.

Thinking in terms of "right and wrong," the decision becomes simple. The "right" thing is to go back to your spouse. But is it "right" to give up this closeness, vitality, and passion? Is it wrong to feel alive and sexual? With Christianity pushing you in a direction that "feels" wrong, but which they define as right, you can't help but feel confused. The confusion is between "do I want happiness" or "do I want to be 'right'" and follow the tenets of the church, sacrificing happiness. Happiness becomes the whore and compliance becomes the nun.

IMPACT ON FEMALE IDENTITIES

Women often see themselves in the role of either the nun or the whore. Others classify women as "good," the nuns, or "bad and sleazy," the whores. These perceptions can have an impact on identity and how women relate to themselves and others.

Wanda came to counseling due to problems in her marriage. It was several sessions before she told us her "true" history. Her family was stable, conservative Christian, but distant. They certainly did not discuss sexual or emotional issues. She finally told us what happened in high school.

> In high school, I became interested in boys. I wanted someone to love me, to think I was special. I went out with several boys and I didn't have—uh—you know—sex with any of them. We did heavy petting. The boys talked and people started saying I was bad and a slut and all of that. I hated it. So I quit dating. I didn't go out with anyone, until I decided to go out with the man that became my husband.

She continued to tell us that she had problems with "that sex thing" with her husband. During our sessions, she commented, "I bet most people use these Kleenex tissues to cry, not to wipe sweat off the palms of their hands!" Although she laughed, it was clear she was very anxious even talking with us about sex. Even after marriage she found no joy or pleasure in sex. She remained the "sexless nun."

In the dating years, women struggle with this identity battle. This simply does not happen with men. Men are not defined as good or bad based upon early sexual experiences. But each of us can think back to middle school and high school and remember the "nuns" and the "whores." This causes massive damage in women. They either become sexually unresponsive or act out sexually. They adopt the label of the identity they have been given. The identity is based upon Christian values.

To begin breaking out of the nun/whore dichotomy, we need to talk about the complexities of our fantasies, our perceptions, and our impulses. People tend to act out their fantasies if they do not talk them out. People display a high level of psychological intimacy and trust when they have the confidence to talk about their fantasies with their spouses.

Like it or not, this ethical dilemma of the nun/whore syndrome has a powerful influence on most of us. We tend to perceive women as nuns or whores and act accordingly. Our perceptions define relationship limits, values, and our reactions to the individuals. We need to think beyond the dichotomous categories of nun/whore and good/bad. Relationships and people are complex and do not lend themselves to such simplistic classifications. There are no "BAD WOMEN." Troubled, needy, and desperate for love, maybe, but not bad.

PREMATURE EJACULATION

"Masturbating when I didn't want to get caught caused my premature ejaculation problem," one of our patients said. "I knew it was wrong. So I was always pushing myself to be fast in case someone came. I learned everything about reaching climax fast and nothing about slowing down."

Guilt, shame, and ignorance about masturbation is, more often than not, the rule rather than the exception. Many men have never been told that masturbation is a normal, healthy expression of sexuality. Reaching climax through masturbation can become a hurried, pressured, guilty affair. Especially when one is ashamed and fearful of being discovered in a "sinful" act. An individual can actually condition himself to ejaculate prematurely. In adolescence, men train themselves to respond to stimulation under pressure, and they deny themselves the opportunity to learn to reach orgasm under less pressured, more relaxed conditions.

After marriage, men with Christian values often refuse to masturbate or put off masturbation because they feel the act is sinful. They really don't know that masturbation is healthy. For these individuals, love-making, within their marriage, may be the only acceptable sexual option. But, when it comes time to make love, the man may be so pent up from suppressing his sexual drive that he has little control. His fear of sexuality and his guilt over sexual enjoyment lead to a sense of urgency which further reduces his control. This is circular because the more out of control he feels, the less control he actually has. With the lack of any "acceptable" sexual outlet, and his bad feelings about sexuality, sex with his wife or any female becomes hurried and tense.

Additionally, the forbidden aspect of sex can add to the urgency and anxiety. The closer a man gets to the forbidden object—the female object of his desires—the more aroused he becomes. As a result, he can orgasm before he gets to actual intercourse. The stimulation of the forbidden adds to the intensity so that he can't control himself. Sometimes a man begins to see sex as something that can save him from his feelings of frustration. This makes control even more difficult. The closer he gets to the source of his salvation, the more out of control. It's over before it actually begins. Once he ejaculates prematurely, he feels even more guilty because he has disappointed the female. The next time he makes love to a woman, premature ejaculation is even more likely to occur. Now he's afraid of failure. The fear that he will disappoint her and humiliate himself simply adds more and more pressure. And, as a result, he has less and less control. The cycle dominates all future sexual relationships. The man begins to worry well before any sexual encounter. He may avoid sex or he may become obsessed with attempts to control his orgasms.

Sexuality could be taught as a beautiful and natural thing. Then it could be enjoyed from the beginning. Instead of feeling so much pressure to reach orgasm, a man should learn to relax and enjoy the touching, the foreplay, and the physical closeness. A couple could talk about their sexual experience together and share their fears. They could work together to increase their mutual pleasure. Unfortunately, Christian values add to the problem rather than help it. As a result, many people must see a therapist before learning how to relax and enjoy their sexuality.

SEXUAL INHIBITION, FRIGIDITY, AND IMPOTENCE

Many women justifiably hold their conservative Christian upbringing responsible for their inability to enjoy sex. We see these women in therapy frequently. They say they were continually reminded as children that sex and their bodies were dirty, nasty, wrong, sinful, and sex was not to be discussed or asked about. Sometimes they were slapped, beaten, yelled at, or threatened by their parents for making sexual comments or gestures. At the very least, their parents and other adults gave them shocked looks when they made sexual remarks or dressed seductively. Thus, they were conditioned to avoid sexual topics, sexual feelings, and to fear their own sexuality.

These young women often learn to consistently suppress their sexual feelings that arise during and after puberty. Fulfilling those sexual desires would be wrong, even thinking about fulfilling those sexual desires would be wrong. Sex only becomes "okay" after she's married.

But somehow, when a woman goes through a ten- to thirty-minute marriage ceremony, that conditioning does not magically disappear. It's too late for some. Already, they have totally squelched their sexual desire. Thereafter, they never experience passion.

Some women are simply unable to let go of the feelings of revulsion and shame they feel in connection with the sexual act. They are tense. They can't relax and experience sexual pleasure. This condition has been described to us repeatedly by female patients such as Rose, who was in counseling after her divorce.

She was 31 and had never had an orgasm. She had been raised in a Southern Baptist family and her mother had never taught her about her body except to caution her as a child, "Don't touch yourself down there." So Rose would not even wash her pubic area for fear of sinning.

Rose's mother vaguely spoke of the things that men and women did as "nasty." When asked a question about her body or about sex, mom acted shocked, embarrassed. Mom communicated to her both verbally and nonverbally that those kinds of thoughts were wrong and sinful. Rose soon learned not to ask mom anything.

Church was no better. The preacher promised hell and eternal damnation to those who "committed adultery in their hearts" or in their deeds. He used the terms "fornicator" and "adulterer" while preaching loudly, red-faced, pointing a finger at the congregation. Therefore, her first sexual feelings were frightening to her and she suppressed them guiltily.

It became easier to make them go away after a while. A sexual thought would enter her head, with a corresponding tingle in her body, and she would visualize God hearing her thoughts, watching her. This made the feelings go away. But she knew that when she married, then it would be okay to be close to a man and allow him to touch her.

In her early twenties she met a nice young man and married him. The wedding night was tense. He was gentle and caring, but she felt only discomfort and guilt. Two children and ten years later, although she knew intellectually that sex with her husband was "right," emotionally she still couldn't lose her sense of wrongness about the sexual act. She couldn't relax, enjoy the experience, or even participate with any enthusiasm. Her husband had become angry and frustrated, and his anger spread to other aspects of their marriage. They separated and divorced. Eventually, through therapy, Rose was able to get in touch with her sexuality and now is happily married.

Many women, who see themselves as good, "clean" people can't maintain that image if they engage in sex. So they eliminate sex from their lives as much as possible. They may even resent the spouse who "forces" them to submit to such "nasty" behavior as love-making. We have even worked with women who avoid sex because they have had a bath before going to bed and don't want to get "dirty."

This phenomenon is not limited to women. Men, too, can translate guilt and "dirty" feelings about sex into impotence, abstinence, or the "need" to shower and clean themselves after sex. Such a man usually has normal sexual desires. When he finds a woman whom he cares about and is attracted to, he wants to be with her. He becomes sexually aroused just by kissing her or touching her body. Normally, if both consent, that arousal leads to love-making and intercourse.

Here is where guilt and negative feelings about sex can interfere. A male who feels evil and unclean about sex may be able to maintain his arousal up until the moment of insertion. However, at that point he may feel a tremendous sense of wrong. If he then loses his erection, he feels horrible. He realizes he has led this woman on. He's embarrassed, ashamed and humiliated, and may not try again. When he finds himself in another potentially sexual situation, he may use tricks or rationalizations or just plain lies to keep himself out of bed with a woman. And, if he does try again, the feelings of guilt, and now a fear of failing again, make it even less likely that he will succeed in intercourse.

ARE YOU SEXUALLY INHIBITED?

A positive response to any of these could indicate you are sexually inhibited.

Do you feel uncomfortable masturbating?

Do you feel uncomfortable undressing in front of your spouse?

Do you have difficulty relaxing during foreplay?

Do you feel ashamed looking at your own nude body?

If you are a female, have you ever examined your own genitals in a mirror? How did you feel?

Do you have difficulty going to the bathroom while others can hear you?

Do you have difficulty going to the bathroom when others can see you?

Do you fantasize about unacceptable sexual adventures in order to overcome your sexual inhibitions?

Do you find the idea of a nudist camp repulsive?

Are you uncomfortable when a nude child runs into the room?

Are you uncomfortable when you see animals copulating?

Do you feel uncomfortable when your child asks, "Mommy, what's that?" referring to your pubic area?

When you take a bath do you have difficulty washing your private areas and allowing yourself to experience pleasurable sensations?

Do you feel that sex is a duty that you are obligated to perform for your spouse?

Do you remember having passionate feelings that you no longer can achieve?

MARITAL RAPE

By law in most states, a woman cannot charge her husband with rape. No matter how much force he uses and no matter how strong her resistance, he is within his legal rights. This perception of a woman as the unconditional sexual property of her husband is strongly seated in Christianity.

Not that Christianity promotes forcible intercourse in marriage, but conservative Christians view women as secondary and they reinforce the husband's rights to receive sexual gratification from his wife. This sets the stage for many males to force the wife's participation in intercourse, or conversely, it places the female in a position of submission to the male.

Grace told us of her experience in a 23-year marriage with a man who repeatedly forced her to have sex with him against her will. They were both Christians and both attended church.

> Many times my husband came home late after I was already asleep. He would take off his clothes and get into bed. After a few minutes he said, "Well, what do you think?"

I said, "About what?"

He got angry then and said, "You know what I mean. What do you think about making love."

I replied, "I don't want to."

He lay there a few more moments and then said, "Well, I do." Then he just rolled over on top of me, forced his penis into me, and did it. It hurt and I hated him for it.

It wasn't the only time it happened, either. But what could I do? It's my obligation to let him. He's my husband and that's what the Bible tells me to do. I would have divorced him but I couldn't because the Scriptures say that I would be forcing him into adultery. I didn't know what to do, so I just put up with it.

This is a mild example. Some women are beaten and physically injured by husbands who, following the Abusive Christian Model, insist on their husbandly rights. Too many men who wouldn't rape another woman will force their wives to have sex with them. The Bible and conservative Christianity tell them that marital intercourse is their right, that the woman is their property to be used as they see fit. She should subjugate her will to his. Such men can easily rationalize their behavior by saying, "The Bible says...."

We don't think this is a confusing issue, at all. It's really pretty clear-cut, in fact. In these modern times, women are partners in a relationship, not a property of the husband. And when a woman says NO to sex, any degree of force used to obtain her cooperation constitutes rape.

Men who force their wives to have sex with them, who demand their rights as husbands, may be acting out their feelings of anger and hostility. Conservative Christian values offer them too few options through which they may meet sexual needs. They become angry and frustrated by a system which is too restrictive. Masturbation is out, pornography is out, sleeping with other women is out, fantasizing about other women is out, polygamy is out.

The only acceptable means of satisfying those needs is through their wives. And if that, too, is denied them, if the wife is angry or hurt and has withdrawn sex, their bad feelings may begin to build. These men usually fail to discuss their emotions or to allow anyone to get close to them. They stuff their feelings, thinking that the bad feelings will go away or disappear. Instead, those feelings explode in aggressive, punishing behavior which is aimed at the wife who "disobeys" them.

The Abusive Christian Model of obey or be punished is dominant here. It would be much more helpful if the man's attitude were one of compassion and understanding. That would make communication much easier. We strongly believe that Christian values and the Abusive Christian Model contribute to marital rape. It's not always the man who forces intercourse on the woman. Many women submit to sexual contact they really don't want because their Christian beliefs obligate them to do so. Their self-esteem is so low because of their Christian beliefs that they feel their own needs are not important in comparison to those of their husbands.

Rigid and restrictive belief systems, like Christianity, produce situations in which people feel trapped, frustrated, and confused. Any time people feel trapped, in a pressured situation where no options are available, aggressive behavior becomes much more likely. Men raping their wives and women submitting to sex they do not want are dramatic examples of the effects of Abusive Christianity.

FEMALE SEXUAL WITHDRAWAL

The most common sexual problem we see in married females is the loss of sexual interest in their husbands after several years of marriage. Even if the marriage started off passionately for both, almost inevitably, the passion will begin to cool. Many things can contribute to the cooling of the original passion in the marriage. That is not unusual, nor is it necessarily pathological. It can, however, point to pathological processes seated in Christian belief systems. Earlier we looked at how women fear their own sexuality because of Christian guilt and shame. Here, we would like to examine how the whole flavor of the sexual relationship can be affected by the woman's perception of the husband as good or bad. In conservative Christian doctrine, everything is either right or wrong, good or bad.

A woman initially is physically attracted to her husband because she sees him as "good," the union "made in Heaven," and "God means for us to be together." But husbands are fallible, and soon the husband will inadvertently hurt his wife in some way. She forgives him, but begins to become aware that he is not "perfect." When he continues to behave in a human manner and do things which hurt her, her perceptions continue to change. Her view of her husband goes not from "good" to "human" but from "good" to "bad." Because conservative Christian ethics have taught her that things and people are either good or bad, she passes up the possibility that he is merely "human" and goes straight to "bad."

She is angry and hurt. She has no idea how to achieve psychological intimacy or talk about her feelings, so she sexualizes intimacy. When she wants to shut him out, punish him, or to protect herself emotionally, she withdraws sex. She withdraws emotionally and stops communicating because she is "angry and hurt." This fits in with the Abusive Christian Model.

When women sexualize intimacy, withdrawal of love equals withdrawal of sex. She punishes him by shutting him out emotionally and physically. Now her perceptions of him have begun to color her feelings about him. He cannot be "good" because if he were, he would not be capable of hurting her repeatedly. So he must be "bad." And how can she possibly allow someone "bad" to come into her body. Wouldn't that make her "bad?"

In some women, this takes on dramatic and concrete proportions. If he enters her she feels defiled by his body. She begins to feel that his sexual needs are "bad." And because she has stopped communicating with him, there is no way for her to express and resolve her negative feelings toward him, so the feelings continue to build and to eat away at her passion for him.

But here's where the whole thing becomes really confusing and conflicting for her. He is still her husband and God and the church say that she must submit to her husband. However, in her perception, her husband and his needs have become bad, and how can she let someone bad into her body, even if he is her husband and even if God says she must. So what does she do? It's a safe bet that she doesn't relax and enjoy her sexuality. In response to this confusion and conflict, the wife may adopt the good girl or "nun" mentality. She becomes sexless.

While we have described sexual withdrawal in terms of the female, we do not mean to suggest that it is only the female who experiences loss of passion in a marriage. Many wives have also complained of similar behavior in their husbands. Men with conservative Christian beliefs may be subject to the same difficulty with incorporating sexuality and "goodness," and they may in turn reject their wives because they are perceived as "bad."

SEXUAL PERVERSIONS

Conservative Christian dynamics contribute strongly to the development of perverse sexual behaviors. Needs for psychological intimacy, which are not satisfied, and normal sexual drives, which are suppressed, cause anxiety. This increase in sexual tension, compounded by an inability to talk about their confused feelings, locks people in a powerful internal struggle. This struggle can become aligned with confused thinking, fear or anger, forming fertile ground for sexual offenses. The anxiety that results sets up a dangerous potential for sexual offense.

These conditions often occur when a man cannot meet his sexual and emotional needs with a female. It may be that the only female he has access to is his wife, and sex with her must be clean and pure, or she may have withdrawn sex. He may be unmarried and his Christian ethics forbid any form of unmarried sexual expression. Or his sexual ethics may be so punitive and "muscle bound" that he has no acceptable means of sexual expression. He suppresses those sexual needs as long as possible. At some point, those needs, having grown powerful from suppression and the resulting anxiety, may well be misdirected toward objects or individuals not normally the focus of healthy sexual behavior, for example, fetishism, pedophilia, exhibitionism, incest, or prostitutes.

He initially finds someone or something to assist him with sexual release. He finds relief in the sexual release associated with that object or person. After several experiences, he learns to respond sexually to that object or person. The forbidden aspect makes the sexual release of tension thrilling and adds strength and urgency to the need. He has done something "bad." He has transgressed his rigid and unrealistic sexual ethic. This causes him to see himself as "bad," eroding his ability to stop himself from committing further unacceptable sexual acts.

We know that a high percentage of sexual offenders are extremely religious, conservative, and uncomfortable with sexual issues. Sexual offenders generally have a lot in common:

1. Men who expose themselves tend to have been reared in a puritanical environment where attitudes about sexuality were oppressive and secretive.

2. Sexual offenders are often males who are unable to consummate sexual relations without experiencing extreme anxiety.

3. Many who engage in sadomasochistic behavior believe that sex is sinful and immoral. Masochistic behavior may help guilt-ridden individuals to relieve guilt. They must first suffer the punishment before they are entitled to experience sexual pleasure. Sadists may focus on punishing their partners for being involved in something so evil as sex.

4. Fetish objects offer a substitute when human contact is off limits. Many times these objects will be dispensed with when an acceptable human partner becomes available, if the individual is able to participate with that partner.

5. Men who molest children are frequently very moralistic, religious, and rigidly traditional. Adult relationships may be conflictual and lack intimacy. Sex with adults may be threatening. Their behavior, performance, and their needs are not as likely to be judged or rejected by a child.

6. Incest often occurs in men who are religiously devout and very conservative. These men see themselves as victims of external forces. These external forces may be past experiences or current situations which they use to rationalize their behavior. They lack a sense of intimacy with others, feel depressed and fearful, and regress from anxiety-producing adult relationships. They may feel shut out by their wives and be experiencing a lack of sexual attention from the wife. Incest may even serve as a way to punish the wife for her wrongdoing.

On the surface, it seems that perverse behavior is contrary to Christian beliefs. Since Christians insist on such rigidly controlled moral behavior, shouldn't perversion be less likely to occur in conservative Christians?

An Associated Press story dated March 20, 1992, reported seven Chicago priests have been removed from parishes or indicted in a nine-month period because of complaints of pedophilia. Cardinal Joseph Bernardino appointed a committee to study the issue only after significant publicity over the Catholic Church's persistent inaction in the matters. It was estimated that, nationally, hundreds of priests have been involved in pedophilia.

We think that the very rigidity of those beliefs actually increases the likelihood of perverse behavior. Control becomes difficult or impossible, due to the anxiety stemming from the rigidity of the beliefs. This results in a compulsive cycle. The guilt, shame, and fear that result from the perverse sexual behavior increase the tension and anxiety. Suppression of sexuality, lack of emotional intimacy, and "bad" feelings which follow the perverse behavior generate even higher levels of anxiety. This anxiety builds to the point that the offender is compelled to repeat the perverse behavior, which has become his only means of release.

An attorney we know handles sexual offenders on a regular basis. She told us that an extraordinarily high percentage of child molesters are Christian ministers or very devout conservative Christians. The last ones you would ever suspect.

How does the minister fall into the pattern of the pedophiliac? When you think about it, aren't ministers under more pressure to be perfect, to be more than human, to be above sin? Aren't their options yet more limited than even a church member, who at least is not in constant public view. While your ordinary conservative Christian can be expected (though not condoned) to err and request forgiveness, the same privilege isn't given a minister.

And isn't it possible that such unreasonable demands on these very human individuals could add intolerable pressure? Given the conditions we have described above, such pressure can be easily translated into perverse behavior.

Have you ever noticed that while sex with females and homosexual behavior is repeatedly addressed in the Bible, there is no direct mention of sex with children, even though society makes it very clear that it is wrong? People who have no choices—all of the choices are wrong—are condemned to follow the path of least resistance. Divorce is wrong. Affairs are wrong. Talking about sexual needs is wrong. Almost every option is wrong. Thus, secrecy is essential, as is ease of gratification. Children offer little resistance and thus are easy prey. Certainly Christian sermons focus on adultery and fornication. They tend to avoid the sensitive subject of pedophilia, and thus facilitate the secrecy.

Child molestation can go on for years in families with conservative Christian ethics. Since it's not okay to talk about sex, neither is it okay to talk about ongoing sexual abuse. They ignore it and hope that it, like all the other untouchable issues, will just go away. Or they just have no idea how to handle the situation because no one ever explained it to them. Or the mothers are passive, submissive individuals who fear challenging the offender who may be head of the house. The family falls into a pattern of keeping secrets, of discouraging communication about powerful issues. They may ultimately even place the blame for the abuse on the child.

How many people have turned their heads to child molestation within their own families? Isn't turning your head to this kind of behavior just as much a sexual offense as committing the behavior itself? We applaud those individuals who finally realize that, and come forward to stop pedophiliacs from abusing again and again.

Joan, the daughter of a Christian minister, initiated therapy as a result of a pattern of relationships in her life that always included sexual abuse. By the time she sought therapy at 37, a health professional by then, she had moved from one sexually abusive relationship to another. Her first experience was with a Christian minister friend of her father, who took every opportunity to hug, kiss, and furtively fondle all the little girls in the congregation. Joan was about six years old when it happened to her the first time. When she came into therapy, she knew of dozens of children who had been fondled by this minister. Yet she had never confronted it, never even told her parents about it.

This man was, as a part of his ministerial duties, driving the church bus. He usually transported the young children of the church on regular outings without their parents. As it turned out later, several of the children had complained of his advances. It was easy to see which of the children quickly backed away when he approached. Even then he would pursue them, insisting that they give him a hug, using the opportunity to run his hands over their bodies. This occasionally took place in front of other adults, who turned their heads or pretended they didn't notice.

During her therapy, Joan informed her parents of the problem. They were understandably shocked, hurt, and claimed they never knew. Yet no one did anything to stop the abusive minister's behavior.

Joan became more and more alarmed at what she knew was going on. She talked to the other women in the church and discovered they had concerns, too. Yet a year passed before Joan finally confronted him. When she did so he denied it, of course, but at least the issue was out in the open. She made sure he understood that others knew about the abuse, too, and that it would be tolerated no longer. The women of the church subsequently removed their children from his care.

He had been abusing children at the church for at least 30 years.

We realize these ideas may be shocking and frightful. We are aware the stance of all Christian churches would be against pedophilia and sexual perversions. However, we strongly feel that these same Christian religions, through their rigid sexual ethics and fear of sexuality, force individuals into the very behavior they condemn.

Children and society must be protected. While perpetrators must often be isolated from society, these individuals need help, not further condemnation and punishment.

SEXUAL ACTING OUT: PROMISCUITY/INFIDELITY

Conservative Christian ministers and evangelists preach against sexually acting out. However, it is well known that ministers are likely to act out sexually. Like the ministers and priests who act out sexually against children, other ministers fall into acting out with prostitutes and women other than their wives.

For example, Minister Jimmy Swaggart, a dedicated Christian, for years preached against and must have denied his sexual urges. We recognize the power that suppressed sexual needs can have and the evidence suggests that Swaggart must recognize them, too. He was discovered twice with prostitutes in his company. Was Swaggart falling into the nun/whore syndrome, seeking out a whore while his wife played the nun? Was he taking the path of least resistance because he felt trapped with no acceptable sexual options? He was not alone in this act, several other evangelists have suffered similar fates.

Such individuals lack psychological intimacy because they have been denied it in Christian families or families with Christian sexual ethics. They are looking for love. They become desperate to find it wherever they can and in whatever form they can. It does not take them long to find out that they can achieve closeness to someone through sexual intercourse. At least for a few moments or hours.

The fact that sexual contact is forbidden adds to the thrill and intensity. It becomes heady and ecstatic. Addictive. And the guilt they feel afterwards actually reduces what ever tenuous control they have.

In fact, that guilt continues to build. It becomes even more likely that they will seek out the forbidden, the intimacy, the relief. They feel intensely guilty about what they have done. They fear damnation. They must relieve the tension they feel. And so, they do it again and again and again...always looking for something outside themselves "to save" them from their fear and guilt...always seeing themselves as "bad" and using that to justify more of the same behavior.

MARITAL INFIDELITY AND THE BREAKDOWN OF THE FAMILY

While infidelity may not qualify as a sexual dysfunction, it certainly does rate as dysfunctional sexuality. It is a form of sexual acting out. There is something unhealthy about a spouse going outside the marriage for sexual satisfaction and intimacy. Having an extramarital affair is probably one of the most stressful things a person can do to himself or herself, not to mention the destructive impact it has on the marriage. Marriages that survive adultery require years to recover and rebuild trust.

What happens when a marriage faces adultery? Loss of trust, fear, tremendous hurt, guilt, break-up of the family, even loss of faith.

And what does Christianity have to do with adultery? Doesn't it forbid adultery? Doesn't Christianity threaten punishment and hint at eternal damnation for those who sin? Doesn't it require public admission and repentance for such sinful acts? And isn't that enough to prevent adultery from occurring in couples who follow conventional Christian ethics? It doesn't work that way. In fact, Christian ethics often set the stage for adultery. We have seen these prohibitions backfire, repeatedly.

In chapter one, Melody described how Abusive Christianity set the stage for infidelity in her family. Melody's father felt it was his responsibility to insure that his wife and his family were shining examples of Christian beliefs. So he watched Lois like a hawk, sure that she in some way would mess up and shame him.

He became more and more rigid in his beliefs and more and more strict with her. He demanded his sexual rights with her, not considering her feelings or desires. He didn't talk with her, he talked at her. He was, after all, the head of the house and she was to obey him. She was sexually unfulfilled, angry at his treatment of her, and emotionally isolated. When she tried to talk to him, he didn't want to hear it. He said they had a perfect family.

And it happened. His wife became desperate for love and intimacy and fell into an affair.

At one time or another in most marriages, the couple will experience a breakdown of intimacy. They may grow apart or shut each other out either because they get busy and neglect the maintenance of the marriage or because they are angry and hurt by unresolved issues. The Abusive Christian Model may come to play here. They may withdraw love and begin to punish with anger. As they do, the passion they shared begins to diminish. The negative feelings eat away at their affection and tenderness for one another.

Often it is because they have been taught, through verbal and nonverbal rules, not to talk about sexual issues. So they don't talk about the loss of passion. The situation grows worse. They become more and more isolated and miserable. Each of them feels sexually suppressed and emotionally unfulfilled, lonely. Each is vulnerable, especially to someone who can offer them the intimacy they need.

At this point, at least one of them is set up to talk to someone. Someone who *does* respond to his or her feelings and who may share feelings of loneliness and isolation. It soon becomes apparent that "this person is giving me love and attention." For a time, at least, people in this situation are experiencing the type of psychological and emotional intimacy they have wanted for a long time. They are getting the closeness that their mate has denied them. Because they relate intimacy to sexuality, they begin to sexualize the intimacy. An affair is born.

Even if the spouse doesn't find out, the marriage will suffer. The "adulterer" pulls away even more, in order to keep the secret. Often the marriage breaks up and the whole process begins again, sometimes with the offender following the same pattern through multiple marriages. They find someone they can be close to, the intimacy breaks down, they look for it outside the marriage, another marriage breaks up.

Or the spouse discovers the affair, the marriage survives, but irreparable damage is done. The spouse, true to the Abusive Christian Model, is angry and punishes. After all, haven't they been wronged? And doesn't wrongdoing require punishment? It is that familiar old abusive conservative Christian philosophy. Punishment precludes understanding.

Sometimes rigid Christian ethics backfire in ironic ways. One young woman we know had an unusual response to her conservative Christian background. Reared in a strict Catholic home, she learned that divorce was unacceptable, a sin. At age 24, she found herself in an unhappy marriage, with a man who seemed unable to achieve intimacy on any level. "But," she said, "I knew I would go to hell if I got a divorce."

She went through three years of therapy and marriage counseling to try to save the marriage. Finally, hopeless and frustrated, she had a sexual encounter with her husband's best friend. Later, she claimed, "I knew if I committed adultery, I had done the worst. So then, what difference would it make if I got a divorce? I had to get out and it was the only way I could see. Just go ahead and be a *real* sinner."

PROMISCUITY

Promiscuity is common in many conservative religious men and women, not just ministers. We especially see the pattern in individuals reared in very moralistic, rigid Christian homes. This differs from the process that facilitates infidelity in that there is no breakdown in psychological intimacy. There may never be any psychological intimacy, because stable relationships may never be formed. Intimacy is sexualized and the rigid ethics break down.

Gerald, a 50-year-old male, related that in his early childhood history, he was deathly afraid of his sexuality because he feared it was a mortal sin. He said he would go out and "hold hands and get an erection. I was in hell."

Weekly, he would go to a priest and confess, "Father, I masturbated fifteen times. I touched a girl's breast eight times." This was seen as extremely sinful and he felt terrible guilt and shame. Of course, he could not talk to his parents about these activities because he would be chastised brutally. He felt ashamed, desperate, and did not know where to turn.

Gerald's family sent him to Catholic school where he said he was raised by "mean nuns." He said there was no love, no compassion, no nurturance, no intimacy, and his problem with sex became even worse. "I made out with every girl I could find. I was doomed and I knew it."

He became obsessed with sex, but the sole activity he would allow himself was touching the female's breast or only looking and having fantasies about touching the female breast. He said this made him feel good. He had no one to talk to. No one to be psychologically intimate with.

He did not even understand psychological intimacy. He became more involved in the secret cycle of shame, which led to a greater need for feeling good. That translated into sexually acting out, which led to more shame, and on and on. As he continued to act out sexually, he started wondering if he would hurt people, if he had ruined his girlfriends, and he felt "horrible." His statement at the end of the session was, "I am in hell with what is left for me."

This phenomenon is not limited to males. Women who lose their virginity to a boyfriend, thinking in their immaturity that he is "the one," often adopt a "whore" mentality once the relationship has ended. Since they have already transgressed, "become a sinner," they continue to act out, falling into the same guilt-shame-anxiety acting out cycle as the male.

One young female client belonged to the religious group of Jehovah's Witnesses. She had intercourse with one boyfriend and she reported, "I'm doomed. My days are numbered." She feared psychological intimacy. She was afraid to discuss her fears with anyone, including her therapist. She'd kept it a secret and felt deeply ashamed. She had abandoned her religion and was terrified that she was indeed doomed to spent her life in living hell, of endless disgrace, going from one male to another.

People rejected by the church may act out their hurt and anger by rebelling sexually. They, too, can eventually fall into the cycle of the sexual addict. A 30-year-old female client stated that she had been married at age 16 and divorced at age 17. She said that, because of her divorce, the church "didn't want me—they had no place for me."

She said that she felt like "a rejected child of God." She said it with a loud, humorless laugh. Furthermore, she was "afraid to go to another church. If I did and made any more mistakes, it would be the some old thing. Sorry, Charlie." She became bitter with religion, seclusive, and started sleeping around with several men. By the time she entered therapy she had spent many years in the secret cycle of shame and sexually acting out.

One young Christian man told us that he had acted out sexually with many Christian women. He reported that it was just as easy or easier to find sexual partners among Christian women. He attributed this to the forbidden aspect of sex in Christian beliefs and the fact that these conservative women were so sexually repressed.

"I went to church to find a girl. I found lots of them. I've had sex with over a hundred women and I've found that Christian women are the most sexually driven women on earth. In fact, get them off the front pew at the Church of Christ. I know because I was reared there, too."

HOMOPHOBIA AND EGO DYSTONIC HOMOSEXUALITY

Homophobia (fear of homosexuality) is another situation where Christianity sacrifices people for principles. Heterosexual sex (male/female) is seen as "bad" but tolerated under specific circumstances (if you are married and procreating). If normal sex is seen as bad, then "abnormal" sex is seen as vile and despicable. Men making love to men and women to women! Christians view the image that homosexual sex creates with horror and disgust.

Homosexual sex has to be evil because it doesn't fit the picture of good husband and good wife producing good children. And anything that isn't "right" must be sinful. Many conservative Christians react to that kind of sin with fear and anger. So homosexuals are feared, tormented, rejected from the church, abhorred, abused, and, at the very least, avoided. In the 1992 General Conference of United Methodists, the vote was overwhelming to retain church policy condemning homosexuality as "incompatible with Christian teaching." Churches show no moral leadership in this area. Most businesses and public institutions, because of nondiscriminatory policies, display greater moral leadership than the churches.

Many Christians cite Scriptures from the Bible to validate their claims that homosexuality is wrong. One Christian group appearing on a talk radio show quoted the first chapter of Romans, saying that it condemned homosexual behavior. They used this as an argument that homosexuals should be prevented from teaching in the public schools. Those same passages also condemned premarital sex and adultery, but the group certainly was not going out of their way to prevent fornicators and adulterers from teaching.

A caller to that same radio show reported that the most bizarre song title he had ever heard was "God Hates Queers and So Do I." It was a credit to the media that not one radio station would accept it. However, we'd bet that if the song had been give air time, quite a few conservative Christians would have sneaked out and bought a copy.

Many Christians tend to cling to that first-century view of homosexuality. They ignore any scientific information that homosexuality is a manifestation of physiological phenomena. They reject the possibility that homosexual behavior occurs naturally rather than being wrong or a "sin." For instance, we know that male homosexuality occurs in animals whose mothers were stressed during certain stages of pregnancy, that anatomical differences exist between the brains of homosexuals and heterosexuals, that homosexuality occurs in certain animal species at the same rate as it occurs in humans and that scientists have recently discovered a genetic component to homosexuality. But when faced with information that conflicts with their preconceived ideas, Christians block out those facts and disregard them.

Christians as a group have limited knowledge of what is included in "normal" sexual behavior. So anything that fails to fall within the boundaries prescribed by the church has to be wrong. Some Christian groups are choosing to take a more accepting stand today by welcoming gays into their churches. Many, however, and we suspect most, maintain a rigid position by refusing to view homosexuality as acceptable. They also seem to feel it necessary to convince the rest of the world to be homophobic as well.

Fear can come from a deeper level. Most Christians don't realize that being attracted to a person of one's own sex is not abnormal or unusual. Normal male children go through a developmental stage of physical interest in other little boys. And at one time or another many adult heterosexuals will experience sexual stimulation from the image or sight of another person's nude body or sexual activity even though that person is the same sex. In fact, a large number of people would admit to being bisexual if it were acceptable. When a conservative Christian individual experiences those thoughts and impulses, it can be extremely frightening, because those thoughts and impulses are seen as wrong.

This fear can be taken to extremes. A male rape victim who sought treatment was traumatized more by the fact that he had become stimulated and had an orgasm during the rape, than by the rape itself. Before the rapist fled, he accused the victim, "You liked it, didn't you?" The young man realized that he had no control over his physical response. Still, he was extremely frightened at the possibility that his reaction somehow might mean he was homosexual.

Fear like this controls many men's social behavior. Some men are afraid to get close to another male because emotional intimacy could have sexual overtones. They fear that someone might think they are gay. And they fear that they might begin to feel attraction to the other male. After all, intimacy is often sexualized in these individuals. They reject or avoid any situation that brings up the dreadful possibility that they, too, could have homosexual feelings.

Gay bashing, physical abuse of homosexuals, is the angry outcome of such fear. And here again, the abusive Christian model demands that homosexuals be punished for their deviance from accepted Christian norms. And it isn't just Christians who act on these fears. As we have said before, these belief systems affect the way our whole society reacts.

A frightening story of gay bashing and the extent to which it can have severe repercussions came to our attention just recently. Apparently an individual who felt it was his duty to punish gays had repeatedly sought out and beat up gay men. He developed AIDS as a result of contact with the blood from an infected homosexual whom he injured. We don't know if this abuser was a Christian. It doesn't matter. He was operating on that age-old conservative Christian view of homosexuality as sinful and deserving punishment.

Homophobia exists in homosexuals as well. We call this condition ego dystonic (meaning foreign to the self, uncomfortable) homosexuality. The attitudes that our society has inherited from Christianity cause many homosexually oriented males to reject and fear the thought of sex with another male. Those thoughts feel foreign to them even though they regularly fantasize about it. They may even find sex with a female distasteful, but still try to force themselves into heterosexual relationships. In fact, some homosexual males enter therapy looking for help in learning to feel attraction to females. Therapy is only occasionally successful and, we suspect, only if they are bisexual to a significant extent.

Others submit to their impulses by engaging in homosexual behaviors. Then they feel so guilty and despondent about it that they often become self-destructive. Some kill themselves as a result of that intense guilt. They fear that they will be found out and rejected, or that they have committed a horrible sin. One of our patients, a young Christian male with a wife and children, committed suicide rather than face the fact that he might go against his conservative Christian values.

These unfortunate individuals may, in reality, be mentally healthy. If they weren't constantly faced with a rejection of what they are naturally, there would likely be no problem. Ego syntonic (compatible to the self, comfortable) homosexuality has not been considered a mental disorder by the American Psychiatric Association for over a decade. Ego dystonic homosexuality continues to be described as a sexual dysfunction in the Diagnostic and Statistical Manual of Mental Disorders. If homosexuality were acceptable, there would be no need for confusion or conflict over the issue. This is one example in which the perception of society resulting from Christian doctrine is the cause of a mental disorder. Christianity is responsible for ego dystonic homosexuality.

Many Christians remain unaware of the impact their Christian organization has on them regarding homosexuality. One couple who recently entered therapy because of sexual problems had to confront the fact that the husband was not attracted at all to females. He just couldn't have sex with his wife, he found it distasteful. She felt rejected and unlovable, and she was angry and punishing toward her husband. When it was suggested to her that she was following the Abusive Christian Model of anger and punishment, she denied it, claiming, "Our church is all love. We don't punish." Then it was suggested that, since her church did not punish, why didn't she and her husband go in front of the church and tell everyone he was homosexual? She was shocked, saying, "We couldn't do that!"

We agree. It would have been a mistake.

Christianity traps people. It blocks options such as divorce, healthy discussion of sexuality, sharing of sexual fears and fantasies. Christian belief systems condition people to fear sexuality and communication about sexual issues.

At the same time, Christianity creates anxiety and pressure through the various dynamics we have described. It's similar to putting a pressure cooker on the burner and turning up the heat.

Anxious people have strong impulses to do something to make themselves feel better. Strong impulses demand, by their very nature, quick and easy solutions, immediate gratification. The shame of being out of control with sexual impulses demands that the solution be secretive.

Secretive sexual behavior helps offenders to avoid the public shame, the complexity, the rejection, and the vulnerability which they risk in resolving sexual problems in healthier ways. In short, Christianity forces people into paths of least resistance, such as adultery, promiscuity, sexual perversion, marital rape, and suicide. Although such solutions have disastrous consequences, they allow for the avoidance of public shame, are fairly simple to accomplish, and they are secretive.

Of course, it may look as though we have blamed Christianity for everything but hangnails and natural catastrophe. Seriously, we feel that our society and its sexual behaviors pivot around and cannot escape the influence of Christianity. In conservative Christian families, that influence will be concentrated with even more pathological effects. However, Christianity's detrimental effects on sexuality are felt by a broad section of our population.

THE REVELATION

ABUSIVE CHRISTIANITY AS PRIMORDIAL FAMILY ABUSE

People who work with victims of sick religions in our culture are respected and praised, as long as society views those religions as "fringe" or cults. Dealing with abusive cults and their victims can be difficult and trying. Just look at the complicated standoff between federal authorities and the Branch Davidian cult in Waco, Texas, with its tragic consequences.

But people who try to say mainstream Christianity is sick or abusive are usually labeled "fringe," "atheist," or "humanist" and ignored. As counselors, we know that dealing with Abusive Christians is difficult, trying work. We will probably be labeled atheist or humanist, or possibly seen as cultist and in need of salvation because our views question traditional Christianity.

Those who question Christianity meet cultural, if not universal, resistance. The response is: "You are attacking my culture. You are wrong. You are bad for doing that." Or: "You are attacking my religion. You are certainly wrong, and you are very bad for doing that." For example, in February 1993, Matthew Fox was kicked out of the Dominican order by the Vatican in order to stifle dissent, the dissent being his views on issues such as feminism and universal theology. We are sure they wish to hear no more from him.

Many find it difficult to resist the tendency to condemn messages which conflict with their religious beliefs. Christians learn that tendency because it is implicit in their religion. Those who do not agree with traditional Christian views are condemned. If they do not believe, they will quite simply go to hell or not be among "the chosen." So Christians can certainly condemn and then ignore their heretical beliefs.

Christianity has molded the beliefs in our culture. In turn, the psychological structure of families is formed and molded by beliefs. This is our hypothesis: Individuals are unhealthy because families are unhealthy. Families are unhealthy because our culture is unhealthy. Our culture is unhealthy because Christianity is unhealthy. The "revelation" in this chapter is that Abusive Christianity is responsible for much of the family and individual dysfunction in our culture.

There is little debate about the pervasiveness of family dysfunction and abuse. Every major city has programs and agencies to combat and cope with this abuse. As counselors, we have been trained to help abused children and sick individuals and lately, training and attention have been directed toward treating sick families. If our ideas are correct—that sick Christianity has caused these sick families—then none of us in the mental health profession has been trained to help "sick cultures" or "sick Christianity."

Writings that focus on childhood abuse and sick families also focus on descriptions of abuse or on descriptions of the abusive or dysfunctional family. All would agree that the behavior patterns in these dysfunctional families simply did not spontaneously happen. There is a pattern to dysfunction in these families. Without a doubt, something initially caused and contributed to the development of the dysfunctional behavior found in families today. As editor David B. Guralnik notes in the historical overview in *Webster's New World Dictionary, Third College Edition*: "All events have their antecedents. Nothing comes from nothing...."

The root cause, the antecedent, of many of the individual and family problems we've presented in this book is Abusive Christianity. There is an obvious connection between historic and current abusive Christian beliefs and practices and dysfunctional symptoms found in families (listed below).

Books on alcoholic families describe dysfunction in terms such as authoritarian, angry, abusive, fighting, and fearful (which is an apt description of some churches). It would be very unlikely that the chemical caused the specific sick behaviors in these families. How could the chemical cause rigidity or perfectionism? Most books on codependency, dysfunctional families, and addictions never mention or guess as to the causes of the pathology. We would like to introduce the cause and the perpetuator of this pathology—Abusive Christianity.

One individual noted that his parents were alcoholic and they followed the pattern described, and they *never* went to church! So, what would make us think that Christianity caused their pathology? Trace your family history. There likely will be Christianity in the background somewhere! Christianity has been the most powerful and dramatic influence on our culture for the past two thousand years. Christianity was influencing our culture before we had a culture, before Columbus discovered the Americas.

What should we do about Abusive Christianity? When counselors see a sick family, they do not say, "This is indeed a sick and dysfunctional family," and then shoot all the family members. Counselors do not condemn them. Counselors help them. Maybe this is the reason Christian religions so fear criticism. Those religions tend to condemn and abandon those individuals they see as doing wrong. Perhaps they fear the same could happen to them. They fear they might be treated as they treat others.

We do not advocate destroying Christianity, although Abusive Christians will perceive this as destruction. We believe in helping people, and we think some Christian beliefs and practices need to change. If Christianity becomes healthy, then our culture will become healthier. The growth in our culture will come from our religions. The growth in our families will come from our religion. We must work for love and health in Christianity and less violent and abusive doctrine. Christianity should display caring and open leadership in all moral areas, including race relations, sexual equality, and sexual education. Sadly, at this point in time, the Christian religion is part of the problem.

Abusive Christianity is still being taught and practiced in our culture. It is still causing damage. The Abusive Christian Model is the prototypic model of abuse in families and in institutions.

Christian attitudes toward science have always been skeptical, aggressive, condemning, and condescending. Consider that the Pope, in 1992, stated that Galileo was correct, that the earth revolves around the sun. Finally—350 years later—the Pope agrees.

During his life, Galileo was condemned and punished for his views. The history of the Inquisitions and early American history has been powerfully and violently influenced by the beliefs of Christianity. Such Abusive Christianity has not gone away. It is still here and it is the root cause of most family violence and dysfunction found in our culture today. It even serves as the model for our dysfunctional schools and penal systems.

Abusive Christianity causes or contributes to:
    Authoritarianism
    Rigidity—in ethics and thinking
    Perfectionism
    Fear of having fun
    Confusion of love and anger
    Withdrawal of love when angry
    Discrimination
    Punishment
    Family violence
    Codependency/boundary issues
    Child abuse
    Sexual rigidity
    Sexual problems
    Sexual affairs
    Marital problems

It may be that the root cause of some of this pathology is an interaction of our unique American history and Christianity, but we strongly think that Christianity and its authoritarian and abusive values contribute to a large part of the violence and anger, as well as the abuse and family dysfunction seen in our culture today. We are certain that Abusive Christianity has led to a myriad of sexual problems, marital problems, and sexual abuse. Abusive Christianity has contributed to discrimination against women, people of color, people of different sexual orientations, and certainly people of different creeds and beliefs because of its rigid demands for conformity.

Therefore, we want to focus our recovery on the cause of this abuse, Abusive Christianity and the Abusive Christian Model. Intuitively, Alcoholics Anonymous has stated that recovery from alcoholism is spiritual. We think the cause of the psychological symptomology is Abusive Christianity, and the damage *is* spiritual. As we said in the first chapter, it is the spiritual nature of man that is injured by Abusive Christianity. The recovery must be spiritual.

FIRST-CENTURY FAMILY SYSTEM

Freud thought that God was a projection of the typical father image. As a result, the characteristics of God were those cultural characteristics of fathers found in the first-century. We believe the same holds true for the way family systems function. The God of the Old and New Testaments functions and treats "His children" much like the typical family system of that time, the first-century family system. As a result, the typical first-century family system and that God were seen as:

> Male and dominant
> Discriminating against women
> Discriminating against races (Tower of Babel)
> Authoritarian
> Rigid in rules and ethics
> Perfectionistic
> Withdrawing of love if not obedient
> Punishment-oriented
> Potentially violent and abusive

Sexually paranoid and abusive (Christ was "born of
a virgin")
Homophobic

That family system, found in the first century and projected into Christianity, influences the families in our present-day culture. The sad fact is many families today follow those same destructive rules and abuse each other and their children in much the same manner. Those who urge a return to "family values" frequently mean that same abusive, dysfunctional family system found in the religion as taught by Abusive Christians.

That first-century family system no longer works in the twentieth century. The old family-interaction model is not relevant to many, if not most, of today's youth. It avoids issues that need to be discussed and talked about by giving simplistic and unrealistic answers. "Abortion is murder." "Just say no to drugs." "To avoid disease, simply do not have any sexual contact."

Usually these rules are followed up with punishment and censure of those that "fall." The family, as influenced by Abusive Christianity, often refuses to help and continues to hurt its own members, be those family members or church members. These families believe you must follow the rules and believe or get out.

These values lend themselves to angry, abusive behavior and, at times, violent behavior. These abusive values poison our culture. In March 1993, a physician who performed abortions at a clinic in Florida was shot and killed by an abortion protester who was a fundamentalist Christian. Managers of the protest stated that at least some babies were saved. Murder for life?

Abusive Christian values are also at best irrelevant and at worst destructive considering today's sexual issues. Abusive Christians attempt to stop the education and teaching of needed sexual information, regardless of whether healthy values are included in that education.

We need to begin to teach a new family system model, based on love, caring, respect for differences, and ethics, that makes sense to today's youth. We need a religion where the values portrayed and practiced are earthy and relevant. We need a healthy religion so we do not worship manipulation and violence.

We need a religion where children will not be sacrificed because they are pregnant out of wedlock or because they disavow rigid and abusive rules. We need to change the social institutions that have been influenced by Abusive Christianity, such as public schools and the judicial system. The punishment-oriented judicial system hurts more than it helps, especially when it deals with first offenders for drug use and prostitution. Certainly we need to be protected from the incorrigible and violent offender. But those that can learn need to learn to care for and help themselves and others. They need to be helped, not punished or "saved."

We need our violence-tolerant churches, with Christ nailed to the cross, to replace that symbol with a Christ with helping hands outstretched—to all people. We need to rise above the first-century abusive family system model.

SURVIVORS AND RECOVERY/ SEXUALITY AND RECOVERY We discussed survivors from Abusive Christianity in Chapters 4 and 5. These individuals have survived by the use of their anger, guilt, and denial. Their childhoods have been damaged, if not destroyed. Many Christian Perpetrators and Angry Rebels are not aware they are injured. They hide behind their anger or righteous indignation, carrying with them pain and fear behind the anger. They hurt others. They need help.

Similarly, many people do not know they are sexually injured. Women believe they are destined not to enjoy sex. Their beliefs control their bodies. Communication shuts down. Affairs begin. They really do not understand why, but they know they cannot tell their spouses. They cannot talk about sex and their sexual attractions. So marriages end. These people need help.

Those who attempt to block the teaching of sexual information that includes healthy values also are injured. They seek to spread the same fear and repulsion of sexuality to others. These people need help, too. But because their behavior is consistent with accepted and cherished beliefs, we ignore the abusive control of others and the pathology in their behavior.

As we have noted, many books have been written about the sexual and relationship dysfunctions found in families and individuals. These books usually cover tasks and exercises to help recover from these symptoms. We urge you to use these books and have included a plan for change you may use and books for reference in Appendix One.

Since Abusive Christianity damages people's spiritual nature, we can't stress enough that spirituality is the key to recovery. Spirituality pulls people together, regardless of religious creeds. Spirituality brings with it a healthy self-love and the ability to transcend worldly problems. But first, let us focus on the practical aspects of recovery.

THE SELF-HELP PLAN

PLANNING FOR LIFESTYLE CHANGE. Our self-help plan focuses on three important principles:

1. Awareness precedes positive action.
2. Information is therapy.
3. Behavioral change is rarely a "one-shot deal."

People cannot help themselves if they are not aware they have a problem. Neither can anyone help stop the abuse of others if they are not aware there is abuse taking place.

Everyone involved in Christianity has a societal obligation to examine Christian beliefs and practices and to be willing to admit to abuses. Abusive Christianity needs reform from its first-century psychological view and belief system. It is important that we replace the Abusive Christian Model commonly found in our culture with a Healthy Christian Model. It is our obligation to help stop the abuse and begin the healing process. Awareness precedes healing, on both the cultural and personal level.

Next, information is therapy. The more you know, the better off you are, the more options you will have. Read about different denominations. Read about different religions and talk to people within those religions, be they Buddhists or Unitarians. Do not be afraid. Information will not injure you, but what you believe can hurt you.

Finally, it is important to realize that recovery from abuse and changing powerful forces in your life is rarely a "one-shot deal." Life is a process and change comes over time. Rarely does one find "salvation," a one-shot happening that totally changes your life. For long-term change, we need the love, concern, and help of others. We need to trust others. Then we need to develop and work on our goals. Give yourself time and be kind to yourself. Do not demand instant change or set rigid goals. Bring your family in on your goals. Let them be a part of your change. After you are aware, have identified the problems, and realize change takes time, then you need goals and a plan.

When counselors attempt to help people, they generally structure their thinking in some order similar to this. When we want to help people change beliefs, attitudes, or behavior, we use the following points.

1. Be aware of and define the problem.
2. Gather information.
3. Identify specific problems.
4. Develop specific goals.
5. Develop plans to reach goals.
6. Take action.
7. Evaluate progress.

You can structure your "self-help plans" in much the same manner. Let's say you follow the Abusive Christian Model in your family. You yell at your children and punish them to correct them. You are aware this is a problem. Start reading everything you can find on anger, love, intimacy. Study the differences between the Abusive Christian Model and our Healthy Christian Model, presented in the next chapter. For help in your reading, consult the section on anger in Appendix One.

Encourage the participation of your family by starting with a family meeting and discussion. Listen to ideas that family members may have. If the primary changes are in your individual behavior, your family can still help you change and encourage you. So the family meeting is important for the entire process. Take time for it.

Set specific goals for your behavior based upon the information you learn. Involve your spouse, your children (if appropriate), and significant others in these plans and in the evaluation of your progress. Remember, goals must be specific. Such as, "I plan to deal with my anger next time without yelling and saying demeaning things."

How will you reach this goal? Take action. Don't wait. Have family, loved ones, and possibly a counselor help you. Do not forget the spiritual aspect to healing yourself and your family.

Next, evaluate. How are you doing? Your beliefs play a part in your behavior, so be willing to examine your beliefs. Do you believe people should be perfect and punish them when they are not? Do you believe you punish or try to control people with your anger? What does your family think? You need feedback. Do not give up. At times change is difficult, but it is possible. Keep working.

Finally, as a part of your recovery plan, you must examine your Christian beliefs and be willing to convert the abusive beliefs to healthy ones. Pay particular attention to the beliefs that contribute to your specific personal or family dysfunction. In Chapter 9, we will describe a healthy Christian model.

PSYCHOLOGICAL BOUNDARIES AND HEALTHY BELIEFS

Secure psychological boundaries form an important part of a healthy personality and healthy relationships. Assume that you have determined at this point that your Christian affiliation has not been altogether a healthy one. And let's assume that you feel that you are benefiting enough from your participation in the group that you do not want to just pack up and walk out. How do you isolate yourself from any negative effects? By establishing secure psychological boundaries.

Some people have developed secure boundaries and a secure sense of personal identity. As one of our patients said, "I go to church. I get out of it what I need and I do not buy into the nonsense." That individual obviously has healthy boundaries, and we would like to make some suggestions about planning for achieving healthy boundaries.

First, let's define and explain the concept of healthy boundaries. If you choose to do this as a therapy plan, go to Appendix One and select some books which deal with "codependence," Adult Children of Alcoholics (ACOA), and family issues. You must be informed and understand what is happening in order to plan to develop healthier behavior. You must have awareness and information.

Boundaries begin soon after birth. When a baby is born, that child has no concept of boundaries, physical or psychological. The child literally does not know itself from its mother. Anyone who has been around a baby has probably watched the baby discover its hands and feet. Babies do not arrive with the information as to what is "me" and what is "not me." They must learn what is "me" and "not me." Thank goodness, we do not have to send them to school for this or we would have a society of people who literally could not find their feet with both hands.

Few individuals have problems with their physical boundaries. Usually, we do not confuse our body with someone else's body. However, our psychological boundaries are never as completely defined as our physical boundaries. This results in confusing our feelings and behavior with the feelings and behavior of others. Our boundaries and the source of our feelings are not clear to us.

Other individuals' beliefs upset you and cause you to become defensive. You cannot express your opinion for fear of hurting others. Or you let other people determine how you feel. The question is, are your boundaries firm enough for you to be secure in your thoughts and feelings? Are they strong enough for you to feel non-defensive about what you believe? Or do others "make you mad" when they question and doubt. We have included a Boundary Check Exercise by Jerry's friend, Pat Love, author of *The Emotional Incest Syndrome*.

See how many of the following scenarios you have experienced:

1. You have a really good day, but when you start to tell your partner about it, he or she is in a bad mood and—poof—there goes your good attitude out the window.

2. You go to a movie and really like it and on the way out the two friends you went with start talking about how they hated it, and you begin to question your own judgment.

3. You're feeling fine, calm, and relaxed and your partner comes home and you sense some anger. You get tense, you ask what's wrong. The response is, "Nothing, I'm fine." Before long your anxiety is so high that you pick a fight just to relieve the tension.

4. A friend calls you and asks to borrow your car. You really don't want to lend it, but you say yes anyway.

5. Your teenager comes home from school in a bad mood; before long, you're in a bad mood, too. You try to get the youngster to shape up, but you only end up in a fight.

6. You tell a friend something in confidence and you find out that the friend told exactly the person you did not want to know.

7. You are dating someone and find out that he or she is dating another person even though you were assured that would never happen. You are angry and hurt, but you continue to date the person.

8. You stay in relationships that you know are not good for you.

9. You attempt to control those around you, believing that you know best for them.

10. You give advice when it is not asked for.

Your recovery and your emotional and spiritual health depend on the development of intact and strong boundaries. A personal goal could be to not become upset when someone questions your beliefs, like this book may, or to give up attempting to control others so they will agree with you. Another goal could be to feel more confident and to allow no manipulation or abuse from others. Goals would also have to include spiritual development and looking at those beliefs that contribute to codependency and boundary difficulties.

Important issues in the development of secure boundaries are an increased feeling of self-esteem and self-worth. It is important to grow confident in your beliefs and your identity. Emphasize the separation between your ideas, beliefs, and feelings, and those of others.

You may need to remind yourself at times that you do not have control over others, their behavior, or their beliefs. Nor do you have to take responsibility for their behavior. You are you and they are they. Both are unique and separate entities. And that is perfectly fine.

Do not hesitate to call a professional counselor, if you feel you need some guidance. The feedback can help. Do not give up on your growth adventure. Be positive. You are worthwhile. With help, you can succeed.

A TWELVE-STEP SPIRITUAL RECOVERY PLAN FROM ABUSIVE CHRISITIANITY

The following program provides guidelines for the recovery of spiritually abused individuals. An important aspect to your recovery is to gain spiritual health. You will notice that this plan is patterned after some other 12-step programs. However, we do not intend to set up any plan as "essential" to your recovery. You are responsible for your plans and your recovery. Gain information, but remember, none of it is gospel truth. Theories, programs and "steps" are intended to help you, to be of use. They are not intended as truth.

1. We became aware that the spiritual aspects of our lives had been manipulated, controlled, and damaged by Abusive Christianity.

2. We were willing to examine and define our concepts of God, Higher Power, and the spiritual to fit our own beliefs and spiritual experiences.

3. We refused to bow to power and tyranny as others attempted to force their concepts of God upon us. Positively, we understood that there exists a "spirit" or "power" within us that cannot save us but

can empower us to transcend petty ideologies and life's turmoils.

4. We were willing to join in spirit with open and loving people who respect the rights of others to define their own beliefs.

5. We were willing to work to let go of inappropriate guilt, anger, and shame in order to free ourselves spiritually.

6. We were willing to transcend original sin and shame and work to accept ourselves as worthwhile and to recognize our strengths as well as our weaknesses, regardless of our race, sex, creeds, or other petty differences.

7. We formed a plan to meet our spiritual needs in a balanced and healthy manner and were prepared to construct our own spiritual rituals.

8. We decided to be honest with ourselves about our doubts and beliefs and to share our honesty with others.

9. We made a decision to make our beliefs contemporary, practical, and relevant and to eliminate punishing and abusive behavior from our lives, concerning ourselves or others, while recognizing that perfection is unattainable. We believe one should understand and help rather than to censure and punish.

10. We took charge of our lives in a constructive manner, letting go of those situations that could not be controlled and working for those goals we believe important.

11. We were willing to assist those in need in a loving and accepting manner.

12. We were willing to stand against religious tyranny without becoming abusive ourselves.

COPING WITH ABUSIVE CHRISTIANITY

RECOGNIZING ABUSIVE CHRISTIANITY. To develop secure and confident beliefs, you must be willing to examine those beliefs. Many of you will discover by reading this book the same thing we did by writing it: That we are survivors of Abusive Christianity. Not the kind of abuse that the world and the media focus on, but abuse that is approved and ignored because all have been afraid to confront and question a philosophy which is so established in our culture, and a Heavenly Father who seems all to willing to punish.

How do we go about healing the wounds of abuse? First by recognizing there is a problem. But we don't want you to stop with just acknowledging the problem. There are many things you can do to stop further abuse and to facilitate your recovery.

We have discussed different ways that Abusive Christianity can harm you. Christian Perpetrators can attempt to manipulate you with Destructive Christian beliefs, such as attempts to "save" you. Belief in doctrine itself, what we call Destructive Christian Beliefs, can injure by influencing your behavior, attitudes, and feelings. Families may be harmed by following the Abusive Christian Model. This model also influences churches, schools, and the judicial system. The following list can help you determine the areas in your life which have been influenced by Abusive Christianity.

Your religion is NOT meeting your spiritual need in a healthy way if:

- You sacrifice people for beliefs.
- You find yourself angry and defensive when confronted with ideas that conflict with your beliefs.
- You adhere to a "packaged" belief system without rationally examining the system (using common sense).
- Your belief system leads to guilt, depression, neglect, and self-abuse or abuse of others.

- Your beliefs lead to unrealistic fears, or fear of eternal punishment, if you do not behave in specific ways.
- Your religion prevents you from accepting current medical and psychological help.
- You conceptualize God as a dictator.
- Your religion encourages you to engage in magical thinking, such as praying for and waiting for success, praying to be healed and avoiding medical treatment, praying or expecting to be saved from an accident or life problem.
- You dread attending church or attend only out of feelings of obligation.
- Your beliefs lead to suicidal or self-destructive thinking in any way—such as physical, financial, spiritual, sexual, social.
- Your beliefs lead to homicidal thinking in any way.
- Your beliefs have no practical application to your personal life, family life, or business life.
- You encounter threats from other believers if you do not believe certain doctrines or behave in certain ways.
- Your beliefs incorporate numerous, rigid, unreasonable rules.
- Your religious values prevent natural and rational enjoyment and celebration, such as no dancing, no television, no Christmas, no birthday celebration.

Abusive Christianity has such a powerful and pervasive influence that people tend to accept the bizarre and petty rules found in certain Christian belief systems. Even though these beliefs hurt people, out of "respect" we do not confront the religions. In fact, we may not even see the abuse. Abusive business practices and abusive families were "not seen" in the earlier part of this century. Sexual and racial abuse in the military was "not seen" until recently. Along the same line, Abusive Christianity is simply not seen.

However, now we are more aware of abusive business practices such as deceptive packaging of food. We attempt to protect people from such abuses. Unfortunately, protective laws do not apply to Christian churches and their massive administrations. "Caution, Christian religion may be hazardous to your mental, physical, and financial health." Wouldn't that be a refreshing warning before the program of a television evangelist or a "hell or damnation" preacher?

Those who have taken courses in statistics may have read the "helpful" and hopefully humorous book *How to Lie With Statistics.* This book discussed ways people can present ideas which are based on statistical "facts." It is often not difficult to manipulate the numbers so that statements you want to make could be "the truth." Or conversely, it is easy to form questions to discredit any research. The statement, "No one has proved that smoking causes cancer in humans" is accurate. Would you donate your children for cancer research?

The adage that "figures never lie but liars often figure" frequently holds true. We must realize that statements and beliefs can be distorted and abusive, even when based on "fact" or "scripture."

Christian leaders, like all of us, have past experiences and views which color their current attitudes and beliefs. Those beliefs affect the people under their ministry and guidance. It is dangerous to automatically assume that Christian authorities are "good" or have your best interests at heart, or that what they say is "Absolute Truth." We must learn to recognize that some of those ideas and beliefs can hurt you, your family, and your friends.

People frequently have a childlike trust of Christianity which prevents them from being aware of possible abuses. Listen to your internal feelings about situations. Use your common sense. If something offends or threatens you, or if something sounds absurd, maybe there is something wrong with it.

Most of us have vague feelings of discomfort at one time or another in various situations. Our gut tightens up or we feel dread or resentment. If we constantly deny and suppress these feelings, we become insensitive to them. For example, Melody had discomfort when her mother was "excommunicated." But instead of listening to her feelings, she assumed that the church leaders were "right" in their perception and she went along with them against her own doubts. It took her a long time and a lot of soul searching to decide that Christian Abuse had taken place.

Maybe you have, in the past, gone along with actions you doubted, because someone in authority told you it was the thing to do. Remember, it's okay for you to make up your own mind about your beliefs, your behavior, and your attitudes. It is time that we stand against abuse everywhere, even in our churches.

Trusting your judgment is often hard to do, especially when that judgment goes against an established Christian religion. Most of us have a good understanding of what is right and what is wrong. Sometimes we need to put aside what everyone else is saying and listen to our inner voices.

Ask yourself: Does my religion indulge in the following destructive beliefs and practices in Christianity?

- Bizarre and petty rules
- Magical beliefs
- Belief in "original sin"
- Belief in salvation
- Conformity
- Authoritarianism
- Perfectionism
- Emphasis upon exclusion
- Emphasis upon punishment
- Obsession with control
- Elitist and entitlement beliefs
- Rigid and unrealistic sexual ethics
- Rigid, simplistic, and one-sided beliefs about abortion
- Overreaction to "normal" sexual behavior, such as petting and kissing
- Overreaction to sexual education and information

- Heaven and hell beliefs
- Holy Spirit or beliefs in "spirits" or
- Beliefs in Armageddon, the Apocalypse, or the Second Coming
- Emphasis upon the death of Christ over the life of Christ
- Discrimination against women, races, and sexual preferences
- Fear of and a lack of tolerance for other religions or different ideas

You have control over what you believe, and you have control of your own emotions, attitudes, and behaviors. You can exercise that control. Give yourself permission to do for yourself whatever you need to in order to stay healthy and maintain a healthy perspective. You are not trapped nor do you have to believe something just because someone tells you to do so. Develop the courage to stand up for what *you* believe to be right and just.

COPING WITH FEAR AND GUILT FROM DESTRUCTIVE CHRISTIAN BELIEFS

One way Christian Perpetrators discourage your independent thinking is to threaten with beliefs which are intended to make you feel fearful and guilty. The hope is that you will leave your independent thinking and conform to the "accepted" beliefs, even if they are destructive and abusive. Christian Perpetrators frequently use Scriptures to "prove" their abusive beliefs.

To a certain extent, learning to cope with Abusive Christianity is learning to cope with your own beliefs, therefore your own feelings and thoughts. Survivors of Christian abuse may learn to fear their own independent thoughts and impulses. Their minds become the battleground where their Christian beliefs wage war with their humanity and their independent thinking. The best way to take the power out of fear is to acknowledge, define, and challenge it. Examine the fear. Try to sort out where the fear is coming from.

Fear and guilt do not "just happen." Fear and guilt are based upon what you think and what you believe. If you feel these feelings, there will be a thought or a belief behind that feeling. Frequently, *Destructive Christian Beliefs* are behind inappropriate fear and guilt.

Guilt is appropriate under certain circumstances. When you experience guilt, the feeling communicates that your actions are not consistent with the way you believe. If you hurt someone and feel guilt, you believe people should not be hurt. Guilt that comes from Abusive Christianity is not appropriate.

With Destructive Christian Beliefs, you may feel guilt when your behavior is trivial, or you may not feel guilt when your behavior is abusive but in line with your church (beliefs). Christian Perpetrators can and will hurt others and feel no guilt. They feel no guilt because they think they are right.

As an example, the religious leaders of the day brought to Christ a woman caught in the act of adultery. The law of the day demanded that she be stoned and women of that era were frequently stoned for adultery. The religious leaders of the day were ready and willing to stone her. To kill her. They would have felt no guilt, because they were right and she was guilty of adultery (John 8).

Abusive Christian leaders of today condemn and threaten people and feel no guilt. Neither do we accuse them, because "they are right." People are thrown out of churches, hurt and not helped, because they are "wrong." These Christian Perpetrators, contemporary "Stone Throwers," can and do hurt people and feel righteous about their behavior.

Most victims of these Stone Throwers end up feeling guilty for trivia. They feel guilty for playing cards. Dancing. Watching TV. Feeling sexual. Being attracted to the opposite, or same, sex. The guilt is the result of destructive beliefs which are imposed by the Stone Throwers. This guilt is counter to spirituality.

How can you relax and feel spiritual if you are feeling guilty over trivia? Some of us may need to unlearn what we have learned by changing these destructive beliefs. This does not mean that we should abandon all beliefs about right and wrong. It does not mean we should feel guiltless if we steal or hurt others. It does not give us license to abuse our fellow human beings for any reason, even a righteous, religious reason.

Abusive Christianity imposes guilt and fear. Letting go of the destructive beliefs and thus the guilt and fear that have been so ingrained in us can be difficult. To release these feelings, we have to let go of the beliefs that lead to those feelings. We can look to two women's issues to show examples of inappropriate feelings based upon destructive beliefs—female sexuality and abusive marriages.

Many of our female patients and women we have interviewed cannot enjoy sex, even within their marriages. They have been taught sex is wrong. Their churches have taught that mixed swimming is wrong. Revealing dress is wrong. The lessons are powerful. So powerful, in fact, that their beliefs have destroyed their sexuality. Giving up that fear and guilt based on those Destructive Christian Beliefs is difficult. These women sincerely believe sex is dirty and wrong.

Women often feel inappropriately guilty about leaving husbands who severely abuse them. Abusive Christianity has taught these women that divorce is wrong and that one should stay married regardless. They are in a double bind. They believe it is wrong to leave and they feel guilty for wanting to leave. And because they stay with their husbands after being abused again and again, they feel guilty and full of shame. They feel guilty if they leave, and they are abused if they stay. The dilemma is due to their beliefs. Beliefs that destroy our humanity and lock us into abusive relationships are destructive beliefs.

All normal people feel guilt appropriately. Even the thought of doing wrong usually creates enough of a noxious feeling within us to prevent us from hurting someone else. If we do behave "wrongly" and hurt another, then we feel guilt. The discomfort that guilt creates is usually unpleasant enough that we learn not to behave "wrongly" again.

Guilt becomes inappropriate when it lingers long after we have learned the lesson it teaches. and long after we have made amends or done what we could to rectify our behavior. It becomes inappropriate when it is attached to behaviors that conflict with destructive and unrealistic Christian beliefs.

CHANGING DESTRUCTIVE CHRISTIAN BELIEFS

Assess your beliefs and ask yourself, "Is this belief rational or irrational. Do I really believe God would punish me for being human? Sexual? Having fun and enjoying myself?"

You are not helpless, but by allowing your fear and guilt to control you, you are giving away your power. The more you embrace destructive beliefs, the more helpless and fearful you become and the more you become trapped by those beliefs. Ask yourself:

What is the worst thing that could happen?

What is the best thing that could happen?

What is the most likely thing?

Is this a Destructive Christian Belief leading to fear and guilt?

Is there anything I can do to change the way I think and believe?

Do I want to change the way I believe and thus change my feelings?

You may be able to understand your beliefs, and thus your fear, more clearly by talking to it or writing about it as though it were a person. Ask your belief what it expects of you and whether it wants to help you or simply make you feel fear. Then step over and become the belief and talk back to yourself. Ask why you intimidate and dominate that other part of yourself. What do you receive from the fear? Why do you want to feel fear and guilt?

It may help to purchase a notebook and use it as a journal to write the dialogue between your beliefs and your fear. Find a counselor, or someone with an open mind who does not want to indoctrinate you, and talk to that person. If nothing seems to help, then you may need to look at what benefits you gain by holding onto the fear. Are you getting some kind of payoff (for instance, getting out of something you don't like to do)? If so, go back to our section early in this chapter on "The Self-Help Plan" and set goals to change. Never overlook the possibility of seeking professional help; just remember, all therapists have their own beliefs, and those beliefs will influence the way they treat you. Do not be afraid to "shop" for a therapist.

It takes courage to challenge your beliefs, and thus challenge your fears and guilt. You are unique. You will not think and believe as everyone else does, at least not to every detail. And that is fine. Have the courage to be yourself and allow others the freedom to be who they are.

To help yourself release inappropriate and burdensome guilt is a two-step process. First you must deal with the destructive beliefs that have produced the feelings. There are many good books, some of which are listed in Appendix One, on dealing with irrational ideas and replacing them with healthy ideas.

Next, you must deal with the powerful feelings that have grown from years and years of destructive thinking. For this, relaxation exercises and guided imagery may help. Try this visual exercise and tap into your creativity and create your own relaxation and visualization. Read them into a tape recorder, then relax and follow the instructions.

> Relax with some peaceful music or in a restful environment. Visualize yourself lying in a bed or on a grassy spot under a tree. Imagine that you can see your guilt feelings forming a black ball that lies heavily on your chest. The ball is suppressing your breathing and weighing your body down heavily. Imagine that the dark dense ball begins to gradually lighten in color and density. It begins spreading out, becoming a thin, dark cloud which floats lightly over your body. The cloud continues slowly to rise and soften, changing from black to gray. It then turns to a luminous white as you allow it to float away from your body. Open your mouth and blow out a breath of air. Watch

the clouds break up and dissipate in the tiny breeze. Focus on the feelings of relief and comfort you feel now that the weight is lifted. Resolve never to allow inappropriate guilt to control you or abuse you.

Releasing shame is similar to dealing with fear and guilt. Instead of suppressing it or ignoring it, we must confront and address it. Express the feelings that go along with the painful memories. Feel them. Share them with a trusted friend, then let them go. Affirm your self-worth. The belief of original sin has influenced almost everyone in the Christian culture.

There is no way around or over feelings. You must go through them. Self-acceptance is the final goal. For help in dealing with shame issues, John Bradshaw has written the definitive work on recovery from shame, *Healing the Shame That Binds You.*

DO NOT ABUSE YOURSELF

Some people have internalized an abusive parent, much like the God found in the Abusive Christian Model. They then set about punishing and chastising themselves. This oppressive internal power constricts their freedom to question and to believe. Frequently destructive beliefs and thoughts come from an angry internal parent or an angry internal god. It is almost as if there were an angry parent shouting inside your head.

Listen to your internal parent, but do not be afraid to question. You have a right to believe the way you want to believe. That is the basis that our nation was founded upon—individual freedom and religious freedom. Destructive Christian Beliefs and the internal Abusive Christian Model can combine in your thoughts and feelings until you are afraid to do anything and feel guilty about everything. The punishing process becomes internal. You become your own enemy.

If this fits you, formulate a plan. Read *Games People Play,* by Eric Berne, *Your Erroneous Zones,* by Wayne Dyer, and books by Albert Ellis. Learn about the abusive internal parent. Talk back to this parent. Work on that issue. Abusive Christianity encourages and feeds on this internal abusive parent.

Make a promise to yourself. Promise that you will at least treat yourself as good as you would treat an acquaintance. Learn to love yourself.

DO NOT TOLERATE ABUSE FROM OTHERS

After you have dealt with your abusive thoughts and beliefs, it is time to learn not to let others abuse you. The more you love yourself, the easier this is to do. Abusive Christians endlessly tell you how you should think, believe, or behave. If you do not behave this way, they will tell you that awful things will happen to you (fear) and that you should feel bad for going against God and the church (guilt). Christian Abusers are controlling and punishment-oriented. They want you to think the way they tell you to think. They demand that you believe and not question. They can then control you with your own feelings.

They attempt to manipulate your fear and your guilt in order to gain your compliance. Frequently they will point out verses in the Bible or church history and tradition to prove their point. (Remember, David Koresh, leader of the Branch Davidians in Waco, constantly quoted Scripture.) Christian Perpetrators are compelling and forceful.

Do not tolerate their abuse. These people are more than willing to throw stones at you and point out your wrongs. If your behavior is reasonable, ethical, and legal, do not be persuaded. Simply state, "I do not believe that." There is no need to fight with them or argue with them, and you certainly do not want to abuse them. In fact, we would encourage you to respect their beliefs, *and insist that they respect your beliefs!* There is no danger in difference. Difference is acceptable, although they will certainly believe that difference is dangerous. Do not allow them to control and manipulate you by forcing you to conform to their beliefs. Do not subject yourself to their tyranny. If they keep preaching, leave.

Practice saying the following: "I do not believe that. I have no intention of ever believing that. If you wish to believe that, that is perfectly fine with me. I respect you. Now, I must insist that you respect me." If you do not believe, there is no basis for fear or guilt. You are free to identify your values and your beliefs. You are free to find your God, your spirituality in your own way.

BE WILLING TO QUESTION RULES AND BELIEFS

It is relatively easy to question others with whom you do not agree. It is much more difficult to question your cherished beliefs. To cope with abusive thoughts and beliefs, and to deal with your own abusive internal parent/god, you must be willing to ask and face the difficult questions:

- Why do things have to be that way?
- Why do I have to do or believe that?
- Is God violent?
- Would God hurt and punish people?
- Would God knowingly allow people to die miserable deaths?
- Would God violently punish sinners, even if they do good?
- Is there a hell?
- Did God create a system of rules that sends people to hell?
- Should you fear God?
- Is the Bible unerring in scientific and eternal truth?
- Is threatening people into belief right and good?
- Should you question God and religion?
- Should Christians punish people before they help them?
- Should Christians threaten or shun people because those people do not act or believe in specific doctrine?
- Should churches and Christians hurt people?
- Do certain Christian doctrines destroy spirituality?

- Is the Christian God the only way to conceive God?
- Are all other religions false?
- Should you fear openly challenging the theology a religious group is presenting?

If your independent ideas are met with censure or anger by the members or leaders of the group, then something is wrong. It is fine if others do not agree with you, but you may want to observe whether you are punished, condemned, or encouraged to feel guilty for your views. If you are, then that tells you a lot about the group's lack of acceptance and the conformity and rigidity of thought that their theology requires. At any rate, you don't have to accept any guilt or punishment for your questioning. There are churches that do not have rigid theologies that require conformity, such as Unitarianism and some liberal Christian theologies.

Christian religions often attempt to separate you from information about other religions and beliefs. Make an effort to find out all you can about opposing ideas and then give yourself permission to make your own choices. You have the power to choose if you will only take it. How can you know what makes sense to you if you have never considered any options? Information should be a freeing and an enlightening thing, not something to fear or to reject without examination.

Not only does Christianity discourage information seeking, it also undermines problem-solving. The rules and beliefs provide answers to issues that we should often decide for ourselves. The way Christianity recommends you solve problems is to adhere to the beliefs or turn them over to God and wait. There's nothing about how to use your own good judgment or work out viable solutions.

Problem-solving requires identifying the problem, listing and discussing options, evaluating pros and cons of each option, and making a final choice. Many of us who have followed Christian ethics closely have never developed good problem-solving strategies.

We continue to depend on beliefs or others' opinions. To solve problems requires information and then testing that information with our reality.

Reality testing is what we do every time we exchange ideas with someone else. We should be willing to listen to and possibly alter our perception of reality based upon what others may think and believe. If you limit yourself to an exchange of ideas within a group where all believe the same thing, your perception of reality will be limited.

Educate yourself in how to solve problems and discuss your issues and problems with others. If your "problems" include a history of Abusive Christianity, consider the following steps to help clarify your ideas and beliefs. Christians have been taught to follow a set of rules rather than to make up their own minds and come up with their own solutions. The first part of this book was dedicated to defining those toxic rules.

PROBLEM-SOLVING EXERCISE

1. Define the problem, whether the problem is a situation, behavior, or belief. Talk it over with someone you respect. Specifically, pinpoint the problem, identify, and define it.

2. List all the possible options. Brainstorm and come up with as many ideas, crazy, practical, and impractical, as you can. Allow yourself to be a little crazy. Have fun and enjoy the process.

3. Begin eliminating options that are clearly unworkable because of unavailable resources, or because you do not have the courage to be that crazy, or the option is not consistent with what you believe.

4. For each of the remaining options make a pro and con list. List all the positives and then the negatives of pursuing that particular option.

5. Make a choice based on which options represent the fewest negatives and the strongest positives.

If the negatives and positives are too close, give yourself some time and wait for your intuition to help with the decision.

6. Follow through by listing logical steps to achieve that option.

7. Develop an "action plan."

8. Realize that different people will come up with different options.

DEVELOP A SENSE OF HUMOR ABOUT GOD AND ABOUT YOURSELF

There is a great deal of health in humor and in being able to laugh at oneself and one's situation. There are instances of people gaining health by simply using humor. Humor can reduce stress for victims of Abusive Christianity who have given up their spirituality. Humor can insulate you from the rigid, self-righteous behavior and thought that go along with Destructive Christian Beliefs. Watch the movie "Oh, God." George Burns does a wonderful job of loosening up a tight subject.

Relax and have fun with a subject that has often been frightening and deadly serious. We think God has a sense of humor, too. If not, we would have been zapped long before this book was published.

FINAL NOTES ON ABUSIVE CHRISTIANITY

Survivors of Christian Abuse may have doubts about their experiences. One part of them says "Something is wrong with what happened to me," and the other part says "Christianity *cannot* be wrong." Other people have had similar experiences and some of them may be willing to talk about them. Seek out or establish your own group of open-minded, accepting individuals. There are various support groups which already deal with issues of abuse. One of these might suffice if nothing else is available. Although the idea of Abusive Christianity is new, many Christians and former Christians will realize that they, too, have survived psychological manipulation and abuse in the name of "Christianity."

People who have been injured by Abusive Christianity need to talk until the power, hurt, and anger are gone from the experiences. Repressed feelings become sources of over-reaction, anxiety, guilt, and depression. When you choose others to confide in, make sure they respect and accept your individuality, your feelings, and your beliefs. It is not necessary that they believe as you do, but it is important that they accept your beliefs. Be cautious. Abusive Christians will try to tell you the error of your thinking and your ways, and they will do so in an abusive and manipulative manner.

Remember, when we repress emotions we give them power. It is as if emotional pressure forms inside of you when you fail to talk about your pain. Your mouth is your pressure relief valve. Talking about experiences and the strong emotions releases that pressure and helps heal the trauma of the experience. You can then recover your strength and comfort.

Another good way to vent the pressure is to write about your feelings. Write a letter to whomever you are angry with and say whatever you need to say. Write a letter to God or your minister and vent your emotions. Then tear it up, toss it, or shred it. Since it will never be mailed, you are free to do a really good job. Write out your fury at the abuser— be it religion or your concept of God, whatever it takes to let off steam. And with it, let go of the anger.

Letting go of pain and anger is not difficult, if you're ready to let go. If you're not, then you may need to prepare yourself. Is holding onto the pain and anger hurting you, physically (headaches, stomach pain, etc.), emotionally (depression, anxiety, etc.), or spiritually (stuck too much in everyday problems while losing sight of the big picture or refusing to admit to any concept of purpose, meaning— the Ultimate)? Then do your writing.

Do not fail to consider professional help. Individual psychotherapy or psychotherapy groups are avenues to consider. We encourage you to attend therapy groups which are conducted by licensed professionals and which have some structure so you will learn what to do to help yourself.

Even though we have spent a lot of time focusing on the negative and abusive aspects of Christianity, holding on to grudges, pain, or resentment certainly will not help you. Holding those feelings over long periods can destroy a person spiritually. We would infinitely prefer that survivors of Abusive Christianity release the anger and hurt, get on with their lives, and define their own spirituality.

CHAPTER 9

THE REFORMATION
A Healthy Christian Model

Spirituality is an integral part of being human. Dictionaries define spirituality as "incorporeal," meaning "not of the body," which is a simple description for a very complex, abstract state of mind. But if you have ever watched a beautiful sunset, become lost in the eternal sound of the ocean, or looked in awe at a range of mountains, then you know the feeling of spirituality. You feel a part of it all, in some way connected to the world. Words simply fail to convey the meaning of this experience of "spirituality." Spirituality in this context brings renewal, hope, and peace.

The spiritual is most often captured by poets, not scientists or ministers. This poem was written by Nadine Stair and was published in a newspaper in Louisville, Kentucky. It later appeared in the *Family Circle Magazine*. Nadine was 85 years old when she wrote it. She was learning the meaning of spirituality.

> **IF I HAD MY LIFE TO LIVE OVER........**
> ....I'd dare to make more mistakes next time. I'd relax, I would limber up. I would be sillier than I have been this trip. I would take fewer things seriously. I would take more chances. I would climb more

mountains and swim more rivers. I would eat more ice cream and less beans. I would perhaps have more actual troubles, but I'd have fewer imaginary ones.

You see, I'm one of those people who live sensibly and sanely hour after hour, day after day. Oh, I've had my moments, and if I had it to do over again, I'd have more of them. In fact, I'd try to have nothing else. Just moments, one after another, instead of living so many years ahead of each day. I've been one of those persons who never goes anywhere without a thermometer, a hot water bottle, a raincoat, and a parachute. If I had to do it again, I would travel lighter than I have.

If I had my life to live over, I would start barefoot earlier in the spring and stay that way later in the fall. I would go to more dances. I would ride more merry-go-rounds. I would pick more daisies.

Spirituality, as Ms. Stair seems to have discovered, requires integration with the whole of the individual. The ancient Greeks believed that human beings needed a balance among the mind, the body, and the spirit. In modern times, we separate the three: Physicians, psychologists, and ministers specialize and they ultimately end up working against each other in attempts to help patients. We leave mental health to the mental health professionals. We leave physical health to the physicians, and we leave spiritual health to priests, ministers, and religious organizations. As mental health professionals, we find that too often we have focused on the emotional issues while neglecting spiritual and physical ones. There is no one to deal with the whole individual, to help a person learn to maintain a balance among mind, body, and spirit. It is no wonder people turn to dysfunctional religions in an attempt to meet their spiritual needs.

Most people feel that organized religion is the *only* way to meet spiritual needs. However, all too often *religion fails to meet spiritual needs.* Thus, people who go to church can actually become spiritually starved.

The problem is that religions have become caught up in legalisms, doctrines, and enforcement of rules. Many people do not believe the doctrines taught by their religious organizations and churches. They go to church for other reasons, such as social, affiliation needs, and often fear of the consequences of not going to church.

There are many other ways to meet your spiritual needs, just as there are many ways to meet your physical and mental needs. For example, consider your physical needs and all the different types of foods there are to enjoy. Consider the different types of exercise, work, and play. A long walk can meet both physical and spiritual needs. Reading can meet both mental and spiritual needs.

In some way, you must attend to the health of your spiritual life. Why? Can people become spiritually sick? We certainly think so. What do you think of when you think of someone who is "sick in spirit"? Depressed. Negative. Controlling. Urgent. Abusive, irritable, and addicted. Lacking in love, affection, and joy.

Spirituality can be a very personal and private part of your life. Others may interfere in this privacy by telling you that you need the structure they impose. However, we think spirituality is between you and your God. Others may certainly be of help, just as we hope we can be of help. But spiritual help should be considered with the same caution you would use in, say, eating wild mushrooms. Some can hurt you and some are delicious.

Some "spiritual leaders" do not have your welfare as their major concern. Instead, they are more concerned with promoting their idea of "right." So, we urge you to be careful when you consider using an intermediary or teacher to instruct and translate to you how to meet your spiritual needs. That includes us. In order to provide the most help we can, we want to offer some guidelines which may help you see if you are meeting your spiritual needs in a healthy way. Then you can make your own decisions.

CHECKLIST FOR HEALTHY SPIRITUALITY

Most of us have been reared in a specific Christian denomination or have a family history of a certain religious affiliation. We have had generation after generation for our beliefs to become a part of us, to integrate into our thoughts and our actions. It may be extremely difficult to step back and look at any set of religious beliefs openly and critically. We think that is necessary if you are to make a good judgment about your spiritual and religious beliefs.

We are not saying that all religion is abusive, we are saying that abuses exist, are widespread, accepted, and performed in the name of Christianity. Here are points to help you evaluate if your church is a healthy one.

YOUR CHURCH MEETS YOUR SPIRITUAL NEEDS IN A HEALTHY WAY IF IT:

- Is energizing.
- Helps you achieve peace of mind, is calming and relaxing.
- Represents a positive rather than negative force in your life.
- Increases your feelings of self-confidence and self-worth.
- Helps you trust and accept others and their beliefs even when they are different from yours.
- Assists you in becoming more open, honest, and emotionally available to others.
- Helps you to handle simple day-to-day stress.
- Provides the means by which to handle major life stress.
- Encourages you to communicate and reach out to others in a sensitive and caring manner and is inclusive and unifying.
- Allows you to deal with feelings of guilt in a healthy way and to use guilt appropriately.

- Helps you fully accept yourself as human.
- Helps you fully accept yourself as a sexual being.
- Builds your resiliency.
- Develops your sense of humor and a broad perspective of life.
- Encourages freedom of choice, creativity, and open questioning of the doctrines and beliefs.
- Provides psychological support when you need it.
- Helps you handle intimacy.
- Helps you reduce pain and release long-held anger by encouraging you to forgive, accept, and let go.
- Is in balance with the other important aspects of your life.
- Brings meaning and purpose to your life, a reason to live, and a reason to go on with life.
- Helps you handle anger toward others in a healthy, nondestructive, and intimate manner.
- Helps you accept life and death in a realistic, healthy way.

You likely received some benefit from your Christian experience or you wouldn't have participated. It was not *all* bad and hurtful. Regardless of how destructive the experience, some of your needs were probably met. This is an important issue in recovery and especially in psychotherapy. Part of the injury of the Angry Rebel and the Disillusioned is they have generally classified all Christianity as "awful" and have rejected everything. This rejection becomes a part of their pain. You may not want to reject the entire experience.

There may be advantages to meeting spiritual needs within a church. Some churches teach ethics in a positive and healthy manner while teaching Bible history and giving direction to adults and children. Good friends in a church can become extended family, organizing retreats for children, softball teams, and outings that are fun and helpful. Some churches are very conducive to spiritual experiences with their beautiful architecture and ambiance.

Churches meet on a regular basis and provide structure and easy access. Churches usually have a long history and stable traditions.

Indeed, Christianity is a religion of rich traditions. Ritual, ceremony, music, and artistry each have a place in the elevation of the human spirit and are almost always provided in a place of worship. These elements offer an opportunity to connect with generations by creating a sense of unity through time. Church traditions become an important part of family life. The best example of this is Christmas which has become not only a family tradition but a boon for the business community. Most people have a feeling of connectedness during the Christmas season. And many people depend upon religious traditions to be the one thing in life that won't change.

So you may want to keep the positive aspects of Christianity while ridding yourself of the abusive elements. When you attempt this, it may be a confusing task. In fact, it can create intense conflict. Letting go of the abusive parts of the Christian belief may set up enough conflict that you feel lost, confused, and fearful. Remember, Christian beliefs have been a part of your life since childhood; you must trust yourself and allow yourself to take your time and use your good judgment.

You may benefit from identifying the positives received in your Christian affiliation. Jot down all the pleasant memories you have about going to church, involvement with other members, and living that lifestyle. You may wish to continue to meet these needs in a healthy manner. For instance, if you received a great deal of satisfaction from fellowship with other spiritual individuals, you may want to remain involved or to involve yourself in a different group that has healthy spiritual values in order to meet that need for yourself.

Now, this time write down the factors that were unpleasant in your Christian affiliation. What things do you want to exclude from your spiritual experience next time? What beliefs do you feel are abusive? What would you want to do about them? If you start eliminating some of your long-held beliefs, what will happen? What will be the foundation of your beliefs?

THE MIRACLE OF BELIEF

Everyone has beliefs. Everyone believes in a god, of one sort or another, be that a Supreme Being, money, sex, or whatever. It's impossible not to believe something about everything, even if your belief is just that "the something" is not worth having a belief about. Beliefs are inherent in the human animal. The moment we become conceptual, we start having beliefs.

Our beliefs range from the negative ("I am a sinner," "the world is a threatening place") to the positive ("I am a good person," "the world is a safe place"). Some of us are more positive in our beliefs, others are more negative. And since our beliefs determine, to a great extent, how we treat others and how we feel about ourselves, it is hard to deny their importance in our lives. We have made beliefs a major point of this book.

As psychotherapists, we find our patients' belief and confidence in us to be very important in the helping relationship. A patient who remains unconvinced that our methods can help with problems will not be helped. Like the shamans of old, the cure depends more upon the patient's trust in the healer than in the treatment. Medical practitioners like author Bernie Segal credit a patient's belief system as critical in the cure of cancer and other terminal illnesses.

Melody's mother conquered a severe type of cancer which the doctors told her was terminal. She will tell you today that it was her attitude and her belief in her own ability to overcome the disease that helped her survive. She is still living and there is no sign of cancer after several years. Certainly, her recovery is a miracle, a miracle which she worked herself through her belief in herself.

Most people feel lost without a spiritual belief system that makes sense to them. Their belief needs to provide practical, day-to-day, realistic direction for their lives. They must be able to connect their beliefs to their everyday actions. These beliefs, if they are positive, nurturing ones, will have a positive and enlightening effect. If they are negative, those beliefs can destroy and negate any good that was the original intent. Our physical and mental, as well as spiritual, health depends heavily upon how we view the world around us.

People need consistency in their beliefs. If their beliefs are inconsistent or conflict with other aspects of their lives, then those beliefs will become destructive. For instance, if people believe in the absolute sanctity of marriage and then divorce, they will feel guilt or project blame. If they believe they can, they often begin searching for answers. They will feel conflicted and confused about their beliefs until they find answers that are comfortable to them or that they can feel confidence in.

Our beliefs about God or a Higher Power form what Paul Tillich, a liberal theologian, called our "ultimate concern." Some may call it the meaning of life. It's what keeps us from feeling empty and directionless. We benefit from having positive and healthy beliefs. And we believe that we don't have to discard Christianity to do so. If we must discard the abusive parts of Christianity, what do we have left to teach?

Dr. Barry Bailey, minister of the 10,000-member First Methodist Church in Fort Worth, Texas, believes in and practices a supportive and gentle Christianity. His views often shock the more traditional Christian. However, people keep coming back to hear him, most likely because he opens the doors to a wonderfully satisfying spirituality.

Dr. Bailey does not believe in miracles, the Virgin birth, Christ's resurrection, the divinity of Christ, a punishing God, or the folly of bringing an unwanted child into this world. He claims that many of our serious social problems are caused by religion. The God he knows is a "loving and redemptive" God "whose grace extends unconditionally to all humans from the greatest saint to Saddam Hussein himself." Bear in mind that Fort Worth sits in the heart of the Bible Belt, where abide the most conservative Christians in the country.

Dr. Bailey's congregation feeds the hungry (in three years, nearly 24,000 children) and clothes the poor (20,000 in 1991), certainly a more constructive use of energy than that wasted in congregations that punish and reject "sinners." This congregation builds on a positive belief system.

Do Christians benefit spiritually from participation in these healthy Christian groups? Tamara, a young professional, reports that she does. She explains how going to a healthy church helps her meet her spiritual needs:

> It's all in what you put into it. The church is more for teaching and instruction. True spirituality comes from your relationship with God. Look at all the times in the Bible when people talked to God, it was when they went off alone into the wilderness. You go to church to learn how to meet your spiritual needs and then you're somewhat on your own.
>
> Church is important, if it's the right kind of church, because it gives you a different perspective on things. These are people who are trying to be better than themselves, to go beyond what they are. They can help each other to grow. They expect more from each other and so they give more. You can do a lot on your own but you can evolve more quickly when others expect you to.
>
> Being surrounded by people who are trying to do good things affects you positively. You have those relationships to fall back on. They give you support when you need it. When I was a child we always went to very small good churches where people didn't judge but accepted and helped each other. There was a lot of joy and caring and little old ladies that just loved us. I always had a feeling that these people were behind me and were there for me. That I was not on my own. I knew I could call on them. It gave me a feeling that I was connected with something bigger and something good. It's always kept me from being afraid, gave me a lot of peace.

Being in the church helps you with your relationship with yourself. Unless you can give love and accept others and see the good in them, you may have trouble loving yourself. You need to love others and yourself as a part of your spiritual pursuit. We're not living in a vacuum, we're molded by the situations around us.

Singing in church also helps you to feel a unity because you are participating with others. There have been different times in my life when the songs would pop back into my head to comfort me. They bring back good memories and good feelings. Singing helps you to create good feelings, to get out of yourself a little and to open up your heart.

Going to church gives you a time when you sit and think about spiritual things. In church, you can take the time to be still and think about what you are going to do and how you can be a better person.

Ultimately, we believe that Christianity can exist and flourish without any destructive, negative, and harmful beliefs. We believe there's a spiritual vacuum in our country and that people are desperate for religion that is healthy, supportive, and positive.

THE NEW "NON-ABUSIVE" CHRISTIANITY

We think Christianity needs to exclude Destructive Christian Beliefs and practices and to use healthier ones. A Healthy Christian Model is based on the following:

1. Understand that people are more important than religious beliefs.
2. Recognize that spirituality is more important than religious beliefs.
3. Stand against tyranny in any religion.
4. Stand against abuse in any form and in any religion.

5. Become the champion for all children and unfortunate individuals.
6. Respect the views and beliefs of others.

We think a "Healthy Christianity" encompasses many elements,
each of which promote, rather than block, spirituality.

FIRST, DO NO HARM

A "Healthy Christianity" would include the message: Help, Not
Hurt. Energy finds no positive direction in punishment, rejection,
and control. Somehow along the way the Christian theology has
turned around so that it is okay to hurt others as long as the purpose
is to get them to believe or to do "right." This is abusive and a poor
excuse to control and injure others. We need not sacrifice people for
religious beliefs.

Every Christian, before they act to help another might ask themselves, "Am I hurting this person in any way?" If the answer is yes,
then it is time to back off and reevaluate.

The next question might be, "Am I helping this person the way
they want to be helped or am I helping this person the way I think
they should be helped?" If it is the second, then perhaps some work
needs to be done on the part of the helper. It may help to identify
whose needs are being taken care of—yours or the person you are
helping. Helping others can only be selfless and genuine when one
truly considers the desires of the needy. Otherwise, it is not helping.
It is manipulation.

FILLING THE EMPTY VESSEL

For centuries, Christianity has promised a philosophy of love,
acceptance, and forgiveness. At the same time, Christianity has
practiced a model of anger, rejection, and divisiveness. There is a
confusing duality here—the message of love and the practice of
hurt. This is why believers often talk about their feelings of emptiness instead of happiness and fulfillment found in Christianity. We
live in a land of plenty, but many people sense an emptiness inside,

a lack of direction and relevant meaning. This is why many people have abandoned Christianity. The promise is not kept. Christians and individuals affected by Christianity have been carrying around an empty vessel. It looks good and sounds good but it does not deliver. The empty vessel carries a lack of spiritual fulfillment and spiritual damage caused by empty promises and abuse.

Our patients often search to fill the emptiness they have inside themselves. They complain that, even when things in their lives are going well, they do not feel content or happy. Sometimes they try going to church or getting involved in church but it does not seem to help.

A Healthy Christian Model would end the duality. It would eliminate the hurtful elements in Christianity while fulfilling the spiritual potential. The simple colloquial phrase for this is "practice what you preach." Each of the positive ideas in healthy Christianity can be carried out in practice. Otherwise, they will be as useless as if they were never known.

This may be the connection that is lost in modern-day Christianity. It is why a Christianity that preaches love and acceptance while practicing racism, sexism, and rejection is impotent for so many in meeting spiritual needs. Healthy Christians have a choice of helping others, loving others, accepting others, and practicing the philosophies that, on the surface, make Christianity so attractive. In doing so they will reach spiritual satisfaction. They will fill their empty vessel.

TRANSCENDENCE

The purpose of any religion is to promote spirituality or, at least. to do nothing to block spirituality. Healthy Christianity teaches, promotes, and enhances spirituality. And does nothing which will endanger or detract from that state! We need not sacrifice spirituality for religious beliefs.

Transcendence is the act of reaching a spiritual state. Transcendence leads us beyond our reality, above the universe, beyond material existence. It allows a detachment from the ordinary, the stressful, the mundane. During transcendence, one achieves a connectedness with a Higher Power. Not a separate Higher Power but a source of strength that already exists within us. You come to learn what you already know. The result is an experience of wholeness, completeness, and peacefulness that separates us from the pettiness of everyday life.

Actually, transcendence is a multilevel phenomenon which can take either of two forms. The first or more frequently encountered level is what we will call attitudinal transcendence. This attitude takes the broadest perspective imaginable—that all is one, that we are all part of a universe that is working as it should. In this way, we keep our perspective by staying above daily hassles and never quite buy into all the rules and demands of society. It requires that we separate ourselves from everyday stress enough to remember consciously that life is not usually as serious as some would have us believe, that money is not the most important aspect of life, and that we probably won't die if we don't get our way. This type of transcendence can be developed as a skill, a type of training that Christian churches could well promote.

The second level of transcendence occurs less frequently, although when it does, it tends to leave a long, cherished memory. The effect is a very personal one—one which can be spoiled by too much description. This type of experiential transcendence is usually brief but ecstatic. We feel extraordinary, uplifted in spirit. It is truly a physical, emotional, and spiritual experience, a sensation of rising above.

Natural phenomena like thunderstorms can stimulate transcendence. We once watched a storm from a mountain as it roared across the valley below, moving over us in a sweep of such power that we felt that we were rising up to join with it, participating in its power. Many people experience this type of transcendence by getting lost in an emotional piece of music. They give themselves over to the music and allow themselves to be carried along by the pure essence of sound.

Because life involves pain and crisis, we seek the relief of transcendence. When we feel haggard or out of control, we need that relief. And when we are ill, either physically or mentally, we first must get all the help we can medically or psychologically; then when we have done all we can, there is still refuge in our spirituality.

People will often go to any lengths to reach such a state. And since most don't know how to get there without help, they use unhealthy means such as drugs, impersonal sex, alcohol, seeking a "high." Movies, television, and ball games have become our mantras, our escape from crisis, stress, boredom, and fear. We use these substitutes for spirituality daily. But such escapes are empty, while transcendence is fulfilling.

The role of teaching transcendence is natural for Christianity. Transcendence represents a much healthier concept than salvation and it is the direct opposite of the rigid rule system of religious legalism. Churches can teach Christians to let go of the aggressive emotions, to accept others, to release control, to broaden narrow views. Christianity could help individuals reach transcendence by ridding themselves of the fear, anger, punishment, resentment, and guilt that block transcendent states. If we could develop the skill in our churches, we wouldn't need to look for our spirituality in an addiction, with a bottle or a pill, in hoping for salvation, or in waiting for a deity to deliver us. Instead, we would find that true transcendence is within ourselves.

ORIGINAL INNOCENCE

Much healthier than the concept that humans are born in sin is the idea that at birth they are blessed with innocence. They have the capacity to become good or evil based on their training and experience and the paths they choose for their lives. We know there are criminals and "bad" people in the world. And, yes, we realize that some of their tendencies may be inherited. But those people form a small minority. It is the rest of the world that we address.

It's funny how we can talk about the "miracle of birth" and the "blessing" of having a child and then turn around and describe that child as "born in sin." In a healthy Christianity, children are born in purity. They are open, they are pliable, they are dependent. No concept or spirit of bad or good invades their beings. They are both a blessing and a responsibility to their parents who must teach them in loving ways how to survive, to transcend, and to love.

The human animal is born with the will to survive and with the capacity to become either destructive or constructive in attempting to make a living and to eat and find shelter. Those who choose to bring children into this world take on the task of helping them positively direct those instincts. They take on the responsibility of nurturing their children emotionally so that their children will be available for their own families.

Children do not do as their parents say, they do as they see their parents do. Therefore the way to teach a child is not to punish harshly or to withdraw love as in the Abusive Christian Model, but to be a model of love and acceptance. Then, with caring, to reinforce the desired behavior and to set limits and logical consequences for the child.

Once we assume that the capacity for good is in the child, then we lovingly expect goodness in the child. Our perspective toward our children, ourselves, and others will change. The way we respond to one another will change. Then, when the child, or anyone else, misbehaves, we do not become excited or overreact; rather, we assume that the child is basically good, is attempting new behaviors, and just needs to be guided. It is the nature of children to explore their environment and to attempt every known combination of behaviors at their disposal (better known as driving their parents crazy). We bestow a blessing on our children when we choose to believe they are good. They are then free to respond positively to those expectations.

Original Blessing is a book by Matthew Fox, a modern-day hero who, as a priest, defied the Catholic Church on its abusive beliefs, especially that of original sin. He was silenced for a year by church authorities. His book covers in depth the idea that we do not inherit sinful natures. The book is currently in print and has sold well over 100,000 copies. That tells us that people are hungry for healthy Christian beliefs and that they welcome a relief from the burdens imposed by ideas such as original sin.

It is the role of our churches to help families change and to respond to each other in healthy, supportive ways based on the concept that most of us have great potential for good. It is the role of our churches to help parents to give up control by anger and manipulation and to become emotionally available for their children.

THE RIGHT TO CHOOSE

People who feel secure in themselves and with their own beliefs can allow others to make their own choices about beliefs. This is opposite of the Christian concept of conversion. In Healthy Christianity, individuals would be encouraged to question their own beliefs, to study and respect beliefs different from their own, and to choose to take part of any belief system that they feel comfortable with and leave the rest. These Christians would respect others' beliefs and the wonderful diversity of viewpoints and perspectives available. In doing so, they might choose to make someone else's beliefs a part of their own beliefs.

There would no longer be a mandate to convert or convince others of the truth of each denominational or religious view; rather, there would be a mandate to allow others to define their own beliefs. The new policy would be to respect and revere others' beliefs. It is the freedom to think and to choose that is sacred.

This new respect would allow each of us to listen to minority and dissenting views within our own groups. Perhaps the dissenters would make more sense than what the leaders are saying. Instead of rejecting beliefs, we would reject prejudice. People would be heard even to the extent of going out of our way to encourage them in their separate views.

The world becomes boring when everything is plain vanilla. The world becomes threatening when we must be right while others must be wrong. When we learn to love the "differences" we become free. We transcend. Once we begin to appreciate others' ideas and values, we can truly touch our spiritual natures.

Acceptance of many belief systems doesn't have to threaten anyone's beliefs in any way. Try saying this to yourself: "It's okay if they believe one way and I believe another as long as neither of us forces our beliefs on anyone else. There is room in this world for many beliefs."

And: "I am right and you are right even if we disagree." We are all "right" as long as we are comfortable with what we believe and our beliefs do not hurt ourselves or others. Instead of teaching others our beliefs and pressuring others to change, we would teach through example. Our daily lives would become a model of our beliefs.

This release of control over others allows us to transcend. "Pseudo-control," or control of things outside of ourselves, is replaced by "true" control, or control of things inside ourselves. Transcendence and acceptance are relaxing and calming. They allow us to achieve control over our bodies, our minds, and our spirits, which is the only control we really have.

Releasing people from control and allowing them the freedom to choose helps them achieve a type of redemption. They are freed from the captivity of distress, confusion, and guilt that occurs when beliefs are forced on them.

Healthy Christianity provides the means by which everyone can define personal values and belief systems. It becomes permissible to ask ourselves: "What do I really believe apart from what I have been told?" This type of Christianity offers exposure to and the choice of new ideas. This may mean that first we have to abandon the old toxic ideas that have bothered us.

A therapist friend occasionally invites a few of her patients to a seminar she holds out in the country. She gives each person a bucket. They spend some time wandering through the woods picking up stones until their buckets are full. Once they reach the river banks, she has them meditate on their past conditioning. They then decide what burden or piece of old "psychological baggage" each stone represents. They name each rock, such as, "this is my fear of being lazy"... "my distrust of others," and so on. They then toss the stone forcefully into the river, symbolically ridding themselves of the harmful beliefs they have carried for years.

To become healthy, Christians must discard old toxic beliefs and practices. Our therapist friend tells us that this is a meaningful experience for her patients. They symbolically "cast off" their problems and go away feeling free and relieved of guilt and fears. We feel it could work the same way for Christianity.

Once the toxic beliefs are addressed, we must reinforce our healthy beliefs. People, especially children, tend to trust adults in authority, like parents and religious authorities. We carry the belief system that was taught us, even when it does not work for us. When our values mature and we trust ourselves, we must ask, "What do I really think?" When we compare our beliefs with those of the church we attend, which of the two make more sense, which are more practical, which seem healthier? In most cases, it's okay to trust our own judgment. Below is an exercise which may be difficult and may take time, but it could help you to clarify your beliefs.

VALUES CLARIFICATION EXERCISE

If no one else cared how I felt about this, what do I believe about these questions:

- What do I believe God is really like (versus what I have been taught)?
- What acts do I believe are really wrong (versus what I have been taught)?
- What do I believe happens to us after death?
- What do I need and/or wish to get out of my religious and spiritual experiences?
- What am I currently receiving emotionally from my spiritual experiences? (Both positive and negative.)
- How should I respond to those who do not share my beliefs?
- How should I respond to those who try to convert me to their beliefs?
- What is my responsibility to others spiritually?
- What does it mean to me to minister to others spiritually?

Some believe that the universe is random and coincidental, that a certain amount of life is under our control and a certain amount is probabilistic. They feel that by taking action you can take control and make things happen that you want to happen. Some believe that we experience heaven and hell here on earth. Some believe that we are reincarnated to learn new lessons in each lifetime. All these beliefs are acceptable and can be consistent with a Healthy Christian Model which focuses on love, acceptance, and helping others rather than on rigid rules, beliefs, and salvation. Most of us want to believe there is purpose in life. But there can be many alternate ways of viewing that purpose.

Healthy Christianity cuts the rules down to the basics: Don't hurt others, do unto others as you would have them do unto you, respect others. A sign we see posted at a nearby business points out the level of the ridiculous to which our society has risen. It reads: "50,000 laws support Ten Commandments!" If we were raised as children with trust and acceptance and responsibility, most of us would not require rigid rules. If we taught love and problem-solving to our children instead of maintaining a complex rule system, they would learn to develop good judgment.

It is essential that we feel comfortable with our own beliefs and know that those beliefs are ours and not ones that have been forced on us by others. It is crucial that we allow others the same respect.

STRONG ENOUGH TO BEND

One woman told us about her father's decision to leave Christianity. He found the doctrines too harsh and punishing and he didn't want his young children exposed. His decision to leave a church with abusive doctrine was healthy and demonstrated his flexibility.

Did he really have to leave Christianity? Probably. The Christianity of previous generations has been relatively unrelenting. Recently, however, healthier movements and attitudes are evolving within Christianity. People know more now. They are more sophisticated about what is hurtful and abusive. They are beginning to understand they have choices and they are developing the courage to make decisions for themselves.

In a Healthy Christian Model, individuals and churches make changes in doctrines and in practices when the old rules cease to work. Nothing is "written in stone." As our culture matures and becomes more sophisticated about mental health, new methods replace old, ineffective ones.

Some will say that changing Christian doctrine indicates weakness and an inability to withstand pressure. We disagree. Like the sapling that bends in the wind and survives the storm, beliefs can be stronger because of their flexibility and because of a willingness to change in healthy ways.

As therapists, we know that secure people are able to be flexible. They deal with change and feel comfortable with it. When conditions change, they approach the situations pragmatically with interest and curiosity. Healthy people and healthy organizations are sensitive to change and welcome it as the natural condition of our world. When sensitive Christians sense the need for change, they alter their beliefs to deal with new information. They know that beliefs can flow and evolve, that perpetually changing belief systems are healthy and rigid ones become stale and ineffective. They have no need to block out information in order to maintain rigid beliefs.

What will this mean in practice? It means that problems and differing points of view will have to be worked out or respected. It means people will disagree. It means people will be expanding their beliefs to allow conditions they themselves feel uncomfortable with. It means people will face the unknown, experience fear initially, and then trust.

Our earth evolves, animals evolve, humans evolve, knowledge evolves. How can beliefs stay constant and thrive? It is only through fear of change and the unknown that rigidity survives. Humans have feared their own sexuality for centuries. Now we are beginning to understand our sexual nature and yet our fearful beliefs of sexuality preclude the use of that knowledge in sexual education. Belief systems must evolve with knowledge in order to remain vital and effective.

Christianity, if it is to be flexible and useful, must evolve in its beliefs to realistically handle issues like alternative lifestyles, extramarital and premarital sex, homosexuality, abortion, and women in roles of authority. As we have previously mentioned, some isolated churches are welcoming gays and working on a modern sexual perspective to deal with these real issues in a realistic and healthy manner. These groups have made successful transitions which will enable them not only to survive in this modern world, but to help set direction in a culture which is spiritually wandering.

THE DIVINITY WITHIN: TAKING CONTROL

Divine intervention is only possible when we draw on the power within ourselves. In a Healthy Christianity, God does not intervene directly and magically in the lives of humanity. Instead, our beliefs of God bring meaning and hope so that we may take control of our lives and act in our own best interests and in the interest of others.

Likewise, Satan does not intervene directly. Rather, Satan or evil is a choice that individuals make when they act in their own selfish interests with no consideration of the harm they do to others or when they act to intentionally harm others. In other words, the devil didn't make you do it, YOU chose to do it.

When we do not take responsibility for our behavior, when we feel out of control, or when we feel confused about what is the right decision, it becomes easy to place responsibility on beings supposedly more powerful than ourselves. We often fear that we will make poor decisions, that we will not do the right thing. Then we may resort to the idea that entities outside of ourselves are better able to make decisions about our lives than we are. The fear of not having complete control allows us to interpret certain aspects of our lives as being controlled by someone or something else.

A rape victim confided in Melody that she couldn't hold the rapist responsible for his crime because she truly believed that Satan was in control of him. She had no one to blame. So, she blamed her employer for not providing enough protection for her and she blamed herself for being sexually assaulted. And, ultimately, she decided that God had caused her to be raped so she could learn some important, but vague, lesson.

It is not likely that evil spirits possess us or that God saves us or teaches us through purposeful trauma. It is not likely that our prayers are magically answered by God or blocked by evil spirits. What is more likely is that we are able in many instances to make our desires come true if we are able to access that power in ourselves. And while we are frequently affected by circumstances which are beyond our control, usually we can transcend or we have options and choices.

Often, situations are beyond our control. Such is the nature of life, to be unpredictable. When things are out of our control, it is then that we learn to accept the things we cannot change and learn true wisdom. We can learn to be happy in spite of our misfortunes and to go on with our lives, or we can learn to satisfy ourselves with responsible choices.

SALVATION OR ACTION

We cannot change others.	We *can* change ourselves.
We cannot prevent disasters.	We *can* take precautions.
We cannot control time (i.e. aging, death).	We *can* use time to act.
We cannot control events.	We *can* control how we act and what we do.
We cannot control some bodily processes and some disease.	We *can* learn behaviors and follow lifestyles which benefit our health.
We will not escape death.	We *can* live with power and grace.

One elderly woman who had been ill for a lengthy period mailed a hefty sum to a TV evangelist asking that God heal her. She became much sicker and eventually sued him. His response? "God didn't heal her. Blame Him. Don't blame me."

We must not give up control of our lives to others, whether they be religious leaders or organizations, or intangible, spiritual beings. We must not wait for magical intervention. We do not need to be saved. We can save ourselves by accessing the power within ourselves. Part of remaining emotionally healthy is taking control of our lives in such a way that we make our own decisions and take action based on rational thought, sound judgment, and good information.

INTEGRITY OF THE BELIEVER: TAKING RESPONSIBILITY

In Healthy Christianity it is permissible to alter your beliefs, to change them so that you feel comfortable with them. And while it is okay to build your belief system and to practice whatever beliefs you choose, the caveat is this: We must take the consequences of our actions. Therefore, if we hurt others, we must be willing to make amends.

There is no need for threat of Hell or damnation; there is no need for punishment or rejection in the Healthy Christian Model. Vague threats or intangible punishments aren't nearly as powerful in shaping behavior as when a person suffers natural consequences. Individuals can learn to accept responsibility for themselves and their behavior.

Instead of teaching fear and guilt, hell and damnation, healthy Christians could teach good judgment. People would never be sacrificed for rules. They would be taught how to think about what they do and anticipate the consequences of their actions. They would learn to trust themselves and to rectify situations where they have caused others pain.

Making amends requires adaptations built on flexibility. When we hurt others we must first admit to our own error and then work to make changes. Ultimately, we will be able to help others to do so.

RITES OF TRANQUILLITY

Healthy Christianity includes a philosophy of spiritual release. As long as we store anger, we create pain and anxiety in ourselves and we focus on our bad feelings toward others. Letting go of anger is hard. It seems a lot easier to stay mad and to hold a grudge. After all, that person shouldn't have hurt you. You feel you were right and the other was wrong.

When asked to let go of their long-held anger, most people reveal their strong misconceptions. "If I let go of the anger, doesn't it make what they (the abuser) did okay?" "Aren't they getting away with it if I stop being angry?" The answer is "NO!" It doesn't make it okay that someone hurt someone else or used them. It is never okay when one human being hurts another human being. Letting go of anger does not absolve anyone of an injury to another. It doesn't even have anything to do with the "abuser," it only has to do with the one who suffers from holding the anger. Releasing negative emotions is something you do for yourself. You let the pain and the anger go. How to do this? Tracy describes how she let go of a lifetime of anger toward her parent:

> My mom drank, and she drank a lot. By the time I was 12, my father divorced her for her drinking and she was out at the bars every night while I stayed home with three younger brothers. I was always afraid, afraid that something would happen and I wouldn't know what to do. I played mother to them, disciplined them, fed them. Until I left home at 18, I felt I had primary responsibility for raising them. My childhood was gone with few good memories.
>
> I married while in college and immediately dropped out after becoming pregnant. I was angry at my mom, furious that I had missed my teenage years and that my brothers had now become drug abusers and one, a drug dealer. I felt that I had somehow failed at raising them and that mom was to blame for my guilt. I seethed with anger.
>
> In my early thirties, after my divorce, I went back to school to get my degree. I saw a therapist for treatment of serious stress-related emotional distress. My anger at mom kept coming up, over and over, draining me. Finally, my therapist suggested, "Maybe you should just give up the anger toward your mother." "How do I do that?" I demanded, somewhat irritated. "You just let it go," he said.

Baffled, I forgot the whole thing. Years later, driving home from school late at night, I thought about my young teenagers home by themselves several evenings a week. I felt guilty and suddenly thought of my mom and how it felt to be without a mother as a child. I cried when it suddenly hit me that she had been coping with her pain the only way she knew, by drinking, just like I was doing by overworking. I sobbed all the way home and forgave her completely. I finally understood that she had done the best she could at the time.

Often, it is necessary that we forgive in order to let go of anger. But forgiveness is not always possible. We have talked with families who will never be able to forgive a murderer for taking their child's life. This is completely understandable. And how do you forgive someone who continues to hurt or kill people? It would be unrealistic to expect people to "forgive" under such conditions. The important thing is that they are able to make peace with themselves, that they release the cancerous emotions inside themselves that eat away at their ability to feel joy and love. Holding anger can only injure the one who holds it.

Letting go of anger sets the stage for inner tranquillity and peace. Forgiveness is spiritual. It relaxes, it calms, it soothes. It separates us from the pettiness and pain of grudges and revenge. It frees us to transcend.

GOD OF THE INNER TEMPLE

God is love. What a concept! Not...God is love, but sometimes God becomes angry and punishes those who disobey Him. Not...God is love, but sometimes He allows bad things to happen for His own mysterious reasons. But...GOD IS LOVE. PERIOD. The existence of a Higher Power that provides refuge and support and comfort for the weary and the fearful will come as a pleasant surprise to many who are weary of the fear and guilt promoted by the Abusive

Christians. It's difficult to continue to fear when one truly embraces the concept of the inner God whose sole basis is love.

Unfortunately, this concept is just too hard for some people to accept. Maybe it is too simple, too contrary to our nature. For some reason, they find it easier to believe in a punishing and angry God who seeks revenge on this world of vulnerable sinners. The Abusive Christian Model flourishes on the concept of a threatening, revengeful deity.

Knowing that God is a loving God allows us to relax and feel free to explore ourselves and our beliefs and our creative abilities. It allows us to accept others regardless of differences and project love ourselves. The idea of a punishing God is so restrictive and fearsome that often creative people must reject the whole concept of God in order to experience comfort in their lives. They sometimes do not realize they have the choice of what kind of god they worship.

God exists in each of us. We don't have to go to church to find God. But if we are in church, God may be found in church. Not the building. Not the structure. We have only to recognize the deity in us all. And knowing that God exists within us makes it natural for us to look inside ourselves for answers. It also becomes natural to ask others for help since God exists within them. In a Healthy Christian Model, Christians work in the image of a God who projects tolerance and ultimate caring for humanity.

THE CHRIST OF DELIVERY

We all realize that the world is full of those who are less fortunate than we are. Often, we forget these unfortunate people in our zeal to convert the rest of the world to our beliefs. Healthy Christianity emphasizes the channeling of our spiritual and physical energies to the relief of suffering in the world. We must help others who are in pain, who are in need, who are hungry, cold or frightened.

Our culture needs to heal. Women and people of color face discrimination on our streets and in our churches. There are uncounted numbers of hungry, alcoholics, and addicts in our cities. We need to reach out to them, invite them into our churches, and treat them as brothers and sisters.

Our energies both as individuals and as groups must be focused on the positive goal of reaching out. In this way, we each become the Christ, the special children of God. We each become the possessor and the implementer of a divine purpose.

THE ILLUSIVE GREAT TRUTH

Most of us are searching for "the truth," the answers in life. Even though various Christian groups and individuals may profess to know the truth, no one person, no one group, no single belief system has exclusive knowledge of *Truth*. If there is a God, certainly no human mortal could comprehend the vastness and complexity of the infinite.

Think, instead, that we all have pieces of that truth. Pieces that when combined will give us direction and meaning. It is in the joining together and the acceptance of one another that we find a Great Truth.

We see a similar phenomenon in psychological training. We study all the theories about why people develop mental problems, choose a theory we like, and then go out into the world, armed with this wonderful knowledge, to single-handedly stamp out mental illness. The problem arises when, as a therapist, we find that one theory fits a certain set of emotional problems, another theory fits a whole different set of problems, and another fits yet another set of problems.

At some point, a revelation occurs when we realize that none of the theories we learned was the truth. Rather, they each had a portion of the truth and it is now up to us to put them together so we can help people. As a result, therapists who start out with a single theory of behavior usually end up using everything they learned. They become "eclectic" in their orientation. And it works, because no one theory can explain everything.

Christianity is no different. No two denominations agree, no two individual churches agree. No religions agree. So this one knows the truth and the others do not? How does that work? Maybe, just maybe, they each have their own perspective. Your "truth" is simply what is truth for you, and my "truth" is my perspective. Maybe, in the joining together we will discover that the Great Truth is unity.

Religions often label individuals outside the group in a divisive way. Labels such as "sinners," "the lost," "infidel," divide and injure people. Individuals may hold different beliefs, but that does not automatically mean they should be labeled "wrong" or immoral or damned. It is never helpful to participate in the "wrong"ing of another individual.

Healthy Christianity recognizes that no one has the Truth. There are no special prophets of "the truth," we all share the truth and most of the time the Truth exists in the perception of the individual's belief. Unity replaces divisiveness, respect replaces rejection.

THE GREAT CHALLENGE: RECTIFICATION

We have been writing about abusive elements found within Christianity. We do not want to rule out conventional Christian churches as a legitimate means by which to meet your spiritual needs. Healthy Christianity could be implemented in any church. It is now the job and the responsibility of the church to make amends by discarding the harmful and reinforcing the constructive.

But what happens when churches will not change? It is much easier to leave an organization than to help that organization change, but sometimes the easy way out is not the best way out for all involved.

Compare a church group to a family system. In many ways a church group becomes an extended family system. When we deal with sick and dysfunctional families, most of us realize it would be much easier to break up the family, to leave. However, if you do this, you lose the bounds, the support, the history, the nurturance, and all the very important values associated with the family. Breaking up the family also brings grief, loss, and injury.

We are not saying, never leave your family or never leave your church. You may need to leave in certain situations, but first encourage growth and change; bring love and concern. The same is true with your church family. Some churches will never change, but there are many individuals who, aware of the abuse that does take place, will want to try to end it.

A PLAN FOR CHANGE

Even liberal churches can wield subtle punishment toward those who disagree with their ideas. It may be as subtle as political posturing or as overt as rejection or eviction. If you feel you must change your existing system and remain in it, here are some guidelines to help you influence change in your church. Remember, churches are made up of people. People with strong ideas and feelings.

First and foremost, show rather than tell. Provide a model of acceptance, flexibility, and good will. Your own positive behavior is the most powerful teacher. Be open in your refusal to punish and reject others who have different beliefs or who have "sinned." Be the first to reach out to those in need. Guide others through your actions. Remember, all the charitable words in the world kneel in shame before one charitable act.

Be vocal about your disagreement. If you remain silent in the face of abusive behavior, that silence may be taken as agreement. You may want to bounce your ideas off others who may share your concern. Always present your ideas in a caring and kind manner. You cannot facilitate change or stop abuse by being negative and abusive yourself.

Organize others who agree with the spirit of acceptance and love. Are they committed to changing the system? One person may be seen as a complainer while several "complainers" tend to give credence to the complaint as being a real problem. Challenge abuse from the position of power you have as a group. There will be many others who will want to support a dissenting group when they might be reluctant to speak out individually.

State your objections and objectives clearly. When you are complaining about a problem or an abusive practice, make certain that you also offer a healthy solution or strategy. Your ideas and alternatives should be well prepared. You may want to take this book and others that describe abusive practices with you. You will want to anticipate traditional "counter-arguments" to your position and be ready for them. The people in your group must clearly understand the issues and the alternatives. Always confront with love and understanding. You do not want to fall into rigid, angry, and punishing approaches. After all, that is part of what you are trying to change.

Chuck, a youth minister at a small Church of Christ, was a kind young man, and members of the church learned to respect him and listen to his ideas. When he began to speak against some of the punishing practices in the church, everyone was surprised. Wasn't it their duty to condemn sinners? He disagreed strongly but gently. He persisted in speaking out when members and clergy spoke of hell and damnation. Many members became fearful. Wouldn't kids fall into sin if they weren't afraid of damnation? He disagreed and, because he believed in them, the kids rarely disappointed him. Using strong positive attitudes of love, attention, and reward, he turned around the attitude of the congregation.

It can be done. With love.

Ultimately, you must be willing to leave. If it becomes apparent that no change is to be forthcoming, then be willing to leave the organization as a group or by yourself. Your group should discuss and plan for this. You can shop around for groups which have broken off because of dissatisfaction with abusive doctrine. We know of at least one such Church of Christ which now focuses on the positives of spirituality and the unity of family and fellowship. Leaving your church may be difficult to do, but staying may condone and enable the abuse to continue. Remember, there are other denominations with less punitive and toxic beliefs. Many times, there is a great variation of practices within the same denomination.

What happens to those who leave their churches because nothing worked to change the system? We know that some do find other churches willing to worship with love and support. The rest discover that there is an infinity of ways to be spiritual.

CHAPTER 10

HEALTHY SPIRITUALITY
They Shall Mount Up
With Wings as Eagles

"And after the earthquake a fire;
but the Lord was not in the fire:
and after the fire
a still small voice."

I KINGS 19: 12

Spiritual needs do not have to want for a church or a worship situation. Some people meet their spiritual needs in church and some do not. Some meet spiritual needs in other ways, yet still want to attend church on a regular basis for education, social, and other reasons. The spiritual is an essential part of being human and, as such, spiritual needs may refuse to be denied.

People who think they have neglected their spiritual needs may actually be fulfilling them in subtle ways. We will explore some of the alternative methods (alternatives to organized religion) of achieving spirituality. There are many choices. Use your creativity and refer to Chapter 9 if you have questions about what a healthy belief system looks and feels like.

NEW RELIGIOUS PHILOSOPHIES

Some people find that Eastern and New Age ideas meet their spiritual needs very well. However, we must caution that some of these religious organizations can be destructive. It is not that the basic philosophy is toxic or abusive, but some organizations have been used in a destructive manner by individuals seeking power and wealth. Therefore, we recommend prudence when participating in Eastern religions. If you keep up with the news, you know of the fleets of Rolls Royce automobiles belonging to one Eastern guru. At times, even a healthy situation and a healthy philosophy can be manipulated by a religious leader into an unhealthy, toxic situation, especially when that leader uses spirituality as another form of addiction. Any religion can be used by an individual as an addictive process. There are people "addicted to" obsessions like work, spending money, chemicals, gambling, sports, sex, exercise, television, and even religion.

Signs of addiction are:

1. Spending a great deal of time in religious activity; for example, meditation, meetings, and religious activities.

2. Increased isolation from family and friends.

3. A change in behavior of the individual. At home less, irritable, verbally abusive.

4. A powerful resistance to spending less time in the religious activity and a denial that the activity is causing any problems.

5. A history of past addictions to any behavior listed above.

6. Resistance to seeking help.

An example of this is Carl, who had a history of alcoholism. He had been married for 20 years and had two children. Although he had stopped drinking, he had not involved himself in therapy or a 12-step program to cope with the psychological and family problems caused by the addiction. He became involved in a New Age religion and began to spend long periods of time in meditation. He became divided and isolated from his family. He became verbally and physically abusive, and his ability to think and rationally solve problems was dramatically reduced. As could be expected, his wife was devastated.

He remained in denial about his problems and refused treatment. As a result of his addiction, his family split up and he became a stranger to his wife and children. Spirituality is not a cure for emotional problems. In fact, when it becomes an addictive process, spirituality becomes a problem.

The caveat is to be very careful in your pursuit of Eastern religions. First, you can be used to make some guru rich. Second, these religions lend themselves to addictive processes. However, Eastern-type religions can be used in a way to meet spiritual needs in a healthy manner. Take the case of Linda, a healthy mental health care professional, who espouses a belief which she describes as a combination of spiritualism, Buddhism, and reincarnation. Linda has had several deaths in her family and has found nurturance and support from her belief system. She is unmarried, lost her fiance last year to cancer, and has only a married brother left in her family, but she functions well both personally and professionally. She credits her religion and her spirituality for this. She maintains balance, shows no destructive effects, and feels a powerful and positive force in her life.

> My belief is a total source of strength. I allow things to run according to Divine Will, even bad things, because there are lessons to be learned. If you think of God as a Divine intelligence, then why should I try to run my own show when there's someone so much smarter. I don't let God do everything for me, I do all the work, but He guides me in the right direction.
>
> When you have big-time forgiveness issues, you can't forgive without spiritual intervention. How can you forgive someone who has done something really abominable without spirituality? Your ego wants to punish and get back at them. The only way to forgive

is to be spiritual and to recognize that one is not a victim and there is a plan in the universe. The focus on spirituality helps one to count one's blessings instead of the negative. It's an outward focus instead of inward.

I believe that we're not just here for one single time. We have to achieve mastery during our time on earth and stop being victims. How do you get the strength to be a master? You meditate, you pray, and you affirm it. Things go well in my life. I don't bring to myself punishing relationships. I don't make so many mistakes.

AMERICAN INDIAN RELIGION

While it is clear that most religions have some aspects of fear, magical thinking, and punishment which we feel are counterspiritual, some certainly appear healthier than others. The American Indian beliefs have recently begun to resurface as an alternative to more conventional religion. These belief systems are powerfully spiritual while managing to avoid many of the pitfalls to which Christianity has succumbed.

Indian spiritual ceremony may involve the use of dance, meditation, pipe smoking, vision quests, and sweat lodges. The philosophy is usually a simple one which involves a focus on healthy, global unity, and a pro-environmental tradition. In their simple ceremonies they seek to find a connectedness that has been lost in the last century.

Balance is the key here. The even number four represents power in terms of four directions, elements, races, etc. To be healthy and at ease one must have all four aspects in balance. Those who place too much emphasis on any one aspect are out of balance.

Spiritual beliefs as such can be very intense. The vision quest involves fasting in a secluded place while searching for the direction life will take. Vision quest searchers may go alone to a secluded woods or hilltop and wait quietly as they focus on their purpose. The sweat lodge is used to help achieve purification. The door to the lodge is made to face east toward the morning star and rising sun. Rocks in the center of the lodge are heated glowing red and cold water is poured over them to create a cleansing steam. Bathed in steam, the participants then offer songs and prayers to the spiritual qualities represented by the four directions and the creatures of the earth.

Thomas, a book distributor, practices the Lakota Sioux Indian philosophy of Chief Black Cloud. In it the Medicine Wheel is a symbolic representation of the Divine.

"It acts as a bridge to access dimensions of being that I can't access through rational mind. It explains humankind's relationship to everything. The truth exists in the understanding that everything is divine. There is no separation of creation and creator. Our creator is in every thing. Worshiping a sunset, therefore, is not idol worship, it is participation in the creation. In this way, you awaken in your own divinity, which makes you strong and loving and gives you power to do good."

As we have discussed, ritual in itself is not necessarily harmful; rather it is the purpose that the ritual fulfills that can be devastating. The American Indian philosophy, while full of ritual, appears in many ways to be a healthy and fulfilling path.

PRIMITIVE PHILOSOPHIES

Kahuna is a ancient Polynesian philosophy currently surfacing among some spiritual seekers in this country. Sharon Rush, a psychotherapist, describes it as a way of life rather than a religion. Since Kahuna has no religious dogma, it doesn't conflict with any religion, including Christianity. Rather than setting up rules and controls, it simply redefines the way one perceives the world. There are seven basic principles designed to promote harmony :

1. The world is what you think it is.
2. There are no limits.
3. Energy flows where attention goes.
4. Now is the moment of focus.
5. To love is to be happy with.
6. All power comes from within.
7. Effectiveness is the measure of truth.

Sharon works with a group of individuals who attempt to use this plan in their lives. She feels that anyone who lives in accordance with these ideas will experience healthy changes in the way they live.

The Kahuna way is to go through the world as an adventure. You will be alert and aware. You will see events as an invitation to learn and experience new things. Therefore, you have fun and take things less seriously. The old way, the unhealthy way, is to go through the world as a warrior, alert to danger, defensive and wasting energy on learning to defend yourself.

There is no separation between you and others. Of course, we still have our boundaries, but only those which are effective. A boundary that separates me from the oneness of the universe is not effective because it causes me to treat others differently from myself. When I am part of the whole, it is impossible for me to see my sisters and brothers as the enemy.

All pain and all illness comes from disharmony. If I have pain then I can look at what beliefs or attitudes I keep doing that are out of harmony. These can be personal beliefs or attitudes about others or about the environment.

We have rituals of sharing. When we meet once a week we share food and water. This refers back to the principle of "there are no limits." If you walk into my house, even as a stranger I am obligated to give you food and water because we are a part of the whole. Following these beliefs has made me more accepting and loving, more at peace, more energized, more spontaneous, more curious. It has helped me to conquer my inner pain.

NATURE

Seeking out nature is another way to get into touch with your spirituality. Although many people are probably not aware of it, activities which involve earth, environment, plants, animals, gardening, and family can be spiritually fulfilling. Nature helps one get in touch with the wholeness of life and brings meaning and peace.

So many of our patients have found peace in landscaping and gardening. They often talk of the peacefulness and fulfillment they achieve by placing their fingers in the earth and by watching nature take over in the growth process. Enjoying a beautiful sunset or sunrise, rejoicing in the delicate beauty of an intricately patterned butterfly or flower, relaxing in the warmth of a spring day, deep breathing the invigorating salt air of the seashore, absorbing the rich green of the forest, all these enhance and fulfill the spiritual part of our natures.

In fact, the loss of contact with nature and the earth's processes may be part of what makes winter so depressing for some. When they move inside for the winter, they fail to substitute another means for maintaining spirituality. Nina talks about how she achieves spirituality through her experience with nature since the church has no longer accepted her:

> My mother taught me both spirituality and religion. I don't know if she knows it, and I'm quite sure I didn't know it until I was a grown woman with children. You see, my mother was and is a religious and spiritual person. I happen to be the youngest of three girls, whom my mother was raising as a single parent. As a child, every Sunday morning we got up and dressed for Sunday school, every evening we went to training union, every Wednesday we went to GA's. This gave me a very solid Southern Baptist background.
>
> However, there were other times that were sacred and seemed special. From my perspective they

seemed more sacred than the days we attended church. These times are many in number, but they involved one common thread. Communing. Being one with your surroundings. Breathing in the air, watching, hearing, seeing pretty things you don't see normally, for example, a wildflower, a lovely colored bird, or butterfly.

Another specific time was when mother would take us to the "country." I thought these ventures were mainly to teach my oldest sister to drive. However, I knew we would wind up at Cope Cemetery. Mother would let us open the big gate and then we got to ride on the hood while she drove to where her father was buried. There were trees and cows and all sorts of stuff we didn't have in the city, so basically the kids went off and explored. It seemed mother was there for one reason. She drew strength from this spot to get through some of the tough, tough problems of being the single parent of three, plus a million other problems.

When I got older I asked her about my observations. She said she just went there to talk with her father. When she was young they used to just sit and talk and she would go to the "country" to just talk and listen. I recall looking at her from a distance and seeing her standing by his grave site. She was sometimes looking at the grave, sometimes looking around at the birds, her hands clasped behind her back. She was simply taking it all in. Looking as I picture the old shaman when he visits the other powers from worlds past and worlds beyond. The pose was one I wish I had a picture of, yet it was too sacred to flaunt by taking a picture of it. The picture remains in my mind. The one thing my mother never was when we left Cope Cemetery was sad. She honestly seemed to have left some burden there or perhaps obtained some renewed strength. Perhaps it was some of both.

As a child, I perceived us on a limited or no budget financial structure. We always went camping. We didn't have a tent, but we had four old Army cots, an old metal ice chest, and a Coleman stove. What more could you need? I look back now and realize it was perfect. The bologna and pork and beans made it seem a treat. Of course, as a young child I got bored on these trips. As I grew older and my sisters grew up and left home we could have afforded much better trips. Those still remained the best. Dangling your feet in a cold, clear stream. Feeding the chipmunks the bacon grease from your morning breakfast. Sitting watching the wind in the trees. Really beginning to notice that it wasn't mother saying so, but there really was a difference in how the air smelled, how your food tasted, how sensitive your ears became, and what beautiful things there were to hear.

Well, I've since remarried and now have two sons. We camp. When possible we camp often. When that's not possible, we visit our local nature center. When neither of those are possible, we all four find ourselves tense, irritable, and somehow needing a nature "fix." As our children were growing up I realized, having quit church, there was a void. I didn't miss church but I sure missed nurturing my spirituality. So we camp.

Going to the woods can make everything okay. I'm not quite sure I understand, perhaps it really doesn't matter. What I do know is the same problems exist when I get home as existed when I left. I simply have a renewed ability to deal with them.

To sit around a camp fire and think that Indians used to sit around their ceremonial fire and thank the deer spirits for deer they had for dinner is an exhilarating experience for me. For some, it's the sound of the sea. Still for others, it's the city park or other nature facility. Nothing brings about a cleansing or more awe-inspiring insight than that nature freely gives. Unconditionally.

When I speak of "nature" I mean many things. I speak of a oneness we all share. We are all part of this living thing we call earth. It is ours because we are it. What concerns me now is our abuse of the earth. If we continue to abuse ourselves and our earth, we will lose our spirituality.

Find a place where trucks and cars can't be heard if possible. A place where you can hear your nature-made noises instead of man-made noises. Take your old clothes, some simple food stuffs like bologna, pork and beans, water and whatever you want for breakfast. Go off the beaten path and find your own sanctuary. Look at the trees around you and notice how many different kinds there are. How oddly shaped their leaves are, yet how intricately the veins, branches, trunks, even bark are made. How very precisely everything works for its continuing existence. What kinds of tundra are around you? How many birds can you hear? What about insects? Sunrise? It's endless. It is freely given.

Now sit back and don't view each of these as a separate entity. View these as a whole. A whole that functions because it is a whole. Every time you commune, your spirituality will grow. I don't believe it is automatic. I achieve spirituality when a cardinal risks his life by letting me get close and then blessing me with the beauty of his song. Not for just a moment, but for several minutes. When a deer wanders into camp to bless you with its beauty and knowledge of all critters. Sort of viewing you as a brother just as you should view it. Spiritually you are one with this world.

I get the same effect from gardening. There is something pleasurable about a handful of good dirt. It has a feel that tells you it is good; however, I find it hard to describe the feel of good dirt from a spiritual avenue. That comes from my chest and a knowing in my mind.

These things my mother taught me long ago. I like them. It means I'm valued. I'm valued because I am one part of our earth, nature, universe. I do not make it work or not work. It works because we are all here and we are all a part of this whole. To this extent, spirituality is as close as your back door.

I can remember feeling the euphoria of being "saved" several times before I actually was baptized. I was just too frightened to walk down the aisle in front of all those people. When I finally did walk down front it was euphoria. So nice, I did it several times after that. I still get my euphoria, I've just found that I can have it daily by nurturing my own spirituality. There is euphoria in a beautiful sunset, a full moon, or even a thunder storm. I don't have to feel guilty about these feelings, either. I don't have to worry if I've done it too many times. I can do it time after time and it gets better and better.

Animals are also an important part of this picture. The miracle of birth in beasts can be just as spiritual as in humans. The lovely simplicity of these beautiful creatures can help us separate from everyday pettiness and competition for money and power. The love they give is unconditional and all they ask is attention and their basic needs met.

THE PHYSICAL UNIVERSE

Christians seem to constantly fight among themselves over one issue or another. And frequently the issues seem to be so trivial and petty. Common sense doesn't go very far where belief is concerned. Tolerance is not a virtue often seen. It is rather easy to lose respect for Christian religion as it is practiced currently. There is very little, if any, reverence and no awe for the beliefs and practices one finds in today's Christian world.

Not so with astronomy and quantum physics. Those areas of science deal with "godlike" aspects of nature. Aspects of nature that invoke awe and a feeling of reverence. The concepts of Albert Einstein challenge and push one's perceptual frame of reference. You must expand the old Newtonian logic of cause and effect, that works well day-to-day, in order to assimilate the new data. For example, nothing can go faster than the speed of light, according to Einstein. That is a set limit. At the speed of light, time stops. The same holds true around massive stars, such as "black holes," where time stops. What does that mean? How can one think of time stopping? What is time anyway? The mystery of the universe.

Another observation made in physics is that light always reaches us at the same speed, regardless if the source is moving away or moving toward us at speeds approaching the speed of light. Our old logic says that cannot be, but the statement is accurate.

We must deal with concepts and ideas in physics which defy our logic. Time stopping. Speed relative to the observer and not the source, the bizarre behavior of light. Nature, or perhaps God, is complex and beautiful, pushing the limits of human understanding and, at times, beyond human understanding.

Quantum physics advances ideas and concepts even more bizarre and compelling. Particles that exist and do not exist. Or they exist if you look for them, as if they understand your act of looking. Virtual particles that behave as if they were waves and as if they were particles, and they are both. Either logic does not work on the quantum level. Strange particle waves that seem to know when you are looking at them.

The bizarre beauty of the universe. More complex than we *can* conceptualize. Any "god" would have to be that complex, or more so. Ideas that are magnificent and stretch the concepts of human understanding. Powers, distances, and behavior of elementary particles that elicit awe. The disciplines of astronomy and quantum physics can inspire and move man to think in terms of ultimates and ask questions such as: What is the nature of matter and time?

Sadly, in comparison, the God of conservative Christianity seems petty and narcissistic. The motivation is out of fear of punishment and obsessive trivial ethics. Perhaps some people can find their god in the ideas and concepts of astronomy and quantum physics. The god of majesty and awe.

DAILY MEDITATION AND RELAXATION TECHNIQUES

Meditation or visual imagery in moderation (30 to 60 minutes per day) can help achieve spiritual satisfaction. Rachel's first successful experience with visual imagery was guided by a friend she trusted so completely she was able to truly let go and achieve a spiritual high.

> Once in a state of relaxation, I mounted, in my mind, a small rocket which propelled me toward the moon and through the center of endless hoops of brilliantly flashing colored lights. Passing through hoop after breathtaking hoop left me feeling awed and reverent. I purposely extended this unbelievable experience even though my friend was calling me back to an aware state. I didn't want to leave the experience for a while and managed to ignore him and continue on my journey for a few more minutes. When I did return, I was totally rested and peaceful, feeling that I had transcended the petty realities of my day-to-day life to discover a separate dimension.

We have included a script (see Appendix Two) if you want some guidance in your meditation. If you like, record it in your own voice, very slowly, and play it for yourself on a regular basis. There are numerous meditations, visual imagery, and musical audio tapes on the market to enhance your relaxation and spiritual experience. You may wish to seek out your inner guide. We have heard this described in many terms—tapping one's imagination or creativity, reaching the subconscious mind, meeting one's spirit guide or guardian angel. Whatever you want to call it, it seems to work for many individuals. Practicing meditation is the first step, followed by the use of visual imagery. Before you attempt this, read the relaxation exercise in the appendix to get an idea of how to visualize an image.

STEPS TO MEETING YOUR INNER GUIDE

1. Place your body in a comfortable position.

2. Use a breathing exercise to begin to let go. Either count your breathing, slowly inhale 1,2,3, exhale 1,2,3 or just stop breathing and let your body take over with soft, slow, deep breaths.

3. Imagine yourself in a peaceful and beautiful setting. Imagine that you can see, smell, hear, and touch everything in that setting and do so in your imagination.

4. Call to your inner spirit or guide. Visualize it coming out to sit by you and comfort you. Ask questions about anything you need to know. Listen carefully to the answers.

5. Once you feel satisfied, bid your inner spirit farewell and begin to allow yourself to return slowly by stretching and opening your eyes and once more focusing on the things going on around you.

ARTS, MUSIC, WRITING

Many individuals express themselves spiritually in their creative efforts. The rest of us just work at it. Have you ever wondered how artists, musicians, and writers tolerate the financial disadvantages of their vocations? It makes sense once you realize that they are able to experience spirituality through their work. Luis, a musician, describes how he meets his spiritual needs through creating music.

> A musician attempts to promote a spiritual response in his listeners and then thrives on their response in a spiritual way. It allows me to experience an undefinable closeness to others when I know that they have heard my message. I cry when I put a beautiful song together, inspired by a power greater than me. It's hard to believe sometimes that something so beautiful could have come out of a human like me. It gives me a swollen feeling in my chest. When it happens like that, I thank that Power for sending it to me and expressing it through me.
>
> In everything else in life there are barriers, things I can't do or can't tolerate. But in my music, there are no barriers. Every time I play a new melody or a new chord structure, a whole new universe opens up to me, with no boundaries. Instead of confinement and the world pressing on me, it is releasing, letting go, pulling out or away from me. It can keep expanding eternally in that state. I can't keep from it. The pressure is reversed, the music pulls it out of you.

Even if you are not a creative person, not particularly good at any one thing, just participating in the enjoyment of others' creative expression can be therapeutic. Listening to certain types of music has been shown to actually affect physical response, reduce blood pressure, heart rate. We suspect that this is related to changes in the brain wave patterns. Beta waves (which are present when we solve problems and are actively involved in tasks) change to alpha-theta waves (which are most prevalent during meditation states and spiritual states).

CREATIVE SPIRITUALITY

Develop your own brand of spirituality! A fellow counselor once told us of a biker who, while in addictions treatment, only felt comfortable defining his Higher Power as his motorcycle. He apparently achieved feelings of peace, freedom, and comfort from cruising on his "hogg."

Another patient chose the ocean as his Higher Power. He was a rebellious teenager who just could not or would not accept the concept of the God that his parents attempted to force on him. But he was able to lose himself spiritually in thoughts of rolling waves while allowing himself to let his fears and concerns go. A competitive motorcyclist we know of feels closest to God only when "tucked into a 90 mph power slide."

Another friend, Ted, describes himself as a thrill seeker and his skydiving pursuits as a thrill seeker's path to spirituality. We feel the importance of reporting, but not recommending, these dangerous activities.

> I saw myself walking on air, felt invincible and powerful, separate from reality. The only time I felt truly peaceful and in control was when I was plummeting toward the earth, in free-fall, at 176 feet per second. It changed me from a meek and timid guy to a self-confident individual who could confront his fear. I knew the rules, that there were things I had to do to live through it. Some of my friends died. We were all dancing with death.
>
> I don't recommend it to anyone else, it was just my own way. Guys who jumped together were bonded in an unexplainable way. We had to count on each other not to do anything that would jeopardize anyone else during team exercises. We developed that trust that only comes with total dependence on another for survival.

12-STEP PROGRAMS

These are support groups aimed at various targets such as alcoholics, overeaters, codependents, narcotics abusers, marijuana abusers, depressives. Twelve-step programs are highly spiritual and in fact based on a releasing of oneself to peacefulness and letting go of control and anger. We highly recommend 12-step programs.

Open Alcoholics Anonymous meetings (open to anyone who wishes to attend) offer wonderful experiences. They can be incredibly uplifting, spiritually and emotionally enlightening, accepting and uniting in a very human way. The whole idea of recognizing ourselves as human, turning our pain over to a spirit stronger than ourselves, and asking help to overcome ourselves can be empowering and relaxing. Such 12-step programs have saved hundreds of thousands of individuals who needed acceptance rather than rejection for their problems.

We do not know of an AA group ever kicking anyone out for failing at their program. They *want* drinkers there, the idea being that eventually the unconditional acceptance and spiritual fulfillment will get through and build strength within the alcoholic. Unconditional acceptance—how incredibly simple and yet how out of reach for most of us.

The only problem we have with 12-step programs is that the use of the word "God" turns some people off, especially those who have been spiritually abused. We prefer the use of the phrase "Higher Power," which is entirely acceptable in these programs. We recently discovered that some new AA groups eliminate references to a spiritual being.

Earl reported that he had been concerned about his spiritual life for several years and, although he described himself as a Christian, had been experiencing a void that he didn't understand. He stumbled onto an answer only after he checked himself into a hospital for chemical dependency treatment and was forced to attend AA.

In AA I got a chance to start from the ground up searching for God. You can get rid of all the negative things you've been taught. You can ask others how they see God. You can get in touch with yourself. If a person is alcoholic and has hit spiritual bottom, they can start off new and, if you are sincere, it helps you spell out what God is. If I went from what I learned from churches, I would have thought He was judgmental. This way I can find out what He is to me rather than what others want Him to be. I think that we are spirits trying to accept that we're human. If you think of yourself as a spirit it puts you above the problems of life. It gives you closer contact with God.

Part of spirituality is saying "I don't know" and feeling good about it. I used to feel uncomfortable talking about spirituality because I couldn't feel good about not knowing. But recently, a friend asked me what happened to people who kill. Now, I don't believe in hell, so I told him "I don't know and that isn't useful to me spiritually, anyway." There's good and bad in all of us and what we seek we find. If we seek out God we will find the good in ourselves—the devil is just the bad side of ourselves. A person creates their own hell.

All these people in AA have feelings in common and when they talk it's like me listening to my inner self. The voice inside me becomes clearer. It's helped me not to feel inhibited about what I feel about my God. It's helped me to explore so that my beliefs become more concrete. I found also that I had a sense of humor and now I am more at ease and don't fear God any more because I've discovered that He has a sense of humor, too.

We practice the 12 steps in all our affairs to help understand how we are and who we are. If you are doing your steps right, you will practice your spiritually in all your affairs and you will get closer to your God.

I used to say AIDS was a godsend. I was so caught up in believing in black-and-white rules that I wouldn't accept the idea of homosexuality. Now my sponsor is gay. That's real growth for me.

AA helps you separate in healthy ways from the problems of others. If you're upset, that's your upset. When someone else is doing something, then that's their problem, not yours. If something goes wrong then it goes wrong, it's not a catastrophe. This helps you in your spirituality because there's not as many things getting in the way of it. One of my favorite stories is about a guy who waited three months for a van he really wanted. The first time he drove it to work, it started acting up, so all day he worried that it was something terribly wrong that would cost a fortune to fix. For a while, he let that van be his God.

The wheels turning in your head can drive you to drink. What I now do instead is hit my knees and pray for God to rid me of my thoughts. I fill my mind with Him and it helps me to get rid of the bondage of self. Self-pity can turn into depression and obsession. I know now that I drank to get rid of the feelings and thoughts. This is another way to deal with it.

EXERCISE AND PHYSICAL ACTIVITY

Exercise can be physical and spiritual. Runners and cyclists often talk about the peacefulness and spiritual fulfillment they achieve, as do those who practice Zen and yoga. Dean talks about the way he uses running and biking to meet spiritual needs.

Ever since I was a teenager I became conscious that there was something else out there—a God or however someone might see it. From that point in time, I have always related it to being by myself and being able to be very open with myself and very calm. The older I get, the more I feel that. I think that if I really want to let down all my defenses and open my mind up and talk to God, so to speak, that being by myself is a prerequisite, as is being outside.

Back when I was younger and started thinking about these things, we lived in Colorado. I could go out and walk into the mountains. I was surrounded by mountains, trees, animals. By myself, it's more one-on-one compared to sitting in a church with 200 other people. There's more of a closeness. Exercise gives me structure, a period of time that I'm outside, I'm by myself and I'm not engaged in anything else. Not working. For the time that I'm exercising, I can look around and notice what's around me more.

I don't know whether it's the endorphins or the fact that I'm not thinking about anything in particular. At times, my mind is clear. I'm very in tune with my own body and what's going on inside me. I've learned a lot about my own body and how it works. The biggest thing is how to relax. I usually have a hard time relaxing. I'm sweating like a pig, but I'm relaxed and comfortable. By the time I hit the driveway just out of the front door, I have already begun to let go.

There is no outside interference. The telephone isn't ringing and people aren't asking you to solve their problems, kids aren't yelling at you. You have a chance to feel more positive about things, time to think them out. You are able to be quiet and put all your thoughts into one thing. I usually come up with new solutions to my problems. And also you know you've done something positive.

I set a little goal—how many miles, how fast I'm going to run. I gauge myself to see if I'm hitting that mark, to see if I've gone beyond myself. It makes me feel good about myself, does a lot for my self-worth. Those times I realize that I can achieve more than I thought. If I set a goal of six miles instead of four and I do it, then it hangs over to the rest of the day. Then I can do other things, too. It motivates me. Exercise gives me the opportunity to set a goal and achieve where it's me and me alone that accomplishes it.

Sometimes it affects how I feel about my wife. Halfway through the run I feel that, gosh, I really want to see her. I've been out and I'm dumping everything that's been built up for the past day or two. It feels like you're cleansing yourself of trouble, bad feelings, anger. There's been times that I've been very angry at people and I have been able to release that while I was running. Anger and hostility are energy and you can focus on that energy while you're exercising. I've usually been able to get rid of it by opening up my mind so that I can see both sides of the story. Then I can understand.

If you really think about it there is something you can do. If you set a goal each time and achieve it, then it will become a habit. Then you find it hard to get through a day without it. And if that goes positively, then it has to overflow into daily life.

BIRTH AND CHILDREN

For many of us, a real sense of the spiritual reveals itself at the birth of our children. Most people feel this more intensely with the first birth, but others continue to re-experience the power of something "beyond self" with each new life we create. We talked to new parents, Al and Joy, eight months after the birth of their first baby.

Having children brings you a new kind of love and understanding and a little mystery. There is something more beyond yourself. It gives you a chance to start over, to experience with your child the things you missed. You have the chance to feel young again and to see things through your child's eyes. You can begin to grow beyond yourself.

You have the opportunity to experience unconditional love. When you walk into their room, their little faces light up just because it's you. They accept you for what you are. That's what we are trying to be like, they teach us what we are supposed to be learning. How can you learn unconditional love unless you experience it? Your children influence you in that way.

It's a powerful feeling when you first realize that a new personality exists in the world. They're not here one day and the next day, there they are, a new human. For nine months intellectually you know there's a baby and you can see the movement but it's totally removed from the actual birth. When you see them born, when they come out and breathe, there's actually a new life where there wasn't before. It's spiritual and wonderful. They have their own character and their own feelings. You have to wonder where that came from. One cell dividing into another along with various chemical reactions just doesn't seem to explain it all. We have to wonder if something else had a hand in it. It causes you to ask what makes this life; it makes you think. Maybe we didn't have everything to do with it. How could this have come from just us? Where was it before and where did it come from? If this soul had not gone into this baby, would it have gone unused? You feel that this is something out of the ordinary.

Babies teach us to feel joy in the things around us. It makes you rethink everything you take for granted if you have to think about making your feet work and if you consider what it would be like not to know what anything is. Kids give you a license to play and to let go. They teach you patience and tolerance. You have to accept them because you can't reason with them. They don't understand. They don't play by your rules.

ELECTRONIC SPIRITUALITY?

We have to mention electronic spirituality because of the potential of some of the new electronic equipment. By passing a small electrical current through the brain, doctors may assist the individual in achieving relaxation by promoting alpha-theta brain wave patterns. Some of these are being used in psychiatric hospitals to reduce and control anxiety. Again, the process seems to be that of influencing brain wave patterns from the stressed-out beta waves to the more relaxed alpha-theta patterns.

TRAVEL

The spiritual effect of travel is one of perspective. This is true especially when one visits foreign countries or rural communities. When Marla lived in a small mining town in Colorado, she saw life in a new way, which helped her spirituality. Poverty was evident and survival took on serious meaning so that the importance of spirituality was exposed. The sameness of the world we live in everyday causes us to lose perspective and to sometimes neglect our spiritual lives.

Travel forces you to examine your beliefs about things you may have taken for granted. God, moral rules, appropriate and inappropriate. You have the opportunity to view for yourself how others are spiritual, to stand in places where others have reached spiritual highs, and to see life and afterlife from other eyes. Travel teaches you to *include* and to *unite* rather than *divide*. It can help you listen to your own voice, take risks, or even start over. You may find yourself letting go of old restrictive attitudes and rigid thought patterns.

In his book *Gypsying After 40,* Robert Harris suggests, "Each of us holds a creed no matter how poorly articulated: My pilgrimage exposed my creed so that, at last, I could examine it and was commanded to 'choose how you will be, who you will be, what gods you worship.' " Harris describes the acceptance he learned during his travels and the sense of peace he achieved from learning that he could survive in new and frightening places. He reports that travel "aids in the completion of unfinished business, renews, refreshes" and that people may find themselves "catching up with old dreams, awake each morning as if it were the shining first day of their lives."

EMOTIONAL INTIMACY/SEXUALITY

Getting out of self and into another's feelings can be spiritually fulfilling. The oneness and closeness of emotional and physical intimacy can work to block out stress and resentment.

Getting and giving love separate us from the pettiness of the everyday world, the trials and tribulations which can occupy our minds in an unhealthy way. In this way we may disconnect from self and connect with something larger. Love is more than just an emotion, it can be a spiritually bonding and liberating experience. In its most powerful state, love transforms life from a drudgery of daily routine and habit to feelings of harmony, receptivity, and sensitivity. We all benefit from both the giving and the getting of love and it is important to have both. But in order to get love, one needs first to give love.

Sexuality is a part of love. It can be a part of loving ourselves or of loving another. It connects us with our basic roots as creatures of a whole living system which is the earth. When we merge with another in the ecstasy of completion we are able to reach a spiritual plane which unifies our emotions, our bodies, and our spirits.

In Eastern cultures, sex has been accepted for centuries as a means of achieving spirituality. Individuals who practice a form of slow, gentle sex without orgasm often report intense spiritual experiences, ecstasy that lasts for hours, and awareness of the presence of spiritual beings (Chop Wood, Carry Water).

How do you meet your spiritual needs? Is it your own combination of the activities we have described? Or do you have some special way to make peace with your Higher Power? We all have different spiritual needs.

What we have suggested here is an incomplete list of spiritual pursuits. We have no concept of how many more there may be. Maybe as many as there are individuals in this world.

CHAPTER 11

SPIRITUAL CHRISTIANITY
The Spirit of Unity and Love

Christianity is sick in two ways—its basic doctrine and its abusive practices. In the past there has been no way out of Christianity's doctrines and beliefs. "God's word" was *unchangeable*. For instance, divorce has not been acceptable unless "scriptural" or "Vatican" conditions were met. Not so any more. We note with amazement that suddenly, as churches face declining membership, unchangeable doctrine becomes changeable and negotiable at the whim of church authorities, rather than the "inspired Word."

The June 10, 1991, issue of *U.S. News and World Report* notes that several mainstream Christian denominations are reconsidering their "unchangeable" doctrines in light of a dramatic loss of members (over half a million just in the Presbyterian Church) over the past two decades. Some groups have considered abandoning condemnations against sex outside of marriage and against homosexuality.

These changes are crucial and necessary. However, the effect on people who have been impacted by "unchangeable" rules is interesting. Bob, a close friend raised in the Church of Christ, discontinued his membership in shame after his divorce, due to the harsh disapproval of church authorities. For 15 years he simply followed his own moral code—not much different than he had done before, just less demanding and abrasive. He was hoping against hope that upon his arrival at the Pearly Gates, somehow God would give him a break based on his generally clean existence.

Imagine his shock and dismay when recently, while driving past his old church, he saw a sign requesting attendance at its "divorcee group." He slammed on the brakes, nearly causing an accident. He got out of the car to swear angrily at the "pompous rigid idiots" who had rejected him by forcing him out of a group that he had depended on for support.

HOW CAN CHRISTIANITY HEAL ITSELF?

We do not intend to denigrate those individuals who seek changes within Christianity through sincere sensitivity for their congregation's spiritual needs. Dr. Barry Bailey, discussed in previous chapters, is a leader in this movement toward healthy Christianity. In his recent book *A Picture of God*, he offers Christians a more spiritually oriented religion. Dr. Bailey rejects the restrictive, negative forces in Christianity, while adopting a positive, constructive approach to worshiping a loving, supportive God.

We applaud these changes. In order to make all Christianity healthy, however, they will need to be made universally. We address those who hesitate to change the destructive doctrines, policies, and practices within Christianity. If, indeed, the unchangeable can be changed, and we think it can, Christian religion must undergo a new Reformation. Here's what could be done:

ELIMINATE PUNISHMENT FROM CHRISTIANITY. Replace rejection, sanction, and disapproval with acceptance, love, and support. If your members fall or fail or break the rules or, God forbid, sin in "unacceptable" ways, then why not lend them a hand? If they refuse help at that time, let them know you are available to them and that there will be no rejection or sanction. If others have different beliefs from yours, cherish and support their happiness in those beliefs.

UN-EMPOWER THOSE IN AUTHORITY WHO WOULD CLING TO RIGID AND PUNISHING DOCTRINE. Seek out, as leaders, individuals who can assist members in meeting spiritual needs in healthy ways.

ENCOURAGE QUESTIONING AND SEARCH BY INDIVIDUALS IN DEVELOPING THEIR SPIRITUALITY. Open communications among members, encouraging questioning, discussion, confrontation, and debate. Effective religion should be able to stand up to inspection.

ELIMINATE RIGID BLACK-AND-WHITE, RIGHT-OR-WRONG THINKING. Instead, promote flexibility and help individuals learn to tolerate "grayness" in our complex society. Clinging to belief systems that are out of touch with the reality of today's world approaches "delusional" thinking.

AVOID PHILOSOPHIES THAT ARE EMOTIONALLY DAMAGING AND ABUSIVE, SUCH AS ORIGINAL SIN. Focus instead on the ability of individuals to change their circumstances and take control of their lives and their destinies. Avoid facilitating the myth of helplessness through doctrine or philosophy.

DEEMPHASIZE RELIGION AND EMPHASIZE SPIRITUALITY. Religion is worthwhile only insofar as it serves to facilitate the fulfillment of spiritual needs. When religion stands in the way of spirituality, it has lost sight of its original goal and, at the same time, its usefulness.

AVOID ANY APPEARANCE OF MANIPULATIVE PRACTICES. People don't have to be manipulated into spirituality. They are naturally drawn to spiritual experiences that are presented in a supportive, caring, and nonthreatening manner.

TEACH TOLERANCE OF DIFFERENCES. Make welcome people of all colors, races, sexual preference, financial, social, and educational levels. Use the power of the church to promote good will among all. Become color blind and prejudice-free and set that example for others.

REJECT MAGICAL THINKING. Instead, help people to understand that they have control over their lives, relationships, emotions, behaviors, and thoughts. Assume that most people are capable of making the necessary decisions in their lives and of learning from their mistakes. They don't need threats of "hell," hopes of miracles, prospects of heaven, or fear of a deity to function normally and morally in this life.

BE CAUTIOUS OF RULES AND REGULATIONS. Question each rule—Does it in a very definite way facilitate the fulfillment of spirituality? Our guess is there will be very few rules that meet that requirement. Rules may not promote spirituality but may actually detract from the mind-set necessary to achieve spiritual experience.

SEEK UNDERSTANDING, CLARITY, AND CONSISTENCY WHILE AVOIDING CONTRADICTION, CONFUSION, AND CONFLICT IN MESSAGES. Everyone realizes that the world is full of contradiction. Confusion should not be created by a system which should help in finding answers. People need a way to make sense out of the world which does not add to their stress.

OPEN YOUR DOORS TO INDIVIDUALS MOVING FREELY IN BOTH DIRECTIONS, IN AND OUT. No one should feel trapped or restrained. If your group focus does not fit an individual, that person should feel free to follow other paths. The ultimate goal should be spirituality for all who seek.

REPLACE SHAME WITH COMFORT, CONTROL WITH FLEXIBILITY, FEAR WITH PEACE, ANGER WITH LOVE, PUNISHMENT WITH

ACCEPTANCE, AND GUILT WITH UNDERSTANDING. Ultimately, a healthy and constructive Christianity could play a powerful role in the emotional, physical, and spiritual health of our society. What other system has such long-reaching arms and such impact?

It is time for Christians to expect and even demand change, to refuse to tolerate abuse from religious leaders and fellow Christians. It is time for Christians to expect that, when they enter a church, they can feel safe. People want their churches. In fact, if they don't have them, they will create them. But they need for their churches to represent safety and security.

So here is our prayer to Christian leaders:

What possible harm would it do for us, and all our sisters and brothers in the spiritual search, to recognize and define "God" in our own unique manner? Rather than focusing on divisive and conflicting theories, why not bond together in the quest for spirituality and the higher purpose of helping others in need?

What would be wrong with the church helping us to recognize that the suffering we experience in this world is often a result of our behavior? We could give up the idea of a Savior and of a Satan. No one is going to punish us but ourselves. No one is going to save us but ourselves.

We will all face death and whatever is on the other side some day, but that is a natural and a normal process that we need not fear. Of course, we will continue to struggle to stay alive because that is our nature. We need help getting comfortable with the certainty of the end of our mortal existence and that of our loved ones. Help us to accept our lack of control over such things and help us to work on controlling that in our lives which can be controlled.

Help us to gain a sense of purpose in our lives. Why can't Christianity give us the opportunity to give of ourselves in a manner that helps us reach beyond ourselves and our own needs? Show us how to extend our love and share our support with those who are less fortunate.

Help us to take the energy wasted in religious conflict, fear of punishment, and feelings of guilt, and use that energy for the betterment of all people. Show us how to feel and express love toward others, our spouses, our children, our neighbors, strangers, right or wrong, Christian or not Christian.

Give us relief from our daily troubles. Help us, at least for a moment, to seek a sanctuary where we can gain perspective over that which is truly meaningful in life, be that different for each and every individual. Help us freshen our outlook that we may face the world with renewed energy and strength.

We may need direction at times. Instead of giving us the answers, help us to find the place within ourselves where our answers already exist. If we need structure, help us to make our own, not yours.

Help us to be comfortable with "gray." Although black and white may be the most simple way to define our world, the consequences of taking the easy way out cannot be escaped. In the long run, we will discover that black-and-white beliefs carry a price that we are no longer willing to pay.

Teach us that we are responsible only insofar as we have control. Therefore, we have no responsibility for the souls of others. This removes the pressure from us to "convert" others. This will not relieve us of the desire to help others in every way. But it does relieve us of the need to control others, to force and condemn others. If we are truly concerned for their souls, then teach us that we only benefit others with love and acceptance, not punishment, fear, condemnation, and sanction.

Help us to learn healthy expression of our emotions. Instead of inspiring us to anger, help us to be comfortable with the emotions we already experience. Instead of promoting fear, recognize our lives are full of fear, that we need to learn trust, and to experience relief from fear.

Give us the chance to experience togetherness and mutual support with those that share our quest. Help us to extend our families by including people we know and trust. Help us develop a sense of community by organizing activities which are constructive, recreational, or educational.

Help us to be comfortable with our humanness, our sexuality, our needs and weaknesses. Help us to forgive ourselves and others for human failings, to let go of negative feelings that would build walls between ourselves and others, to let go of negative feelings that would build walls within ourselves.

Show us how to exist within our environment...to join with the earth and our universe...to become a part of all that surrounds us...to exist peacefully in the wholeness, the oneness, the unity.

Help us to break the cast iron chains which bind us in a philosophy that hurts and scars us emotionally and spiritually.

Help us to find a Gentle God.

Help us to be free.

FURTHER READING

ADULT CHILDREN OF ALCOHOLICS
Co-dependent No More. Melody Beattie
Beyond Co-dependency. Melody Beattie
Choice Making. Sharon Wegscheider-Cruse
Guide to Recovery. Herbert L. Gravitz and Julie D. Bowden
It Will Never Happen to Me. Claudia Black
Repeat After Me. Claudia Black
Struggle for Intimacy. Janet Woititz
The ACOA's Guide to Raising Healthy Children.
    Jim Mastrich with Bill Birnes

ANGER
The Dance of Anger. Harriet Lerner
Do I Have to Give Up Me to Be Loved by You?
    Jordan and Margaret Paul

DYSFUNCTIONAL FAMILIES
Adult Children: The Secrets of Dysfunctional Families.
    John and Linda Friel
An Adult Child's Guide to What's "Normal." John and Linda Friel
Stage II Relationships: Love Beyond Addiction. Earnie Larsen
Healing the Child Within. Charles Whitfield
A Gift to Myself. Charles Whitfield
Healing the Shame That Binds You. John Bradshaw

Toxic Parents. Susan Forward

The Emotional Incest Syndrome. Patricia Love

COGNITIVE MANAGEMENT

Your Erroneous Zones. Wayne Dyer

How to Stubbornly Refuse to Make Yourself Miserable About Anything, Yes Anything. Albert Ellis

INCEST

Conspiracy of Silence. Sandra Butler

Kiss Daddy Goodnight. Louise Armstrong

Kiss Daddy Goodnight, Ten Years Later. Louise Armstrong

Quest for Respect. Linda Braswell

The Courage to Heal. Ellen Bass and Laura Davis

Healing the Incest Wound. Christine Courtois

MARRIAGE/ FAMILY

Bradshaw on the Family. John Bradshaw

The Dance of Anger. Harriet Lerner

Do I Have to Give Up Me to Be Loved by You? Jordan and Margaret Paul

Getting the Love You Want. Harville Hendrix

Is it Love or Is It Addiction? Brenda Schaeffer

OTHER

Healing Your Sexual Self. Janet Woititz

Women Who Love too Much. Robin Norwood

Woman's Experience of Sex. Sheila Kitzinger

I Hate You, Don't Leave Me. Jerold Kreisman and Hal Straus

Don't Call It Love, Recovery From Sexual Addiction. Patrick Carnes

RELAXATION EXERCISE

The instructions for recording this script are in parentheses.

(When recording this exercise, be sure to count slowly from one to ten after reading each sentence in order to pace the recording correctly. Read slowly, softly, clearly, and in a monotone.)

Place yourself in a comfortable position. Take a deep breath and let it out very slowly. Take another deep breath and let it out even more slowly. Take a third deep breath and let it out so very slowly. Now, stop breathing and gently allow your body to breathe for you. It will do so slowly, gently and deeply. Watch your abdomen as it rises and falls, rises and falls. Just observe your abdomen as it takes over the job of breathing for you. Rising and falling, rising and falling. Good. Allow all your muscles to let go while your body breathes slowly and deeply. Let go of any tension and allow yourself to let go as you begin to feel heavy and warm. Heavy and warm and peaceful.

(Allow about 30 seconds to pass before
you begin reading the next paragraph.)

You may notice that there are sounds around you. Some coming from inside the room, some from without. Those sounds will only serve to allow you to relax more completely. As you hear the sounds, they will remind you to let go more and more. The sounds will actually help you to let go. Now, just remind yourself that you have plenty of time. Plenty of time to allow yourself to let go of all your tension. You have plenty of time to flow with the good feelings inside yourself. Plenty of time. Plenty of time.

(Allow 30 seconds to pass.)

You are feeling warm and calm and peaceful. Heavy and quiet, warm and calm, peaceful and relaxed. Just enjoy these feelings of comfort. Remember that you can reproduce them any time you choose just by going through this exercise. Heavy and quiet, warm and peaceful. Remember that the more you practice this, the easier it becomes and the deeper you can relax. Now, just lie there for as long as you like, allowing yourself to enjoy the peace and calm. And when you do arise, you will feel refreshed, with renewed energy and a sense of inner strength.

BIBLIOGRAPHY

American Psychiatric Association. *Diagnostic and Statistical Manual of Mental Disorders.* Third Edition, Revised. Washington, D.C.: American Psychiatric Association, 1987.

Armstrong, Louise. Kiss *Daddy Goodnight: A Speak-out on incest. New* York: Hawthorn Books, 1978.

Armstrong, Louise. *Kiss Daddy Goodnight: Ten Years Later. New* York: Pocket Books, 1987.

Arterburn, Stephen, and Jack Felton. *Toxic Faith: Understanding and Overcoming Religious Addiction.* Nashville: Thomas Nelson Publishers, 1991.

Augustine Fellowship. *Sex and Love Addicts Anonymous.* Boston: Fellowship Wide Services, 1986.

Bailey, Barry. *A Picture of God.* Nashville: Abingdon Press, 1991.

Bass, Ellen, and Laura Davis. *The Courage to Heal: A Guide for Women Survivors of Child Sexual Abuse.* New York: Harper and Row, 1988.

Beattie, Melody. *Beyond Co-dependency: And Gettng Better All the Time.* San Francisco: Harper and Row, 1989.

Beattie, Melody. *Co-dependent No More: How to Stop Controlling Others and Start Caring for Yourself.* San Francisco: Harper and Row, 1987.

Beck, Aaron T. *Love Is Never Enough: How Couples Can Overcome Misunderstandings, Resolve Conflicts, and Solve Relationship Problems Through Cognitive Therapy.* New York: Harper and Row, 1988.

Black, Claudia. *It Will Never Happen to Me.* Denver: M. A. C. Printing and Publications, 1982.

Black, Claudia. *Repeat After Me.* Denver: M. A. C. Printing and Publications, 1985.

Booth, Father Leo. *Breaking the Chains: Understanding Religious Addiction and Religious Abuse*. Long Beach, California: Emmaus Publications, 1989.

Booth, Father Leo. *Spirituality and Recovery*. Deerfield Beach, Florida: Health Communications, 1985.

Booth, Father Leo. *When God Becomes a Drug*. San Francisco: J. P. Tarcher, 1991.

Bradshaw, John. *Bradshaw on the Family: A Revolutionary Way of Self-discovery*. Deerfield Beach, Florida: Health Communications, 1988.

Bradshaw, John. *Healing the Shame That Binds You*. Deerfield Beach, Florida: Health Communications, 1988.

Bradshaw, John. *Homecoming: Reclaiming and Championing Your Inner Child*. New York: Bantam Books, 1990.

Braswell, Linda. *Quest for Respect: A Healing Guide for Survivors of Rape*. Ventura, California: Pathfinder Publishing, 1989.

Brown, Stephen. *No More Mr. Nice Guy*. Nashville: Thomas Nelson Publishers, *1986*.

Brown, Stephen. *When Being Good Isn't Good Enough*. Nashville: Thomas Nelson Publishers, 1990.

Burzon, Betty, editor. *Positively Gay*. Berkeley: Celestial Arts, 1992.

Butler, Sandra. *Conspiracy of Silence: The Trauma of Incest*. Volcano, California: Volcano Press.

Byrne, Eric. *Games People Play*. New York: Grove Press, 1964.

Carnes, Patrick. *Don't Call It Love: Recovery From Sexual Addiction*. New York: Bantam Books, 1991.

Cermak, Timmen L. *Diagnosing and Treating Co-dependency: A Guide for Professionals Who Work with Chemical Dependents, Their Spouses and Children*. Minneapolis: Johnson Institute Books, 1986.

Courtois, Christine. *Healing the Incest Wound*. New York: Norton, 1988.

Dyer, Wayne. *Your Erroneous Zones*. New York: Avon Books, 1976.

Ellis, Albert and Harper, Robert A. *Guide to Rational Living*. Englewood Cliffs, New Jersey: Prentice-Hall, 1961.

Ellis, Albert. *How to Stubbornly Refuse to Make Yourself Miserable About Anything, Yes Anything*. New York: Carol Publishing Group, 1988.

Enroth, Ronald M. *Churches That Abuse*. Grand Rapids, Michigan: Zondervan Publishing House, 1992.

Evans, Christine B. *Breaking Free of the Shame Trap: How Women Get into It, How Women Get Out of It*. New York: Ballantine Books, 1994.

Fields, Rick; Taylor, Peggy; Weyler, Rex and lngrasci, Rick. *Chop Wood Carry Water.* Los Angeles: J. P. Tarcher, 1984.

Forbush, William B., editor. *Fox's Book of Martyrs: A History of the Lives, Sufferings and Triumphant Deaths of the Early Christian and the Protestant Martyrs.* New York: Holt, Rinehart and Winston, 1926.

Forward, Susan, with Buck, Craig. *Toxic Parents: Overcoming Their Hurtful Legacy and Reclaiming Your Life.* New York: Bantam Books, 1989.

Fox , Matthew. *Original Blessing.* Santa Fe: Bear & Co., 1983.

Freud, Sigmund. *The Future of an Illusion.* Translated and edited by James Strachey. New York: Norton, 1961.

Friel, John and Friel, Linda. *Adult Children: The Secrets of Dysfunctional Families.* Deerfield Beach, Florida: Health Communications, 1988.

Friel, John and Friel, Linda. *An Adult Child's Guide to What's "Normal."* Deerfield Beach, Florida: Health Communications, 1990.

Gravitz, Herbert L., and Julie D. Bowden. *Guide to Recovery: A Book for Adult Children of Alcoholics.* Holmes Beach, Florida: Learning Publications, 1985.

Greven, Philip. *Spare the Child: The Religious Roots of Punishment and the Psychological Impact of Physical Abuse.* New York: Vintage Books, 1990.

Harris, Robert W. *Gypsying After* 40. Santa Fe: John Muir Publications, 1987.

Hendrix, Harville. *Getting the Love You Want: A Guide for Couples.* New York: Henry Holt and Company, 1988.

Jeffers, Susan. *Feel the Fear and Do It Anyway.* New York: Fawcett Columbine, 1987.

Kaufmann, Walter A. *Faith of a Heretic.* Garden City, New York: Doubleday, 1961.

Kitzinger, Sheila. *Woman's Experience of Sex.* New York: Penguin Books, 1983.

Kreisman, Jerold, and Hal Straus. *I Hate You, Don't Leave Me: Understanding the Borderline Personality* New York: Avon Books, 1989.

Kushner, Harold. *Who Needs God?* New York: Pocket Books, 1989.

Larsen, Ernie. *Stage 11 Relationships: Love Beyond Addiction.* San Francisco: Harper and Row, 1987.

Lerner, Harriet. *The Dance of Anger: A Woman's Guide to Changing the Patterns of Intimate Relationships.* New York: Harper and Row, 1985.

Lord, Janice H. *No Time for Goodbyes: Coping with Grief, Anger, and Injustice After a Tragic Death.* Ventura, California: Pathfinder Publishing, 1987.

Love, Patricia. *The Emotional Incest Syndrome*. New York: Bantam Books, 1990.

Mastrich, Jim, with Birnes, Bill. *The ACOA's Guide to Raising Healthy Children: A Parenting Handbook for Adult Children of Alcoholics*. New York: Collier Books, 1988.

Mundis, Jerrold. *How to Get Out of Debt, Stay Out of Debt and Live Prosperously*. New York: Bantam Books, 1990.

Norwood, Robin. *Women Who Love Too Much: When You Keep Wishing and Hoping He Will Change*. New York: Pocket Books, 1985.

Paul, Jordan, and Margaret Paul. *Do I Have to Give Up Me to Be Loved By You?* Minneapolis, Minnesota: CompCare Publications, 1983.

Peck, M. Scott. *The Road Less Traveled: A New Psychology of Love, Traditional Values and Spiritual Growth*. New York: Simon and Schuster, 1978.

Schaef, Anne Wilson. *Co-Dependency: Misunderstood — Mistreated*. Minneapolis, Minnesota: Winston Press, 1986.

Schaeffer, Brenda. *Is It Love or Is It Addiction?* San Francisco: Harper Collins, 1987.

Sheler, Jeffery L.; Schrof, Joannie M. and Cohen, Gary. "Sex and Religion." *U.S. News and World Report* (June 10, 1991): 60-66.

Tillich, Paul. *What Is Religion?* Translated by James L. Adams. New York: Harper and Row, 1969.

Watters, Wendell W. *Deadly Doctrine: Health, Illness, and Christian God- Talk*. Buffalo, New York: Prometheus Books, 1992.

Wegscheider-Cruse, Sharon. *Choice Making: For Codependents, Adult Children and Spirituality Seekers*. Pompano Beach: Health Communications, 1985.

Weiss, Douglas and DeBusk, Dianne. *Women Who Love Sex Addicts*. Fort Worth, Texas: Discovery Press, 1993.

Whitfield, Charles. *Healing the Child Within: Discovery and Recovery for Adult Children of Dysfunctional Families*. Deerfield Beach, Florida: Health Communications, 1987.

Whitfield, Charles. *A Gift to Myself: A Personal Workbook and Guide to Healing My Child Within*. Deerfield Beach, Florida: Health Communications, 1990.

Woititz, Janet G. *Adult Children of Alcoholics*. Pompano Beach, Florida: Health Communications, 1983.

Woititz, Janet G. *Healing Your Sexual Self*. Pompano Beach, Florida: Health Communications, 1989.

Woititz, Janet G. *Struggle for Intimacy*. Pompano Beach, Florida: Health Communications, 1985.